TIME FOR KIDS

ALMANAC 2014

D0058050

Produced by

DOWNTOWN
BOOKWORKS INC.

PRESIDENT: Julie Merberg
EDITORIAL DIRECTOR: Sarah Parvis
EDITORIAL ASSISTANT: Sara DiSalvo
SENIOR CONTRIBUTORS: Beth Adelman, Susan Perry, Thea Feldman
SERIES CONTRIBUTORS: Kerry Acker, Marge Kennedy, Jeanette Leardi, Lori Stein
SI KIDS PHOTO RESEARCH: Marguerite Schropp Lucarelli
SPECIAL THANKS: Julie Merberg, Lorin Driggs, Krissy Roleke, Lynn Messina, Emily Simon, Patty Brown, Stephen Callahan, Jessica Kaplow Applebaum, Morris Katz, Nathanael Katz, Kal Katz, Janice and Jeff Wilcoxson

Designed by
Brian Michael Thomas/Our Hero Productions

TIME FOR KIDS
PUBLISHER: Bob Der
MANAGING EDITOR, TIME FOR KIDS MAGAZINE: Nellie Gonzalez Cutler
EDITOR, TIME LEARNING VENTURES: Jonathan Rosenbloom

Time
HOME ENTERTAINMENT
PUBLISHER: Jim Childs
VICE PRESIDENT, BRAND & DIGITAL STRATEGY: Steven Sandonato
EXECUTIVE DIRECTOR, MARKETING SERVICES: Carol Pittard
EXECUTIVE DIRECTOR, RETAIL & SPECIAL SALES: Tom Mifsud
EXECUTIVE PUBLISHING DIRECTOR: Joy Butts
DIRECTOR, BOOKAZINE DEVELOPMENT & MARKETING: Laura Adam
FINANCE DIRECTOR: Glenn Buonocore
ASSOCIATE PUBLISHING DIRECTOR: Megan Pearlman
ASSISTANT GENERAL COUNSEL: Helen Wan
ASSISTANT DIRECTOR, SPECIAL SALES: Ilene Schreider
SENIOR BOOK PRODUCTION MANAGER: Susan Chodakiewicz
DESIGN & PREPRESS MANAGER: Anne-Michelle Gallero
BRAND MANAGER: Jonathan White
ASSOCIATE PREPRESS MANAGER: Alex Voznesenskiy
ASSOCIATE PRODUCTION MANAGER: Kimberly Marshall
EDITORIAL DIRECTOR: Stephen Koepp

Special Thanks
Katherine Barnet, Jeremy Biloon, Rose Cirrincione, Jacqueline Fitzgerald, Christine Font, Jenna Goldberg, Hillary Hirsch, David Kahn, Amy Mangus, Amy Migliaccio, Nina Mistry, Dave Rozzelle, Ricardo Santiago, Adriana Tierno, Vanessa Wu

For information on TIME FOR KIDS magazine for the classroom or home, go to **TIMEFORKIDS.COM** or call 1-800-777-8600.

For subscriptions to SI KIDS, go to **SIKIDS.COM** or call 1-800-889-6007.

Published by TIME FOR KIDS Books,
an imprint of Time Home Entertainment Inc.
135 West 50th Street
New York, New York 10020

ISBN 10: 1-60320-952-2
ISBN 13: 978-1-60320-952-6

TIME FOR KIDS is a trademark of Time Inc.

We welcome your comments and suggestions about TIME FOR KIDS Books. Please write to us at:

TIME FOR KIDS BOOKS
ATTENTION: BOOK EDITORS
P.O. BOX 11016
DES MOINES, IA 50336-1016

If you would like to order any of our TIME FOR KIDS or SI KIDS hardcover Collector's Edition books, please call us at 1-800-327-6388 (Monday through Friday, 7:00 a.m.–8:00 p.m. or Saturday, 7:00 a.m.–6:00 p.m. Central Time).

1 QGT 13

CONTENTS

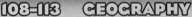

A Hurricane Came Ashore

Millions of people in the Northeast and the mid-Atlantic states were hit hard by Hurricane Sandy. One of the largest storms ever to reach the East Coast, Hurricane Sandy stretched nearly 1,000 miles (1,609 km) wide. Offically deemed a "post-tropical cyclone," it brought pounding winds, rain, and flooding to some of the most heavily populated areas in the nation. The center of the storm came ashore on October 29, 2012, near Atlantic City, New Jersey. Coastal areas, including parts of New York City and New Jersey, were flooded by huge surges of seawater, made worse by high tides and a full moon. The storm caused at least 130 deaths in the United States and Caribbean, and billions of dollars in damage. President Barack Obama declared New York and New Jersey disaster areas, which made federal aid available to the states for rebuilding. "All of us have been shocked by the force of Mother Nature," Obama said.

A neighborhood in New York after Hurricane Sandy

Teachers Walk Out

On September 10, 2012, thousands of teachers in one of the nation's largest school districts left their classrooms. After 10 months of discussions, the Chicago Teachers Union (which represents the teachers) and the city government could not agree on a contract. So about 26,000 teachers went on strike. Classes were canceled for more than 350,000 students in the city's public schools.

Chicago teachers march in protest.

The teachers were protesting what they called unfair work conditions. They said the biggest issues were health benefits, job security, poor classroom conditions, and teacher evaluations. After a week, union leaders agreed that a proposed contract had enough changes for teachers to return to work. The school district made changes to how closely teacher evaluations were tied to student test scores, and offered better opportunities for teachers who are laid off due to budget cuts. The new contract also included a longer school day and pay raises for teachers.

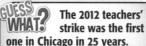
GUESS WHAT? The 2012 teachers' strike was the first one in Chicago in 25 years.

Longer School Day

Starting in 2013, 40 public schools in Colorado, Connecticut, Massachusetts, New York, and Tennessee will each add at least 300 hours of learning time to their calendars. "Adding meaningful in-school hours is a critical investment that better prepares children to be successful in the 21st century," said U.S. Secretary of Education Arne Duncan.

Four More Years

In November 2012, U.S. citizens reelected President Barack Obama and Vice President Joe Biden to a second term. They triumphed over Republican presidential candidate Mitt Romney and vice presidential candidate Paul Ryan. When all the votes were counted, President Obama had won 332 electoral votes to Romney's 206, well over the 270 electoral votes he needed to win. He had a total popular vote count of more than 62.6 million votes to Romney's 59 million.

Congress at a Glance

The 113th Congress of the United States began its term on January 3, 2013. These senators and representatives will remain in office together until January 3, 2015. As of February 2013, this Congress consisted of 232 Republicans and 200 Democrats in the House of Representatives; and 53 Democrats, 45 Republicans, and 2 Independents in the Senate.

GUESS WHAT? President Obama was able to declare a decisive victory on the evening of Election Day, November 6, 2012. But it took the state of Florida four days to count all its votes. When it was done, its 29 electoral votes went to Obama. The President won Florida's popular vote by less than 1%.

Mighty Math Museum

The National Museum of Mathematics (MoMath) opened in December 2012. Its mission? To develop stronger future mathematicians across the nation. Throughout the museum, visitors take part in various games and programs. The museum's founders hope that by having guests participate in the exhibits, they will better understand mathematical concepts. An example of this hands-on method of learning is a ride called The Coaster Roller. Visitors glide in a rounded triangle cart across an acorn-shaped track that miraculously creates a smooth surface. According to MoMath associate director Cindy Lawrence, "The triangular balls [on the cart] have a constant diameter that are even on all sides that simulate a smooth feel."

At MoMath, visitors can ride a tricycle with square wheels.

Many school lunch menus have gotten a lot healthier.

Obesity Rates Falling

For decades, childhood obesity rates have been on the rise. Now some U.S. cities, including Philadelphia, New York City, and Los Angeles, are seeing progress in their fight against fat. Declining childhood obesity rates have also been reported in parts of Mississippi, the state with the highest obesity rate in the nation.

Civil War in Syria

At the end of 2012, a civil war had been raging for 22 months in Syria. More than 60,000 people from both sides had reportedly

Many Syrian families have left their homes and are staying in refugee camps to avoid the civil war.

been killed in the battle for control of the country. The opposition party, seeking to end the rule of Syrian President Bashar al-Assad, gained control of several cities. In 2012, U.S. President Barack Obama endorsed the main Syrian opposition group, known as the Syrian National Coalition, calling it the only "legitimate representative" of Syria's people. Great Britain, France, and Turkey are some countries that had previously made a similar declaration.

In fall 2012 trade union members staged a 24-hour general strike.

Economic Woes in Greece

Greece has been in a severe debt crisis since 2009. Part of the European Union, it shares the euro as its unit of currency. To avoid running out of money completely, Greek leaders accepted money from the European Union and the International Monetary Fund. In exchange for bailout money, Greece enacted a series of extreme measures, known as austerity (aw-*ster*-ih-tee) measures, to control its spending on public programs. Pensions and wages have decreased, and many people have lost their jobs. Fees have been added to hospital visits that used to be free, and the retirement age has been raised. The government also hoped to bring in more money by raising taxes. But few people wanted to live with fewer services and higher taxes. The Greek people, already suffering from the global recession, took to the streets in protest.

South Korea's First Woman President

In 2012, South Korea, which is a democratic republic, elected Park Geun-hye as its first woman President. The 60-year-old is no stranger to the presidency. Her father was President of the country from 1961 to 1979. He first gained that office by seizing power in a military coup and was assassinated 18 years later by his own chief spy!

GUESS WHAT? North and South Korea are technically still at war, because no peace accord has ever been reached since their armed conflict in the 1950s.

Meteor Blast Over Russia

At around 9:20 a.m. on February 15, 2013, people in the town of Chelyabinsk, in central Russia, heard an explosion and watched a big streak of light burst across the sky over the nearby Ural Mountains. A 10-ton (9 metric tons) meteor, moving at a speed of 33,000 miles (53,108 km) per hour, had exploded 12 to 15 miles (19 to 24 km) above the surface of Earth. The explosion was as powerful as dozens of atomic bombs. It was the largest recorded space rock to hit Earth in more than a century. (For more on meteors, see page 184.)

Fragments of the meteor fell to Earth in a low-population area of the frigid Chelyabinsk region. The blast injured nearly 1,500 people and damaged buildings and other property. Governor Mikhail Yurevich estimated the damage would cost about $33 million to repair.

Scientists searched for major fragments of the meteor for testing. Within days, they found more than 50 tiny fragments (about 0.5 in/1.3 cm each) in the Ural Mountains' ice-covered Chebarkul Lake, where the meteor left a hole in the ice 20 feet (6 m) wide.

A driver captured this image with his car's dashboard camera.

Are Space Rocks Dangerous?

Tons of space debris flies around Earth every day. On the same day as the Russian meteor, a 150-foot (46 m) asteroid (see page 184) flew past Earth and came within 17,000 miles (27,359 km) of the surface. That's closer to Earth than some satellites. According to astronomers, this asteroid and the meteorite that landed in Russia are unrelated events.

NASA keeps a close eye on the skies for all near-Earth space objects, in case any threaten our planet. The space agency—and others—are working on ways to redirect incoming asteroids away from Earth.

Tragedy and Triumph in Pakistan

In October 2012, 14-year-old Malala Yousafzai was attacked on her way home from school in Mingora, Pakistan. She was shot by a group of fighters called the Taliban. The group's members follow a strict version of Islam. They believe girls should not go to school. Yousafzai was targeted because she writes about girls' rights and children's education in Swat Valley, one of the most dangerous and remote places in Pakistan.

Pakistan's Prime Minister and President, President Obama, and many world leaders immediately said the attack on Yousafzai was wrong. Support for the girl poured in over social media and from members of the international human rights community.

After two major operations, Yousafzai left a London hospital in February 2013. She told reporters, "I want to serve the people. I want every girl, every child, to be educated." She continues to give hope to millions of people around the world who are working for good causes.

Free-Falling to Earth

Felix Baumgartner is a pilot, skydiver, and high-altitude jumper. Nicknamed "Fearless Felix," Baumgartner has jumped from some of the world's tallest bridges and buildings. But on October 14, 2012, the Austrian daredevil made the jump of a lifetime. He leapt from a space capsule 128,100 feet (39,045 m) above ground. That's about 24 miles (39 km)—a world-record-breaking height! At that distance, Baumgartner stood on the edge of space, in the stratosphere, which is the second layer of Earth's atmosphere. About nine minutes after he jumped, he landed safely on his feet in Roswell, New Mexico.

Baumgartner also broke the record for fastest jump, by reaching speeds up to 833.9 miles (1,342 km) per hour during his free fall back down to Earth. For comparison, an average Boeing 737 airliner flies at 40,000 feet (12,192 m) at 600 miles (966 km) per hour.

Baumgartner and a team of scientists, engineers, and doctors spent five years preparing and training for the project, which is called Red Bull Stratos after the project's sponsor. A helium balloon carried Baumgartner and the Red Bull Stratos capsule up to space. The balloon was the largest ever used for a manned flight. The ascent took nearly three hours. A special suit kept Baumgartner safe during his bold skydive.

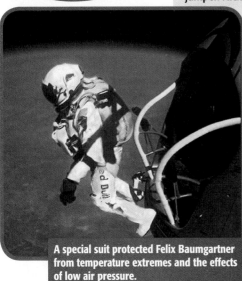

A special suit protected Felix Baumgartner from temperature extremes and the effects of low air pressure.

GUESS WHAT? Cameras attached to Felix Baumgartner's suit recorded his historic space jump. His free fall was watched by millions.

Dragon takes off

Special Delivery

The International Space Station (ISS), a floating lab in space, is home to astronauts and scientists. When those astronauts need groceries and other necessities, they cannot stop by a local supermarket. Instead, they rely on shipments from Earth. Since NASA retired its shuttles in 2011, only Russia, Japan, and Europe have been transporting cargo to the ISS. That changed on May 22, 2012, when the American company SpaceX launched a supply ship called Dragon. The unmanned Dragon took supplies to the ISS and brought back about 1,400 pounds (635 km) of science experiments and old equipment. It was the first time that a company—instead of a government—made a delivery to the space station.

Super Salmon

What kind of FISH is THIS ?! ?!

In the wild, a salmon takes 30 months to grow to full size. Scientists have found a way to make the fish grow twice as fast and to make it grow year-round. They inject it with a gene from a Chinook salmon and a gene from an ocean pout, a large eel-like fish. The Chinook gene makes the salmon grow to full size in about 15 months. The ocean pout gene makes the salmon grow in summer and winter. The result is a genetically modified, or GM, fish. Some crops have been genetically modified to resist pests. But GM salmon is the first GM animal that people can eat.

Some people think genetic modification is a useful new technology. Others are worried about how these new foods could affect our health. Right now, the U.S. Food and Drug Administration does not require GM foods to be labeled, but many food-safety advocates want to make sure these "frankenfish" are clearly labeled so that consumers will know what they are eating.

Up in the Air

Helium is the second-most-abundant element in the universe. Without it, life would be very different. And birthdays and parades just wouldn't be the same. But helium supplies are running low.

Helium is used for much more than just inflating balloons. The gas has scientific, medical, manufacturing, and military applications. One of its most important uses is in hospitals. Helium cools the magnets found in MRI machines.

The very thing that makes helium float is what makes it hard to store. As one of the lightest gases, helium floats right out of Earth's atmosphere. And just as with fossil fuels (see page 98), there is a limited amount of helium. Eventually—in hundreds of years—Earth will run out of the gas. The helium shortage isn't affecting hospitals yet, but prices are going up. Until new helium plants open up in the next few years, consider skipping the balloons at your next birthday party.

GUESS WHAT? One-third of the world's supply of helium comes from production plants in the United States. The gas is mostly found in Oklahoma, Kansas, and Texas.

Brain-Powered Bionic Leg

A prosthetic (pross-*thet*-ik) device is designed to take the place of a missing leg, arm, hand, or foot. And scientists at the Rehabilitation Center of Chicago have developed an incredible new type of prosthesis—one that responds to the wearer's thoughts. It reacts to electrical impulses sent from the nerves to the muscles around the robotic limb.

In November 2012, Zac Vawter, who had lost a leg in a motorcycle accident, used the mind-controlled bionic leg to climb all 103 floors of the Willis Tower in Chicago. He explained, "With my standard prosthesis, I have to take every step with my good foot first and sort of lift or drag the prosthetic leg up. With the bionic leg, it's simple. I take stairs like I used to and can even take two at a time."

The Hunger Games Is a Hit!

The Hunger Games and its stars Jennifer Lawrence, Josh Hutcherson, Liam Hemsworth, and Alexander Ludwig won Teen Choice and People's Choice Awards for their portrayal of young people fighting for survival in a harsh future society. The rest of the tale, based on a trio of novels by Suzanne Collins, will unfold in three more movies released in 2013, 2014, and 2015.

Pint-Sized Powerhouse

For her inspiring turn as a character named Hushpuppy in *Beasts of the Southern Wild,* Quvenzhané Wallis became the youngest actress ever to be nominated for an Academy Award.

South Korean Superstar

Psy, the South Korean pop star behind the song "Gangnam Style," has taken the entertainment world by storm. The video went viral, setting off a dance craze in the United States. Psy performed at the 2012 American Music Awards.

The Only Direction Is Up

Singers Harry Styles, Niall Horan, Liam Payne, Zayn Malik, and Louis Tomlinson each competed individually on the British TV show *The X Factor*. They didn't win, but they did take the advice of one of the judges, who said they should join forces. They formed the band One Direction and have been releasing songs, winning awards, and selling out tours ever since.

GUESS WHAT? With the release of *Up All Night* in the United States in March 2012, One Direction became the first British band to hit Number 1 on the U.S. charts with their first single.

Golden Slam

In the 2012 Olympics, Serena Williams competed against Maria Sharapova in the women's singles tennis final. Williams won the gold, becoming only the second female tennis player to achieve the Golden Slam by winning singles titles in all four major tennis tournaments and the Olympics.

Gymnastics Dynamo

At the 2012 Olympic Games, sixteen-year-old Gabby Douglas became the first American woman to follow up her team gold medal with a victory in the individual all-around. She also became the first woman of color, of any nationality, to win the all-around.

Fastest Man Alive

Jamaican Usain Bolt raced to the top for the second Olympics in a row, successfully defending both his 100-meter and 200-meter sprint gold medals—the first time any man has ever done that. At 100 meters, he set an Olympic record of 9.63 seconds. Bolt was also part of Jamaica's world-record-setting 4x100-meter relay team. He currently holds the world records in both 100 meters and 200 meters, too.

GUESS WHAT? For the first time in Olympic history, there was a female athlete from every country participating in the Games.

An Olympic First

Nineteen-year-old Sarah Attar, of Saudi Arabia, competed in the women's Olympic 800-meter race, on August 8, 2012, becoming the first Saudi woman to compete in an Olympic track-and-field event. As she crossed the finish line—last in the race—many people in the crowd rose to their feet to give her a standing ovation. The London 2012 Olympics marks the first year that women from Saudi Arabia, Qatar, and Brunei competed in the Games.

FROM TIME FOR KIDS MAGAZINE

Not Extinct!

By TIME For Kids Staff

Good news! Experts have found that some species that were thought to be extinct are not. The species were able to survive problems such as natural disasters, habitat loss, and hunting.

The woolly flying squirrel is 2 feet (0.6 m) tall, with a bushy 2-foot (0.6 m) tail. It is one of the tallest squirrels that can glide through the air. It was thought to be extinct for more than 70 years until it was found in Pakistan in 1995.

Lonesome George was thought to be the last of the Galápagos tortoises. New evidence shows there are more of them in the Galápagos Islands. The tortoises can survive for years without food or water.

The Javan elephant was thought to be extinct until 2003. Centuries ago, elephants were given as gifts among rulers. A sultan from Sulu may have helped these elephants survive when he shipped them to Borneo as a gift.

Since 2005, Miller's grizzled langurs were thought to be extinct. Scientists said it was a result of forest damage in Indonesia. But in June 2011, cameras in the jungle snapped photos of them and proved they still exist.

The Laotian rock rat was thought to have become extinct more than 11 million years ago. That is, until it was found being sold in food markets in Laos. The rodent has the body and whiskers of a rat and the thick tail of a squirrel.

Miller's grizzled langur

Galápagos tortoise

Laotian rock rat

ANIMAL GROUP NAMES

Herd of buffalo? Of course you've heard of herds, but how many of these unusual animal group names do you know?

Animal Name	Group Name
Alligator	Congregation
Ferret	Business
Hippo	Bloat
Hyena	Cackle
Kangaroo	Mob
Otter	Romp
Parrot	Company
Rattlesnake	Rhumba

A mob of kangaroos

ANIMAL HABITATS: THERE'S NO PLACE LIKE HOME

A habitat is the natural home for an animal. And animals have habitats in every corner of the globe. Monkeys, snakes, toucans, and more live in **rain forests.** Camels, fennec foxes, and scorpions live in **hot deserts.** Deer, squirrels, and raccoons call **temperate forests** home. The **tundra** is the habitat for wolves, polar bears, and snowy owls. In the **grasslands,** you will find elephants, lions, and ostriches.

An animal is able to survive in the physical environment of its habitat. It can find food, water, mates, and shelter, and deal with the weather conditions. Let's take a quick look at some of the more unusual habitats that animals call home.

SHRUBLANDS

Shrublands, true to their name, have a lot of shrubs. Shrubs are strong, woody plants that are smaller than trees. A shrubland has four seasons, including hot, dry summers and mild, rainy winters. These habitats are home to many animals, such as insects, like bees and butterflies; reptiles, including pythons, boas, tortoises, and rattlesnakes; birds, like mockingbirds, eagles, and quail; and mammals, including antelope, wild boar, sheep, and goats.

Antelope in the shrubland

TIDE POOLS

A tide pool forms in rocks along the shoreline in coastal areas around the world. When the ocean is at high tide, which generally happens twice a day, water fills up around the rocks. When the tide goes out (also twice a day), the water level in the tide pools gets lower. Animals that live there have to be able to adjust to these daily changes in water level and temperature, as well as changes in amount of salt and sunlight.

To survive in this habitat, sea stars attach themselves to the rocks so they don't get swept out to sea during low tide. Clams use their shells to dig holes in the sand and into rock for the same reason. Other tide pool animals include jellyfish, sponges, anemones, and a variety of fish, such as the sculpin.

Sea stars in a tide pool

THE BATHYPELAGIC ZONE: THE DEEP, DARK SEA

There is life at various levels in the sea, including the completely dark zone that starts at about 3,300 feet (1,006 m) below the surface. Not only is it hard to see in the bathypelagic zone, but it is dangerous as well. The water exerts a crushing force of 5,800 pounds per square inch (408 kg per square cm)! And the temperature hovers around a chilly 39°F (3.9°C). Giant squid, some kinds of sharks, and some eels call this place home, as do bioluminescent creatures—animals that make their own light using special light-producing organs. The anglerfish makes light in order to attract mates and to lure in prey. The gulper eel also uses its light to draw in curious prey.

Deep-sea anglerfish

ANIMAL CLASSIFICATION

Scientists use many different indicators to group, or classify, animals. One way that animals can be classified involves their body structure. Animals that have backbones are called vertebrates. Animals without backbones are known as invertebrates.

VERTEBRATES

AMPHIBIANS are cold-blooded and begin life in the water, breathing through gills. When they are fully grown, they breathe through lungs and can walk on land. They lay eggs. Some examples of amphibians are frogs, toads, newts, and **salamanders.**

MAMMALS are warm-blooded and, with the exception of the platypus and the echidna, give birth to live young. Mammal mothers breast-feed their young. Most mammals have hair or fur and live on land (except for porpoises, dolphins, and whales, which live in the water). Wolves, pandas, orangutans, bears, **meerkats,** dogs, elephants, tigers, seals, horses, and humans are all mammals.

BIRDS are warm-blooded and have wings and feathers. All birds lay eggs and most can fly (though emus, cassowaries, and penguins cannot). Some other examples of birds are ducks, vultures, egrets, macaws, woodpeckers, wrens, **puffins,** orioles, eagles, and peacocks.

FISH are cold-blooded and live in water. They have scaly skin and breathe using gills. Most fish lay eggs. Betta, catfish, koi, mako sharks, pufferfish, **stingrays,** and trout are examples of fish.

REPTILES are cold-blooded and have lungs. Their skin is scaly. Most reptiles lay eggs. Reptiles include alligators, crocodiles, **tuataras,** iguanas, rattlesnakes, and tortoises.

INVERTEBRATES

COELENTERATES

(sih-*len*-teh-rates) have stinging tentacles around their mouths. They use their mouths not only to eat with but also to eliminate waste. Examples of coelenterates are **jellyfish**, corals, hydras, sea wasps, and sea anemones.

ECHINODERMS

(ih-*ky*-nuh-durms) live in the sea and have exoskeletons, which means that their skeletons or supporting structures are located on the outside of their bodies. Echinoderms include sand dollars, sea stars, sea cucumbers, and **sea urchins**.

MOLLUSKS (*mol*-usks) have soft

bodies. To protect themselves, some have hard shells. Oysters, **snails**, octopuses, slugs, clams, scallops, squid, and mussels are all mollusks.

SPONGES

live in water and are immobile. They get their food by filtering tiny organisms that swim by.

ARTHROPODS have bodies that

are divided into different parts, or segments. They also have exoskeletons. Arthropods include crustaceans (such as prawns, crawfish, shrimp, and barnacles), arachnids (tarantulas, mites, and scorpions), centipedes, millipedes, and all insects (such as **butterflies**, maggots, katydids, wasps, cockroaches, ants, and earwigs).

WORMS live in a variety

of places, including underwater, in the ground, and even inside other living creatures. Examples of worms include hookworms, earthworms, **leeches**, peanut worms, and tapeworms.

TOP 5 Biggest Spiders

Take a look at the biggest spiders in the world, measured by leg span.

1. Huntsman spider	11.8 inches (30 cm)
2. Brazilian salmon-pink spider	10.6 inches (27 cm)
3. Brazilian giant tawny spider	10.2 inches (26 cm)
4. Goliath birdeater	10 inches (25 cm)
5. Wolf spider	10 inches (25 cm)

Huntsman spider

Source: Scienceray.com

TOP 5 Most Popular Pets

Cats are chasing dogs in this race! More homes in the United States have a dog than any other pet. Here are the top pet picks in the country. What's your favorite pet?

1. Dogs — 46.3 million U.S. households
2. Cats — 38.9 million U.S. households
3. Fish — 12.6 million U.S. households
4. Birds — 5.7 million U.S. households
5. Small animals — 5 million U.S. households

Source: APPA's 2011–2012 National Pet Owners Survey

TOP 10 Most Popular Dog Breeds

1. Labrador retriever
2. German shepherd
3. Golden retriever
4. Beagle
5. English bulldog
6. Yorkshire terrier
7. Boxer
8. Poodle
9. Rottweiler
10. Dachshund

Source: American Kennel Club

Labrador retriever
Beagle
German shepherd
Golden retriever
Yorkshire terrier
English bulldog
Boxer
Poodle
Dachshund
Rottweiler

SILLIEST PET NAMES

Every year, the Veterinary Pet Insurance Company does a survey of pet owners to find out the most popular names for cats and dogs. Bella, Bailey, Max, Lucy, and Molly topped the most recent list. Here are some of the wackiest names that pet owners supplied.

CATS

1. Pico de Gato
2. Dingleberry
3. Dumpster Kitty
4. Schnickelfritz
5. Koobenfarben
6. Sassy Pants Huska
7. Vincent Van Furrball
8. Kitty Gaga
9. Beefra
10. Mister Bigglesworth

DOGS

1. Chew Barka
2. Nigel Nosewhistle
3. Sir Maui Senqkey Schwykle
4. Spark Pug
5. Agent 99
6. Stinker Belle
7. Vienna Sausage
8. Furnace Hills Dante
9. Senorita Margarita
10. Trigonometry

A VERY CATTY YEAR

Clips of cats doing a lot or a little have long been among the most popular online videos. In the summer of 2012, the Walker Art Center, in Minneapolis, Minnesota, decided to embrace the trend. It hosted the first ever Internet Cat-Video Film Festival.

An estimated 10,000 people, and even some cats, packed the lawn outside the museum, where a giant video screen was set up. The eager audience viewed 79 videos in 75 minutes. The museum chose the videos based on submissions from the public. Selected clips were put into the categories documentary, art house, lifetime achievement, and foreign. The videos included fan favorites, such as Maru, the cat from Japan who loves to squeeze his round body in boxes. The Golden Kitty Award, chosen by visitors to the museum's website, went to the silly, subtitled video *Henri 2: Paw de Deux,* which features a black-and-white French cat with lots of worries.

Cats and people arrive at the Walker Arts Center for the first ever Internet Cat-Video Film Festival.

Animals

TOP 10 Most Popular Cat Breeds

1. Persian
2. Exotic
3. Maine coon
4. Ragdoll
5. Sphynx
6. Siamese

7. Abyssinian
8. American shorthair
9. Cornish rex
10. Oriental

Source: Cat Fancier's Association

Siamese

Persian

GUESS WHAT? A study conducted by researchers at Hiroshima University, in Japan, concluded that watching cat videos can make a person more productive at work. They concluded that watching cute faces makes people want to care for others and slow down and focus more.

THE KITTY-CAM PROJECT

Scientists at the University of Georgia conducted a study to see what domesticated cats really do when they're out on the prowl. During the study, 60 pet cats in Athens, Georgia, wore lightweight kitty cams around their neck. The cameras were made especially for the animals by National Geographic, which makes many larger "critter cams" for wildlife field-research projects. None of the cats appeared to be bothered by their cameras.

The goals of the study were to see how much the cats attacked native wildlife and also to determine how much being outside put the cats at risk. After compiling 2,000 hours of footage, the study found that 44% of the cats did try to kill small reptiles, mammals, and invertebrates. As much as 85% put themselves in harm's way by doing things like crossing two lanes of traffic, eating or drinking things from an unknown source, or wandering into spaces, like storm drains, where they could get trapped. Four of the cats in the study were also leading double lives, spending time with other families.

KNOCK, KNOCK, ANYBODY HOME?

Some animals move into already existing structures, such as a knothole in a tree or a crevice in a rock. Others build their own places.

Using its powerful front legs, the **African aardvark** digs underground burrows. Sometimes they are big enough for a person to sit in.

The **clownfish** makes its home within another animal: the sea anemone. Unlike other fish, the clownfish has a mucus covering on its body that protects it from the anemone's swaying, stinging tentacles. This living home provides not only protection, but food as well—clownfish like to eat the plankton and algae that get caught in the anemone's tentacles.

The world's largest bird's nests are built by tiny brown birds called **sociable weavers.** Found in southern Africa, their nests are like giant apartment buildings with dozens of different compartments—each pair of birds that lives in the nest gets its own. Because the nests are so big, they are built only on very sturdy trees— or sometimes on telephone poles.

In Africa, Australia, and South America, some types of **termites** use mud, saliva, and chewed wood to build skyscraper-like structures called termite mounds. The mounds, which can reach heights of 30 feet (9 m) or more, contain an elaborate maze of specialized rooms. Although the queen gets her own room, most of the termites live in a nest that's just under the mound.

ANSWER ON PAGE 244

Best Friends Forever

By Carl Zimmer for TIME

Since 1995, scientist John Mitani has been going to Uganda, in Africa, to study chimpanzees. He likes to tell the tale of two males that researchers named Hare and Ellington.

Hare and Ellington weren't related. But when they went hunting, they would share food with each other. They would spend days traveling through the forest together.

Their friendship lasted until Ellington's death. What happened next was surprising and sad. Hare had been an outgoing ape. But when Ellington died, Hare went through a sudden change. "He just didn't want to be with anybody for several weeks," says Mitani.

Not all animal friendships occur between creatures from the same species. Owen and Mzee are a hippo and a tortoise that struck up a wonderful friendship at a wildlife sanctuary in Kenya.

Animal Pals

For a long time, friendship was considered an important trait of only one species: humans. Scientists now know better. Animals can make friends too.

Animal friendship is not just about dogs playing together at the park. It is about lasting bonds defined by sharing, sacrificing, and, sometimes, grieving. In humans, friendship has been linked to good health and longer life. But scientists have often wondered why. Recent studies of animals provide some answers.

Researcher Lauren Brent spent four years on an island off the coast of Puerto Rico, studying a group of rhesus monkeys. Brent measured the monkeys' levels of a chemical that the body produces in response to stress. She then compared the chemical levels of those monkeys in friendships with monkeys not in friendships. The monkeys with friends were less stressed. Stress can lead to health problems. So friends were keeping friends healthy!

Chimpanzee friends spend time together, sharing meals, grooming one another, and playing.

MYSTERY PERSON

I was born on March 30, 1820, in Norfolk, England. I wrote the classic children's book *Black Beauty*. It is told from the point of view of a horse that has careless and unkind owners. The book made people aware of the mistreatment of animals.

Who Am I?

ANSWER ON PAGE 244

WORLD'S BIGGEST CROCODILE CAUGHT

In September 2011, after a three-week hunt, villagers of Bunawan, in the Philippines, along with local wildlife officials, successfully captured a saltwater crocodile suspected of killing two people and attacking several more. They didn't know if they had caught the right predator, but they quickly realized that they had caught an enormous one.

The crocodile, named Lolong in honor of a crocodile hunter who died shortly before the critter was captured, measures 20.24 feet (6.17 m) long and tips the scales at 2,369 pounds (1,075 kg). These stats make it the largest crocodile in captivity, and, in July 2012, Lolong's size was recognized in the *Guinness Book of World Records*. Before Lolong, the record holder was an Australian-caught saltwater croc that was 17.97 feet (5.48 m) in length.

Lolong lived out his days being cared for in an ecotourism park in Bunawan, becoming the biggest tourist attraction in the area before his death in February 2013.

Villagers with Lolong, the world's biggest saltwater crocodile

A MATCH FOR THE WORLD'S SMALLEST CHAMELEON

In 2012, four new species of tiny chameleons were identified. Found on a tiny island off the coast of Madagascar, the smallest of the four, named *Brookesia micra,* grows to be, on average, just 1 inch (2.5 cm) long. How small is that? *Brookesia micra* can fit comfortably on the head of a matchstick. It is one of the smallest vertebrates (see page 18) ever found on Earth.

Brookesia micra is one of the smallest animals with a backbone. It's tiny!

How did researchers locate lizards so little? They had previously found tiny chameleons on neighboring Madagascar, and they knew that the animals were active during the day. So they searched tree branches on this island at night, when the animals were sleeping. *Brookesia micra* climb up into tree branches to sleep, but because they are so small, these lizards only climbed about 4 inches (10 cm) off the ground!

A GIANT PANDA MYSTERY

In 2012, paleontologists at a dig site in Zaragoza, Spain, found a piece of a jaw belonging to an 11.6-million-year-old species of bear. They determined that this fossil was from a newly discovered ancient bear species called *K. beatrix*, and that *K. beatrix* is a relative of the giant panda in China. Before this, the oldest known panda relative was "only" 7 to 9 million years old!

Scientists can tell a lot from the fossils they found. The jawbone indicates that *K. beatrix* probably ate tough plants, much like today's bamboo-munching giant panda does. They also believe that *K. beatrix* weighed about 130 pounds (59 kg), making it smaller than any of the bear species that exist today. Its size, however, would have made it easier for *K. beatrix* to climb trees to avoid the bigger predators of its time.

What scientists haven't figured out yet is how *K. beatrix* made it from Spain all the way to China. Or whether it had the same black-and-white markings that modern-day giant pandas do.

Giant panda eating bamboo

THE FROZEN ARK

While researchers are still discovering new species, according to the United Nations Environmental Program, upwards of 150 species go extinct every day. Enter the Frozen Ark, a worldwide association of institutions, including the Natural History Museum, in London; the Zoological Society of San Diego, in California; the Dublin Zoo, in Ireland; and the Center for Cellular and Molecular Biology, in Hyderabad, India. The Frozen Ark, based within the University of Nottingham, in England, is saving the DNA (see page 174) and some cells of the world's animals. One day, this material might be used to keep species alive through cloning. The Ark currently has 48,000 samples of more than 5,500 animals, including both endangered and non-endangered species.

A zoologist (scientist who works with animals) at London's Natural History Museum will take DNA samples from an endangered Polynesian tree snail and store them in the Frozen Ark.

25

A JUMBO YEAR FOR ELEPHANTS

Elephants have been making headlines lately. Here are just a few of the stories featuring these huge land mammals.

WHAT DID YOU SAY?

Koshik, a male Asian elephant at the Everland Zoo, in South Korea, can speak. Scientists aren't sure exactly how the pachyderm is producing the sounds, but he does put his trunk inside his mouth before "talking." He can say the Korean words for *hello*, *good*, *no*, *sit down*, and *lie down*, in a tone that is shockingly similar to a human's voice. The words and phrases are ones Koshik's keepers use with him, so he is likely just imitating them and does not understand the meaning of what he's saying.

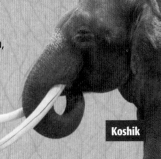

Koshik

GUESS WHAT? Scientists think Koshik is vocalizing to bond with people.

WOULD YOU LIKE SUGAR WITH THAT?

The Golden Triangle Asian Elephant Foundation, in Chiang Rai, Thailand, sells a unique blend of coffee for about $50 a cup. To create this coffee, elephants eat coffee beans. They can't digest the beans and they don't absorb any of the caffeine or get sick from eating them, but they do give the coffee a special flavor. Workers at the sanctuary wait for the beans to come out in the elephants' dung. Then they collect the beans, clean them off, and ship them to a gourmet coffee roaster. Eventually, the beans wind up as a coffee blend called Black Ivory. The pricy coffee is a treat for the wealthy, but it also provides much-needed income for the care of the elephants.

A cup of Black Ivory coffee

GUESS WHAT? It can take from 15 to 30 hours for the beans to pass through an elephant. They swallow the beans with fruit and sugarcane, which give a fruity flavor to the final brew.

A Human Threat

Elephants are sometimes killed for their tusks, because the tusks are made of ivory, which commands a high price on the **black market**. According to conservation groups, 2012 was the worst year since they began keeping records for elephants being illegally killed. In one case, officials in Malaysia found 1,500 tusks that had originated in Togo, in West Africa, and were on their way to China. According to Save the Elephants, an estimated 1.3 million elephants lived in Africa in 1979. That number fell dramatically to 450,000 by 2007.

The term *black market* refers to the buying and selling of illegal goods.

Malaysian officials display the confiscated tusks.

GUESS WHAT? Both male and female adult African elephants have tusks, which are teeth, but only adult male Asian elephants have them. An adult male African elephant tusk can weigh more than 110 pounds (50 kg) and be more than 7 feet (2 m) long.

TIME FOR KIDS GAME

CREATURE CROSSWORD

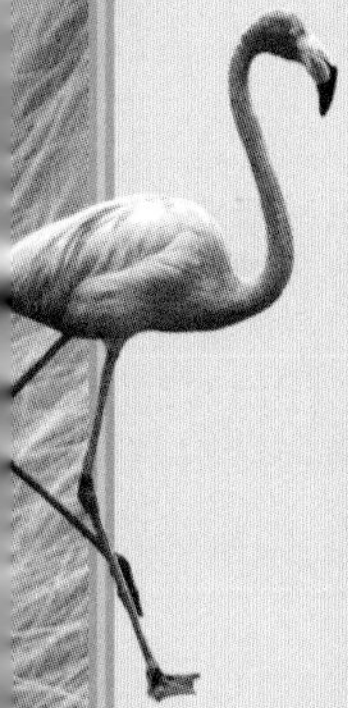

ACROSS

2. You can find this big, green reptile in the swamps of Florida.
5. This pet swims around in a bowl.
7. A male sheep is a ________.
8. A _________ is an enormous ocean-dwelling mammal.
10. This insect flies around and loves to land on food. It also likes to land on animal droppings. Yuck!
11. A type of small salamander is called a ________.
12. This famous black-and-white bear likes to eat bamboo.
14. An electric _____ has a shocking way to hunt and keep predators away.
15. This small animal likes to eat eucalyptus leaves. Most people think it is a type of bear, but it is actually related to kangaroos.
16. These wriggly animals live in the dirt. When fishing, some people use these critters as bait.

DOWN

1. *Tyrannosaurus rex* is a famous _____________.
3. A snake is a type of ________. Lizards, turtles, crocodiles, and alligators also belong to this group.
4. This wise bird is a hoot!
5. You might recognize this African mammal by its long neck.
6. This pink critter is often seen standing on one leg.
9. This is the short version of the name of a huge African mammal that spends its days in rivers and lakes. It is often seen wearing a tutu in cartoons. But in real life, it is an incredibly dangerous beast.
13. These insects work together in huge groups. You might even see one try to carry away your picnic lunch.

ANSWERS ON PAGE 244

PAINTING
THROUGH THE AGES

Art has always been a form of communication and expression for people. The world's oldest paintings date back 40,000 years. Found on the walls of caves, these paintings often featured large animals. Finger flutings are another type of cave art. They are impressions in the walls of caves made by people's fingers.

Over the years and centuries, there have been many different styles of painting. Here are just a few examples. Check out a museum near you to see more!

ITALIAN RENAISSANCE PAINTING

The Last Supper, by **Leonardo da Vinci**

Renaissance means "rebirth," and the Renaissance in Europe, which lasted from the 14th to the 17th century, was a time of great growth for all kinds of learning, culture, and art, including paintings. The city of Florence, Italy, was considered the birthplace and center of the Renaissance art movement. Many Renaissance paintings were commissioned by the Catholic Church and feature religious themes. One of the most famous of these paintings is *The Last Supper,* by Leonardo da Vinci, painted on a convent wall. Visitors to Milan, Italy, can still see it today. Wealthy families also commissioned portraits of themselves and family members. Some paintings, such as *The Birth of Venus* by Sandro Botticelli, captured themes from classical literature. Even when showing fictional characters, Renaissance paintings portrayed people and other subjects as realistically as possible.

THE DUTCH GOLDEN AGE OF PAINTING

In the 17th century, the Dutch Republic (which is now the Netherlands) was the richest country in Europe. During this time, Dutch painters were known for several different kinds of paintings. Many depicted scenes of middle-class and peasant life, such as *The Milkmaid* by Johannes Vermeer. Other themes included landscapes, townscapes, still lifes, and the sea. Wealthy families commissioned many family portraits. Rembrandt van Rijn painted individual as well as group portraits, such as *Night Watch.* Painters from this period often emphasized light and shadow.

The Milkmaid, by **Johannes Vermeer**

GUESS WHAT? More than 5 million paintings were created by Dutch artists during the Dutch golden age of painting. There were so many canvases done that individual paintings didn't sell for very much money most of the time. Today, many of the works of these artists hang in museums and are considered priceless.

IMPRESSIONISM

Paris, France, was the center of the art world in the mid to late 1800s, when a new painting style called Impressionism was created. These paintings featured ordinary people, scenes of everyday life, landscapes, and still lifes. Impressionist artists painted with a brighter range of colors than a lot of previous artists. This is evident in many paintings, including Claude Monet's *Water Lilies.* Painters also used shorter brushstrokes, which are visible to the viewer, such as in Vincent Van Gogh's *The Starry Night* and in portraits by Auguste Renoir, including the *Portrait of Madame Charpentier and Her Children.* Impressionistic works were often less realistic looking than those of painters who had come before them.

There were about 250 paintings in Claude Monet's *Water Lilies* series.

GUESS WHAT? Today, museum exhibits of Impressionist paintings are among the most popular with the public. But when the Impressionists began painting, their work was not appreciated. Art patrons and members of the art community did not like the new style.

MODERNISM

Modernism is less a style of art than an entire movement. Modern art is all about an artist's individual experimentation with and interpretation of objects and emotions. That explains why these works of art are incredibly varied and inventive. Some modern artists include the early-20th-century painters Henri Matisse and Pablo Picasso, as well as Piet Mondrian, who worked mostly in the 1930s, and Jackson Pollock, who painted in the 1940s. Two famous modern artists from the 1960s are Andy Warhol and Roy Lichtenstein.

GUESS WHAT? Researchers have found cave paintings on the walls of Rouffignac cave, in France, that were done 13,000 years ago by children as young as 3 years old. They figured out the ages of the artists by measuring the finger flutings found there.

Artist Jackson Pollock was known for his unique style of dripping and splashing paint onto a canvas.

CRAZY, COOL ART PROJECTS

Sculpture, photography, and printmaking are just a few kinds of art other than painting. More and more artists' work cannot even be put into one specific category, but the results are often unique creations that engage and delight audiences around the world.

INFLATABLE ART

Kurt Perschke describes himself as a sculptor who is interested in architectural spaces and the relationship of people to these kinds of spaces. His *RedBall Project* began as a public art commission for the Arts in Transit program in St. Louis, Missouri. The *RedBall* is an inflatable ball that, when inflated, is 15 feet (4.6 m) high. It weighs 250 pounds (113 kg), and it is impossible to miss when it is wedged under a bridge in St. Louis or blocking street access in an old section of Barcelona, Spain. The *RedBall Project* has rolled its way into more than 12 cities around the globe.

GUESS WHAT? It takes about 40 minutes to inflate the *RedBall* once it reaches its destination. It is always inflated and deflated at the site where it will be exhibited.

The 250-pound (113 kg) *RedBall* is perched above the pedestrian walkway on the Golden Jubilee Bridge in London, England.

PUPPY LOVE

Another sculpture sure to bring a smile to people's faces is *Puppy*, by Jeff Koons. It is part of the permanent collection of the Guggenheim Museum in Bilbao, Spain. Created in 1992, *Puppy* is nearly 41 feet (12 m) tall by 27 feet (8 m) wide and is 29 feet (9 m) deep. It is made of a stainless steel frame shaped like a West Highland terrier and covered in soil and tens of thousands of flowering plants. Before settling in at the museum, *Puppy* traveled around the world, visiting Germany, Australia, and the United States.

Jeff Koons's *Puppy*, in New York City in 2000

ART ON THE MOVE

Dutch artist Theo Jansen combines artistry with science to create fantastic beach animals from plastic tubes, ties, and fabric. The beasts look like giant dinosaurs come to life. Powered by the wind, the sculptures appear to be walking. Each sculpture is able to create its own energy. The plastic tubes fit inside each other and slide back and forth. This forces air in and out of the tubes and builds pressure. The pressure creates movement. "I didn't try to make something beautiful," Jansen says. "I wanted to make things that function." He did both.

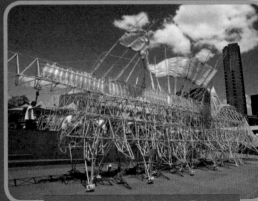

A Theo Jansen creation in Australia in 2012

POLKA DOTS EVERYWHERE

When artist Yayoi Kusama, now in her 80s, began to paint at around age 10, her work made use of polka dots. Throughout the decades, these little spots have become the signature feature of her work, which includes videos and soft sculptures. She created the *Obliteration Room* in 2002.

The *Obliteration Room* began as a stark white room. The walls, ceiling, floor, furniture, and decorations were all white. Once the exhibit opened to the public, visitors were given a sheet of round, colored stickers in different sizes. They were invited to place the stickers anywhere they wanted in the room. Over the next few weeks, thousands of stickers were placed all over, transforming the room into a riot of dotted color. It is an excellent example of interactive art.

A visitor adds stickers to the *Obliteration Room* installation at the Wilhelm-Hack-Museum in Germany in 2012.

TIME FOR KIDS GAME

MORPHING MURAL

This young artist is making lots of additions to her mural. But they aren't the only changes you'll see in this pair of pictures. Can you spot all 10 changes?

ANSWERS ON PAGE 244

Sweet on Sugar

By Suzanne Zimbler

Can you imagine eating 20 teaspoons of sugar? The typical American kid gets that much sugar every day. Eating too much sugar can lead to serious health problems.

According to a recent report from the National Center for Health Statistics, kids get about 16% of their calories from sugar that has been added to food. "It's one of the major problems with our diet," Dr. David Katz, a nutrition expert at Yale University, told TFK.

Vending machine snacks are often high in sugar and fat.

Sugar in Disguise

Much of the sugar that kids eat is hidden. Food companies add sugar to many items, from ketchup to crackers. "There are pasta sauces in every supermarket in the country with more added sugar than ice cream toppings," says Katz. As a result, many people are used to eating very sweet foods.

In 2012, three health researchers published an article in the magazine *Nature*. They said that the government should help people cut down on the amount of sugar that they eat. These scientists suggest banning the sale of sugary drinks to kids and removing sugary products from schools. They also think the government should charge extra taxes for heavily sweetened foods. "We need to unsweeten our lives," Dr. Robert Lustig, one of the scientists, told TFK.

Chew on This

What can kids do to cut down on extra sugar? Katz suggests looking at the ingredients list printed on food packages. Added sugar goes by many different names. Ingredients that end in *ose*, such as sucrose and fructose, are sugars. So are those that have the word *syrup*. "Make sure the only foods [you eat] that have added sugar are foods you actually care about being sweet," says Katz. Lustig says to choose natural instead of processed foods whenever possible. "[Eat] food that came out of the ground or animals that ate food that came out of the ground." Now *that's* food for thought.

SWEET WORDS

Do you want to find out if a food has sugar added to it? Take a look at the ingredients list on the package. Added sugars go by many different names.

Agave nectar	Evaporated cane juice	Maltose
Brown sugar	Fructose	Malt syrup
Cane crystals	Fruit juice concentrates	Molasses
Cane sugar	Glucose	Raw sugar
Corn sweetener	High-fructose corn syrup	Sucrose
Corn syrup	Honey	Sugar
Crystalline fructose	Invert sugar	Syrup
Dextrose	Lactose	

HEALTHY HABITS

Kicking a bad habit can be tough. Sometimes, it is easiest to start by making small changes. Try out a few of these ideas for improved health.

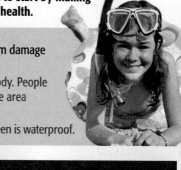

WEAR SUNSCREEN Sunburn hurts, and it can do long-term damage to your skin.

* Be sure to apply sunscreen everywhere on your body. People often forget to cover the backs of the knees, the ears, the area around the eyes, and the neck.
* Reapply at least every two hours, even if the sunscreen is waterproof.

GET ENOUGH SLEEP We need sleep to keep our bodies healthy, and we don't learn as well when we're tired. Students who are well rested tend to score higher on math and writing tests. Kids who don't get enough sleep have a harder time paying attention in class. This can affect future test performance.

☾ Try to go to bed at the same time every night.
☾ Remove all electronics from your room so there are no distractions.

GUESS WHAT? Kids who drink caffeinated beverages throughout the day get less sleep than kids who don't. To get as much sleep as possible, switch to water or milk after 2 or 3 p.m.

MAKE HEALTHY MEAL CHOICES Apples, strawberries, cucumbers, eggs, and steaks are examples of fresh or whole foods, which often have more health benefits than processed foods.

Eat a good breakfast. Studies show that kids who eat a balanced breakfast do better in school. Also, people who eat breakfast tend to take in more vitamins and minerals. They eat less fat and cholesterol. They aren't as likely to overeat later in the day.

Always read the nutrition labels on packaged food. Remember that the labels show the amount of carbohydrates, fat, and nutrients in a single serving. If there are three servings in a bag of pretzels and you eat the whole thing, you must multiply all of the values by 3.

Limit the amount of sugar in your diet, and beware of hidden sugars.

TURN OFF THE TV AND GET ACTIVE! The more TV you watch, the less physically active you are. Exercising is one of the most important ways to keep your body healthy. When you exercise, you strengthen your bones, muscles, and heart. You also burn off extra fat, improve your balance, improve your mood, and regulate your body's metabolism, which is the process that turns the nutrients in food into energy and heat.

* To stay healthy, everyone should try to do about one hour of exercise a day, in four 15-minute periods.
* Find a workout that is fun for you. Jumping rope, playing soccer or basketball, doing jumping jacks, taking a dance class, swimming, playing tag, or practicing yoga are just a few great workout ideas.

FEEL THE BEAT

Nurses and doctors take your pulse to see how fast or slow your heart is beating. It can help them determine how healthy you are. Kids' heartbeats when they're sitting or resting usually range from 60 to 130 beats per minute. Adults have slower heartbeats: usually no faster than 100 beats per minute. Babies have very fast heartbeats: up to 150 beats per minute.

You can take your own pulse. One of the best places to find your pulse is on your wrist. That's because the blood vessel in the wrist that carries blood away from the heart (known as the radial artery) is located very close to the surface of the skin.

TO TAKE YOUR PULSE . . .

♥ Place the pads of two fingers against the outer edge of the wrist on your other hand, just below the base of your thumb.

♥ Slide your fingers toward the center of your wrist.

♥ Apply a little bit of pressure until you feel beats of blood pulsing underneath your skin. You may need to slide your fingers around a bit to find and feel the beats.

♥ Using a timer or a clock with a second hand, count the beats for 30 seconds.

♥ Multiply the number of beats by two. That will give you your pulse.

Don't use your thumb to feel your pulse. It has a pulse of its own!

Try taking your pulse after different activities. How does it change?

Your pulse while sitting: ⬜

Your pulse while standing: ⬜

Your pulse after lying on the floor for 3 minutes: ⬜

Your pulse after doing 25 jumping jacks: ⬜

Goals for Good Health

TOP 5

TFK and KidsHealth.org questioned more than 10,000 kids about health. We found out that kids know a lot about healthy living and that they want to learn even more. We asked kids what health goals they'd like an adult's help to achieve. The bar graph on the right shows what they said.

1. **Learning how to cook**
   4,450 kids

2. **Getting more exercise**
   3,280 kids

3. **Eating healthier foods**
   3,242 kids

4. **Learning how to play new sports**
   2,990 kids

5. **Losing weight**
   2,579 kids

COMMON ILLNESSES

The most common illnesses are **infectious** ones. That means they're contagious. They can be passed from one person to another.

Infectious illnesses are spread by microscopic organisms, usually **viruses** and **bacteria.** These organisms are most likely to enter your body through your eyes, nose, or mouth. To protect yourself, wash your hands often and keep your hands away from your face. Here are some facts about common infections.

❀ More than 200 different viruses cause **colds.** Because of these illnesses, kids miss a whopping 189 million school days each year in the United States.

❀ You don't catch an **ear infection** from another person. But a cold caught from another person can lead to an ear infection.

❀ When kids get **diarrhea,** it's usually because a virus has gotten into their gut, or intestines. The intestines are lined with millions of tiny, fingerlike things called villi, and certain infections make the villi unable to absorb and hold water like they usually do. That means more water flows out with your bowel movements, making them mushy and runny.

❀ **Pinkeye (conjunctivitis)** is a highly contagious infection that will make your eyes red and itchy, but it won't permanently hurt your ability to see.

Body and Health

Noninfectious illnesses can't be passed from one person to another. People sometimes inherit these diseases from their parents. Or something in the environment may trigger the disease.

❀ A person develops **diabetes** when the body has trouble using a type of sugar called glucose.

GUESS WHAT? Diabetes has been around for a long, long time. The first description of its symptoms is on a piece of ancient Egyptian papyrus that was written about 3,000 years ago!

❀ **Allergies** are very common. You have an allergy when your body overreacts to a substance that is harmless to other people. That substance, called an allergen, can be plant pollen, pet dander, mold spores, an insect sting, a food, or something else. Some people are even allergic to money! They break out in a skin rash when they touch coins (or other objects) that contain a metal called nickel.

❀ **Asthma** is an illness that occurs when the tubes that take air into your lungs become swollen and narrow, making it hard to breathe. Special medicines can help keep those tubes open.

GUESS WHAT? Asthma is very common—even among athletes. In fact, about 8% of the athletes who participated in the last five Olympic Games had asthma.

CURIOUS QUESTIONS ABOUT THE HUMAN BODY

HOW DO BROKEN BONES HEAL?

Bones are natural healers. When you fracture a bone, a blood clot starts to form between the bone's broken ends. Within days, new tissue begins to replace the clot. That tissue, called a callus, is like bone but without the mineral calcium. The callus can be easily broken. That's why doctors often put a cast around a bone when it's healing. The cast keeps the bone safe and in place.

Slowly, over a few weeks, the callus is replaced with new bone. That new bone is usually just as strong as the old one.

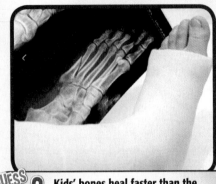

GUESS WHAT? Kids' bones heal faster than the bones of adults. That's because kids' bodies are already hard at work making new bone. Kids need to be constantly producing new bone in order to grow taller and bigger. So when kids break a bone, their existing bone-building process simply goes into overdrive.

WHAT MAKES PEOPLE BURP?

Burping is your stomach's way of getting rid of unwanted air. When you swallow food or liquids, you also swallow some air. Air contains gases, like nitrogen and oxygen. Your stomach can't work properly if it has too much gas in it. So it forces any excess gas back up through your esophagus (the tube that carries food into your stomach). The gas then shoots out of your mouth as a burp!

Burping is sometimes caused by a stomach-related illness, but that is rare in children.

Things that can make you burp:
Eating too fast
Talking while you eat
Drinking sodas and other carbonated beverages
Chewing gum
Sucking on hard candy
Drinking through a straw

WHAT HAS PEE BEEN USED FOR IN THE PAST?

Throughout history, people have used urine in many strange ways. It was once used in medicine, for example. That's because urine is usually free of germs when it leaves the body. Doctors discovered that it was often safer to use on wounds than water. Unless properly processed, water can be full of bacteria and other infectious organisms. Urine was also used in the past to make the following products:

Household cleaning fluids
Leather and wool clothing
Toothpaste and mouthwash

Cosmetics
Gunpowder

TOILET

WHY ARE SOME PEOPLE LEFT-HANDED?

The main part of the human brain—the cerebrum—can be divided into two halves, or hemispheres. The left hemisphere controls movement on the right side of the body. And the right hemisphere controls movement on left side. Most people have a stronger, or more dominant, left hemisphere. So those people prefer to use their right hand when, say, writing with a pencil or throwing a baseball. But in about 10% of people, the right hemisphere of the cerebrum is more dominant. They are left-handed.

Handedness—left and right—tends to run in families. For that reason, scientists think genes are probably involved in determining which hand people prefer to use.

FAMOUS LEFTIES

Here are just a few of the left-handed people whose name you might recognize.

President Barack Obama

Prince William

Angelina Jolie

Oprah Winfrey

Tom Cruise

Paul McCartney

WHAT ARE THOSE TINY BUMPS ON MY TONGUE?

They're called papillae. Some of them are there to help you grip your food and move it around in your mouth while you chew. Others contain taste buds. Each bud has special cells with microscopic hairs called microvilli. These hairs send messages to your brain. They tell you if something you're eating is sweet, sour, salty, bitter, or umami (which is a savory taste, like meat).

Your taste buds help you enjoy food. But they also help protect you from foods that might harm you. Your taste buds alert you, for example, when milk has turned sour and is no longer good to drink.

Taste buds can become weakened or damaged—when you're sick, for example, or when you burn your tongue while drinking a too-hot cup of cocoa. But the damage is almost always temporary. The taste buds will soon repair themselves, or new ones will form.

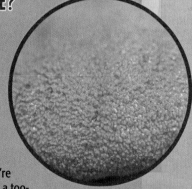

SUPERTASTERS

The average person's tongue has 2,000 to 10,000 taste buds. Some people have even more. Scientists call these individuals supertasters. They taste things more intensely. But that can sometimes be a problem. It can make them dislike healthful foods. For example, supertasters tend not to like green vegetables because those foods taste extra bitter to them. Some research suggests that one in every four people is a supertaster.

BOOKS AND LITERATURE

AWARD-WINNING BOOKS AND AUTHORS

2013 NEWBERY MEDAL
The One and Only Ivan,
by Katherine Applegate

2013 CALDECOTT MEDAL
This Is Not My Hat,
by Jon Klassen

2013 CORETTA SCOTT KING AUTHOR AWARD
Andrea Davis Pinkney,
author of *Hand in Hand: Ten Black Men Who Changed America*

2013 ROBERT F. SIBERT INFORMATIONAL BOOK MEDAL
Bomb: The Race to Build—and Steal—the World's Most Dangerous Weapon,
by Steve Sheinkin

2013 PURA BELPRE AWARD
Aristotle and Dante Discover the Secrets of the Universe,
by Benjamin Alire Sáenz

2013 SCOTT O'DELL AWARD FOR HISTORICAL FICTION
Chickadee,
by Louise Erdrich

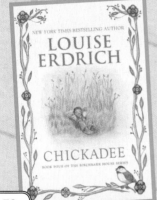

2013 YALSA AWARD FOR EXCELLENCE IN NONFICTION
Bomb: The Race to Build—and Steal—the World's Most Dangerous Weapon,
by Steve Sheinkin

2013 MARGARET A. EDWARDS AWARD

Tamora Pierce,
author of Song of the Lioness series and
The Protector of the Small quartet

2012 NATIONAL BOOK AWARD FOR YOUNG PEOPLE'S LITERATURE

Goblin Secrets,
by William Alexander

GUESS WHAT?

The Margaret A. Edwards Award honors an author, as well as a specific portion of his or her work, for a "significant and lasting contribution to young adult literature.

2012 INDIES CHOICE AWARD FOR YOUNG ADULT BOOK OF THE YEAR

Between Shades of Gray,
by Ruta Sepetys

2012 EDGAR ALLAN POE AWARD, BEST JUVENILE

Icefall,
by Matthew J. Kirby

Books and Literature

TOP 5

Largest U.S. Libraries

The Library of Congress, in Washington, D.C., has the largest collection of any U.S. library. Check out other big U.S. libraries in the chart below.

1. Library of Congress
33,515,702 volumes

2. Boston Public Library
24,079,520 volumes

3. New York Public Library
16,640,294 volumes

4. Harvard University
16,557,002 volumes

5. University of Illinois at Urbana-Champaign
12,780,067 volumes

Source: American Library Association

39

GET LOST IN A BOOK!

There's nothing like the feeling of picking up a book and getting so swept away by its story or information that you lose all sense of everything but what you're reading. And there are so many great books to choose from. Check out one of these fiction or nonfiction books and see where it takes you!

FICTION

***Liar & Spy,* by Rebecca Stead** In this mystery, seventh grader Georges and his family move to a Brooklyn apartment, where he makes friends with Safer, a self-proclaimed spy. Safer recruits Georges to find out what the mysterious Mr. X, who lives upstairs, is up to. But there's much more than the mystery of Mr. X for the boys to figure out.

***The Mighty Miss Malone,* by Christopher Paul Curtis** Set in the 1930s, this novel stars Deza Malone, the smartest girl in her class in Gary, Indiana. Deza's family is hit hard by the Great Depression and is forced to separate to find work. Despite the challenges and hardships, Deza maintains her hope for a better future.

***Crunch,* by Leslie Connor** This lighthearted novel is set in the not-too-distant future, when severe gas restrictions and shortages have become a reality. Dewey Marriss and his siblings must take care of themselves and run their father's bicycle repair shop when their parents are stranded without any gas on the way home from a car trip.

***From the Mixed-up Files of Mrs. Basil E. Frankweiler,* by E.L. Konigsburg** Eleven-year-old Claudia Kincaid and her younger brother run away and hide in the Metropolitan Museum of Art in this timeless, Newbery Award–winning novel from 1967. But, when they encounter a marble statue of an angel in the museum and meet Mrs. Basil E. Frankweiler, their adventures really begin.

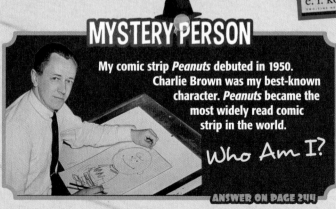

MYSTERY PERSON

My comic strip *Peanuts* debuted in 1950. Charlie Brown was my best-known character. *Peanuts* became the most widely read comic strip in the world.

Who Am I?

ANSWER ON PAGE 244

NONFICTION

The Elephant Scientist, **by Caitlin O'Connell and Donna M. Jackson** This book is packed with stunning photos and fascinating information about elephants. You'll get an inside look at the state-of-the-art methods scientists use to study animals in the field.

Chuck Close: Face Book, **by Chuck Close** In this unique, highly visual autobiography, wheelchair-bound artist Chuck Close candidly addresses his life and his work. There is even a section where readers can mix and match the artist's self-portraits.

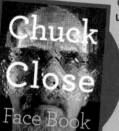

The World Record Paper Airplane Book, **by Ken Blackburn and Jeff Lammers** A combination of how-to and hard science, this book is chock-full of everything you ever wanted to know about paper airplanes. It comes with 112 ready-to-fold planes.

Energy Island, **by Allan Drummond** Illustrated with whimsical artwork, this book tells the true story of how citizens of Samso, an island in Denmark, harnessed the wind, built solar panels, and did a lot more in order to make the island virtually free from the need for nonrenewable sources of energy.

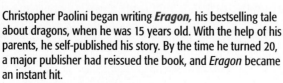

Want to be a published novelist? You can! And you don't have to wait until you're an adult to become one. Start writing now.

Walter Farley began writing his famous novel while he was still in high school. *The Black Stallion,* published in 1941, is about a shipwrecked young boy named Alec Ramsay and a spirited stallion, who has become one of the most famous horses in fiction. Farley followed up with *The Black Stallion Returns, Son of the Black Stallion,* and others.

S.E. Hinton sold *The Outsiders,* a modern classic of young adult literature, when she was 17 years old. Other popular books by Hinton are *That Was Then, This Is Now* and *Rumble Fish.*

Christopher Paolini began writing *Eragon,* his bestselling tale about dragons, when he was 15 years old. With the help of his parents, he self-published his story. By the time he turned 20, a major publisher had reissued the book, and *Eragon* became an instant hit.

BUILDINGS AND ARCHITECTURE

BUILDING PARTS

Architects—people who design buildings—have figured out many ways to use windows, walls, doorways, roofs, and other features to make buildings both strong and beautiful.

ARCH A curved or pointed ceiling that bridges a gap. An arch can bear more weight than a flat roof or a bridge can. Before 1100 A.D., arches were always shaped like rounded curves. In the Gothic period, architects first used pointed arches, which they found could support even more weight than rounded arches. This allowed them to use heavier materials and to design and build taller structures.

Canterbury Cathedral, Canterbury, England

BUTTRESS A stone support that projects outward from a wall

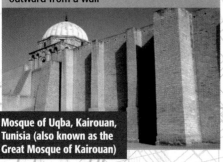

Mosque of Uqba, Kairouan, Tunisia (also known as the Great Mosque of Kairouan)

COLUMN A pillar made of stone or concrete that supports an arch or roof, or that stands alone

Temple of Apollo, Delphi, Greece

DOME A rounded roof of a building

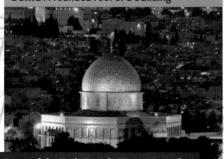

Dome of the Rock, Temple Mount, Jerusalem

FLYING BUTTRESS A buttress that forms an arch, connecting a main wall with another structure

Washington National Cathedral, Washington, D.C.

GARGOYLE A carved figure of a person or animal that is usually made of stone and is placed on the gutters of a building. Some gargoyles are placed just for ornamentation. Others are actually spouts. Rainwater flowing from the roof can escape through the mouths of these decorative beasts.

St. Mary's Church, Melton Mowbray, England

LATTICEWORK A framework of crisscrossing metal or wood strips. Latticework can be used as a support structure or just for decoration.

Eiffel Tower, Paris, France

PORTICO An entrance porch, usually supported by columns

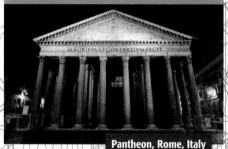

Pantheon, Rome, Italy

SPIRE A tower shaped like a cone that was developed in Europe and is usually the top of a place of worship

Town Hall, Brussels, Belgium

STORY Any level of a building that can be inhabited by people. In the United States, the ground floor is typically not considered to be a story, nor is the basement.

Willis Tower, Chicago, Illinois (formerly known as the Sears Tower)

VAULT An arched ceiling; the inside of a dome

St. Peter's Basilica, Vatican City

TYPES OF COLUMNS

DORIC

This is the most common type of column. It is also the simplest. It has a smooth, rounded top (also called a capital). Doric columns do not have a base at the bottom. The Parthenon, in Athens, Greece, features Doric columns.

IONIC

Ionic columns are known for the scroll-like decorations on their capitals. They have grooves cut into them from the top to the bottom, so they appear fluted. The base of an Ionic column often looks like it is made up of a stack of rings.

CORINTHIAN

These columns are fluted like Ionic columns and rest on similar bases, but they feature more intricate designs on the capital. Inspired by Egyptian architecture, these columns often feature olive, laurel, or acanthus leaves on their capital.

43

SKYSCRAPERS

Supremely tall buildings present architects and engineers with special challenges. How will the building stay upright and not sink into the ground or blow over in a strong wind?

TECHNOLOGY THAT CHANGED CONSTRUCTION FOREVER

Before the late 1800s, the tallest buildings were rarely higher than 10 stories. The solid brick walls at the bottom needed to be very heavy and thick to support the weight of the upper floors. And thick walls used up a lot of space. Once advances were made in the iron and steel industries, architects were able to plan for taller buildings. Builders could use long beams of solid iron and then beams of solid steel (which is stronger and lighter than iron). The development of fire-resistant building materials and the invention of a passenger elevator also changed the future of architecture. Elevator shafts take up a lot of space. In modern skyscrapers, people going to the top floors will often take one elevator part of the way up and then switch to another.

GUESS WHAT? Above street level, the Petronas Towers, in Malaysia, are 1,483 feet (452 m) tall. They have a foundation that is 394 feet (120 m) deep.

MOVING AND SWAYING

All buildings sway a little bit in the wind, but this motion can make the people inside feel uncomfortable. A building's structure must be tight so the whole thing moves together. This prevents different floors from moving differently or twisting, which might weaken the building. Some tall buildings have enormous weights at the top that shift depending on the wind outside to keep the structure from swaying too much and making the people inside feel queasy.

At the Shanghai World Financial Center, in China, there is a large hole built in the top of the building, which allows wind to flow through the building rather than just push on it.

SUPPORTING STRUCTURES

Builders must know a lot about the land that will support a building. In New York City, much of the ground below skyscrapers is bedrock, the solid, sturdy rock that makes up Earth's crust. This makes laying a **foundation** simpler. In Chicago, the ground is clay, which is softer. So it is more expensive to create solid foundation there.

The vertical beams of a structure attach to an underground plate made of cast iron. This plate sits atop groupings of heavy horizontal steel beams, called **grillage.** Each layer of beams in the grillage is wider than the one above it, making a hefty underground pyramid. The grillage rests on an even wider concrete pad. The tallest building in the world is the Burj Khalifa, in Dubai, United Arab Emirates. It is 2,722 feet (829.7 m) tall above street level and has a foundation that's 164 feet (50 m) deep.

Burj Khalifa

BRIDGES

Bridges have been around for thousands of years. Some of the earliest ones were just logs across streams. As time passed, engineers created better designs and found stronger building materials.

TYPES OF BRIDGES

Today, bridges can generally be grouped into three categories:

The simplest type of bridge is a **beam bridge**. It is a beam or plank with two or more columns at each end for support. Many of the bridges you see while on the highway are beam bridges.

An **arch bridge**, such as the Bayonne Bridge, in New Jersey, has a roadway supported by an arch, from which it gets strength. Because of the additional support, arch bridges can be much longer than beam bridges.

The world's largest, and typically most famous, bridges are **suspension bridges**. A suspension bridge has a roadway that is suspended or hung from cables. The cables are attached to two or more towers at the edges of the middle section of the bridge and then to large concrete structures at each end of the bridge. The longest suspension bridge in the world is the Akashi-Kaikyo Bridge, in Japan. Engineers look at the location and the load a bridge will need to support before deciding which type is best.

STRENGTH AND BEAUTY

When building bridges, it is important that engineers consider the forces that will act on them. The two most important are tension and compression. **Tension** is a force that pulls objects apart. **Compression** is the force that squeezes them together. Bridges must be strong enough to resist these forces without cracking or falling down. While some bridges aren't particularly decorative, others are intended to be beautiful and to enhance the landscape.

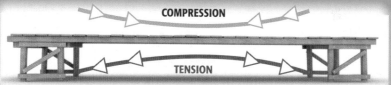

COMPRESSION

TENSION

SPOTLIGHT ON SANTIAGO CALATRAVA

Santiago Calatrava is a Spanish architect, sculptor, and engineer known for blending the lines between sculpture and architecture in his bridges and buildings. His plans often resemble things found in nature, such as the curves of wings, the bones of a skeleton, or the motion of waves. He is especially well known for his bridges, which often feature cables that are lit up at night to add neat curves and striking angles to a city's skyline. He has designed more than 60 bridges across Europe, including the Alamillo Bridge, in Seville, Spain. In 2004, Calatrava completed the Sundial Bridge at Turtle Bay, located in Redding, California–his first bridge in America. He is currently working on the Trinity River Bridges, a series of three bridges in Dallas, Texas. The first of the series, the **Margaret Hunt Hill Bridge**, opened for traffic in March 2012.

AMAZING PLACES

Architects and designers have created wonderful buildings all around the world in many different styles and for many different uses. Read on to learn some fascinating facts about a few famous buildings. What cool features would you add to your own construction?

The **Alhambra** palace complex, in Granada, Spain, was mostly built between 1238 and 1358. An additional palace was built in 1527 during the reign of Charles V, the Holy Roman Emperor. Parts of the Alhambra were restored by Jose Contreras in 1830.

» The oldest part of the Alhambra is the Alcazaba fortress, which dates back to the 9th century.

» Mohammed I was the first royal resident of the Alhambra.

» The Alhambra palace complex is a stunning example of Moorish architecture with its high domes, soaring arches, open courtyards, and decorative tiles.

» At its height, as many as 40,000 people lived and worked in the Alhambra.

The Alhambra palace complex

The palace of **Versailles**, in France, was designed by architect Le Vau, interior decorator Charles Le Brun, and landscape architect André Le Nôtre. It was completed in 1710.

» Beginning in 1682, the palace was the official residence of Louis XIV.

» Approximately 5,000 noblemen and women lived in Versailles's hundreds of rooms.

» Versailles is an excellent example of Baroque architecture. It is filled with flowery details and flashy decorations.

» Inside the palace, the Hall of Mirrors features 17 huge mirrors along one entire side of a 240-feet-long (73 m) hallway. The mirrors face 17 large windows, which look out over the garden.

Versailles

Angkor Wat, in Cambodia, built by King Suryavarman II, was completed in the early 12th century. Originally built as King Suryavarman's personal tomb and to honor the Hindu god Vishnu, Angkor Wat became a Buddhist temple beginning in the late 13th century.

» The temple was designed to represent Mount Meru, the home of the Hindu gods. The five towers, shaped like the buds of a lotus flower, represent the five peaks of the mountain.

» Sandstone was the main building material.

» The temple's surfaces are covered with miles of **bas-relief** sculptures depicting Hindu stories of warriors, dancing girls, dragons, unicorns, and more.

Angkor Wat is one of the largest temples in the world.

Bas-relief is a sculpture technique in which figures and other design elements jut out a bit from a flat background.

The **Space Needle,** in Seattle was designed by John Graham. It was completed in time for the 1962 World's Fair.

» When it was built, the Space Needle was the tallest U.S. building west of the Mississippi River.

» The structure weighs 3,700 tons (3,357 metric tons).

» The Space Needle is fastened to its foundation with 72 bolts, each 30 feet (9 m) in length.

» High-speed elevators go from the ground to the 520-foot (158 m) high observation deck in 43 seconds.

» The Needle is built to withstand winds of 200 miles (322 km) per hour.

The Space Needle's observation deck and restaurant are open 365 days a year.

The **Tower of Pisa,** in Pisa, Italy, was completed in 1399. The designer of the tower is unknown.

» The tower, a freestanding bell tower of the cathedral in Pisa, began to lean during construction because of the soft ground on which it was built. The name *Pisa* comes from a Greek word meaning "marshy land."

» The tower, originally 196 feet (60 m) high is now about 186 feet (56.6 m) high.

» There are 297 steps from the bottom to the top.

The Leaning Tower of Pisa is in the Square of Miracles, in Pisa, Italy.

The **Guggenheim Museum,** in New York City, was designed by Frank Lloyd Wright. It was completed in 1959.

» Most of the building's exterior was created without corners.

» Visitors never need to retrace their steps. They can take an elevator to the top floor and walk down in a circular path, seeing each object of art as they go.

Guggenheim Museum

CONTAINER HOUSES

One of the latest eco-friendly trends in housing is to convert old shipping containers into homes. The dimensions of one intermodal steel building unit (ISBU) shipping container are 40 feet (12 m) long by 20 feet (6 m) wide and nearly 9 feet (3 m) tall. This can make for a comfy home that can be renovated to include all the necessary amenities for a fraction of the price of buying or building a larger property. These homes are catching on around the world. Some homes are made out of two or more containers put together in a variety of ways. There are restaurant kiosks made out of old shipping containers, and there are even container hotels, including one in London that has 120 bedrooms.

CALENDARS AND HOLIDAYS

2014

January

S	M	T	W	T	F	S
			1	2	3	4
5	6	7	8	9	10	11
12	13	14	15	16	17	18
19	20	21	22	23	24	25
26	27	28	29	30	31	

February

S	M	T	W	T	F	S
						1
2	3	4	5	6	7	8
9	10	11	12	13	14	15
16	17	18	19	20	21	22
23	24	25	26	27	28	

March

S	M	T	W	T	F	S
						1
2	3	4	5	6	7	8
9	10	11	12	13	14	15
16	17	18	19	20	21	22
23	24	25	26	27	28	29
30	31					

April

S	M	T	W	T	F	S
		1	2	3	4	5
6	7	8	9	10	11	12
13	14	15	16	17	18	19
20	21	22	23	24	25	26
27	28	29	30			

May

S	M	T	W	T	F	S
				1	2	3
4	5	6	7	8	9	10
11	12	13	14	15	16	17
18	19	20	21	22	23	24
25	26	27	28	29	30	31

June

S	M	T	W	T	F	S
1	2	3	4	5	6	7
8	9	10	11	12	13	14
15	16	17	18	19	20	21
22	23	24	25	26	27	28
29	30					

July

S	M	T	W	T	F	S
		1	2	3	4	5
6	7	8	9	10	11	12
13	14	15	16	17	18	19
20	21	22	23	24	25	26
27	28	29	30	31		

August

S	M	T	W	T	F	S
					1	2
3	4	5	6	7	8	9
10	11	12	13	14	15	16
17	18	19	20	21	22	23
24	25	26	27	28	29	30
31						

September

S	M	T	W	T	F	S
	1	2	3	4	5	6
7	8	9	10	11	12	13
14	15	16	17	18	19	20
21	22	23	24	25	26	27
28	29	30				

October

S	M	T	W	T	F	S
			1	2	3	4
5	6	7	8	9	10	11
12	13	14	15	16	17	18
19	20	21	22	23	24	25
26	27	28	29	30	31	

November

S	M	T	W	T	F	S
						1
2	3	4	5	6	7	8
9	10	11	12	13	14	15
16	17	18	19	20	21	22
23	24	25	26	27	28	29
30						

December

S	M	T	W	T	F	S
	1	2	3	4	5	6
7	8	9	10	11	12	13
14	15	16	17	18	19	20
21	22	23	24	25	26	27
28	29	30	31			

Calendars and Holidays

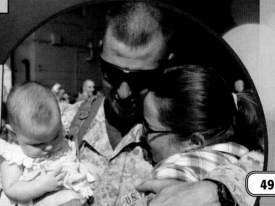

GUESS WHAT? There are 2.2 million members of the armed services in the United States. They and their families are recognized during Military Family Month, which is celebrated in November.

Time to Celebrate!

January 1: New Year's Day
January 20: Martin Luther King Jr. Day
January 31: Chinese New Year
February 2: Groundhog Day
February 14: Valentine's Day
February 17: Presidents' Day
March 4: Mardi Gras
March 9: Daylight saving time begins
March 17: St. Patrick's Day
April 1: April Fools' Day
April 15-22: Passover*
April 20: Easter
April 22: Earth Day
May 5: Cinco de Mayo
May 11: Mother's Day
May 26: Memorial Day
June 15: Father's Day
July 4: Independence Day
September 1: Labor Day
September 25-26: Rosh Hashanah*
October 4: Yom Kippur*
October 13: Columbus Day
October 31: Halloween
November 2: Daylight saving time ends
November 11: Veterans Day
November 27: Thanksgiving Day
December 17-24: Hanukkah*
December 25: Christmas Day
December 26-January 1: Kwanzaa

*All Jewish holidays begin at
sundown the evening before.

Every Month Is Special

Presidents, government agencies, and nonprofit groups have worked hard to designate certain months for the observation of a specific theme, medical condition, or group of people. Here are a few.

January
National Mentoring Month
National Braille Literacy Month

February
American Heart Month
Black History Month

March
Women's History Month
Irish-American Heritage Month

April
National Poetry Month
National Child Abuse Prevention Month

May
National Bike Month
Jewish American Heritage Month

June
National Oceans Month
Caribbean-American Heritage Month

July
National Culinary Arts Month
National Park and Recreation Month

August
National Water Quality Month
National Immunization Awareness Month

September
National Wilderness Month
National Preparedness Month

October
National Disability Employment Awareness Month
National Bullying Prevention Month

November
Military Family Month
Native American Heritage Month

December
Universal Human Rights Month
Read a New Book Month

President George W. Bush signs a 2007 presidential proclamation to declare February American Heart Month.

A boy prepares to dance during a Native American Heritage Month celebration.

51

HOLIDAYS AND CELEBRATIONS AROUND THE GLOBE

Burns Night is enjoyed by Scottish people all over the world. They gather together for a feast, music, and poetry readings on January 25 to remember the famous poet Robert Burns, who was born on January 25, 1759. Participants often eat haggis—a Scottish dish made of sheep organ meat and spices served in a sheep's stomach—and they read Burns's poem "Address to a Haggis." Celebrations end with a rousing round of the song "Auld Lang Syne," which is a Burns poem set to music.

Día de los Muertos, or the Day of the Dead, is celebrated on November 1 and 2. Mexicans gather on these days to honor loved ones who have passed away. They visit cemeteries, build colorful altars, and offer gifts to the dead. Sometimes, they bring pillows and blankets with them and stay all night, talking, singing, and remembering.

Holi is a Hindu celebration that marks the beginning of spring in India and is known as the Festival of Colors. People celebrate in the streets. They wear white clothing, smear paint on each other's faces, and throw *gulal* (colored powder) into the air. Some people even fill squirt guns with paint to spray on friends and strangers.

Holi begins with the lighting of bonfires on the evening of the full moon in the lunar month Phalunga (which falls in late February or early March). The next morning, the *gulal* tossing begins!

Tanabata, or the Star Festival, is celebrated in Japan. It usually takes place on or around July 7 or August 7. According to legend, this is the one day a year when a pair of star-crossed lovers can be together. People write their wishes on colorful pieces of paper called *tanzaku* in hopes that they will come true. The *tanzaku* and other decorations are hung from bamboo branches.

Santa Lucia's Day marks the beginning of the holiday season for Scandinavians. Celebrated on December 13, it commemorates an Italian girl who lived in the 4th century and died for her Christian beliefs. On the morning of Santa Lucia's Day, the oldest daughter of each household portrays Lucia. She wears a long white nightgown with a red sash, and a a wreath with candles around her head. She wakes her family and brings them sweets. Other girls and boys act as Lucia's helpers, walking with her in local processions.

People put candles, flowers, decorated skulls, and food atop Day of the Dead altars, or *ofrendas.* They make special food such as *calaveras,* which are sugary treats in the shapes of skulls, and *pan de muerto,* which is a sweet bread covered in sugar.

MYSTERY PERSON

In 1621, I helped the Pilgrims survive winter. I helped colonists and Native Americans make peace. Thanksgiving might not exist without me.

Who Am I?

ANSWER ON PAGE 244

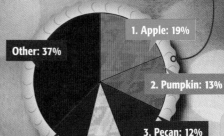

TOP 5 Holiday Pies

There is nothing more American than apple pie! The American Pie Council asked people which pies they eat during the holidays. Guess what came out on top?

- 1. Apple: 19%
- 2. Pumpkin: 13%
- 3. Pecan: 12%
- 4. Banana cream: 10%
- 5. Cherry: 9%
- Other: 37%

Source: Crisco and the American Pie Council

TIME FOR KIDS GAME

MERRY MAZE

Rudolph can't remember the way back to the North Pole. Can you help him out?

NORTH POLE

ANSWER ON PAGE 244

Do Kids Need Their Own Cell Phones?

By TIME For Kids Staff

Two recent studies have people talking. They are debating whether kids need their own cell phones. According to a July 2012 study, 56% of parents of children ages 8 to 12 have given their kids a cell phone. A recent YouthBeat survey says 12 is the most common age for kids to get their first cell phone. But 13% of children ages 6 to 10 already have a mobile phone.

Those who support kids having cell phones say the devices help kids keep in touch with their friends and families, and are an important tool in an emergency. Many people who oppose kids having phones are worried about the effect of the phones on kids' health and safety.

What do you think? Do kids need their own cell phones? Here are two opposing viewpoints.

NO!
Lauren Wahl, 9, San Diego, California
Kids should not have cell phones. Cell phones are expensive. When kids spend time talking and texting, they have less time for other activities, like playing outdoors with friends. Kids might be tempted to use their phones while they are doing homework, which can distract them. Using a cell phone in class can lead to big trouble. There's also the risk that cell-phone use may not be good for kids' health.

YES!
Sofia Calayag, 10, Foster City, California
Responsible kids need their own cell phones. Owning a cell phone helps kids learn about responsibility. It also lets parents and kids stay in contact. Some parents believe that because they didn't have a cell phone when they were younger, their kids should not have one. Parents didn't have a computer growing up either. That doesn't mean their kids don't need a computer. A cell phone is an important tool.

GUESS WHAT?

TIME For Kids likes to find out how its readers feel on all sorts of topics, so the magazine's editors conduct polls on topics that range from whether the electoral college should choose the President to whether or not science students should be given reduced school tuition. Check out the polling site at *timeforkids.com/debate*.

MYSTERY PERSON

I was born in Houston, Texas, on February 23, 1965. In 1984, while in college, I launched a computer company called PC's Limited. Today, my company, which carries my name, is a top seller of computers.

Who Am I?

ANSWER ON PAGE 244

WEBBY AWARDS

In 1996, when the International Academy of Digital Arts and Science began giving out yearly awards for excellence on the Internet, 603,367 websites existed. Sixteen years later, that number has increased by more than 1,000 times—but fear not! Thanks to the 16th Annual Webby Awards, held on May 21, 2012, you don't have to look hard to find the best the Internet has to offer.

Best Use of Animation or Motion Graphics
drawastickman.com

Music
spotify.com

Cultural Institutions
United States Holocaust Memorial Museum
rememberme.ushmm.org

Personal Blog/Website
Clouds 365 Project
clouds365.com

Education
khanacademy.org

Social
Skype

Education and Reference
The Human Body App

Sports
espn.com

Food and Beverage
foodily.com

Tourism
NYC The Official Guide
nycgo.com

Web Services and Applications
dropbox.com

Webby Breakout of the Year
Instagram

Youth
Sesame Street Muppets
sesamestreet.org/muppets

Games
Androp "Bell" Music Video Game
award.aid-dcc.com/androp_bell/en/

Government
nasa.gov

THE MOST-WANTED LIST
A 2012 study by Nielsen of kids ages 6 to 12 revealed which items they hoped to buy or receive within the next six months.

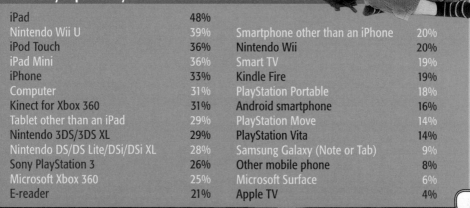

Item	%	Item	%
iPad	48%	Smartphone other than an iPhone	20%
Nintendo Wii U	39%	Nintendo Wii	20%
iPod Touch	36%	Smart TV	19%
iPad Mini	36%	Kindle Fire	19%
iPhone	33%	PlayStation Portable	18%
Computer	31%	Android smartphone	16%
Kinect for Xbox 360	31%	PlayStation Move	14%
Tablet other than an iPad	29%	PlayStation Vita	14%
Nintendo 3DS/3DS XL	29%	Samsung Galaxy (Note or Tab)	9%
Nintendo DS/DS Lite/DSi/DSi XL	28%	Other mobile phone	8%
Sony PlayStation 3	26%	Microsoft Surface	6%
Microsoft Xbox 360	25%	Apple TV	4%
E-reader	21%		

MAKE BEAUTIFUL MUSIC . . . WITH YOUR COMPUTER

Music at Your Fingertips

Dozens of sites exist online where you can download your favorite songs. Or you can tune in to one of hundreds of streaming music stations through your computer, tablet, or phone. There are also a number of software programs that help users create their own compositions. For example, the Sibelius Groovy Music Series is software geared especially toward kids in elementary and middle school. It teaches the basics of sound, rhythm, pitch, composition, and scales, and lets users create their own music.

For the more advanced musician, there are programs such as the Apple Logic Pro 9, which lets you record yourself or your band and then build arrangements and edit the music.

Video Chatting

Computers let you reach out, talk to, and see friends and family who live all over the world—for free. All you need to do is check the clock to make sure you and your friend are both awake at the same time. Google e-mail has a video-chat function. Google also offers Google Talk for PCs, which allows users to chat and to send and receive files. Skype is a downloadable app that lets users video-chat from computers, tablets, mobile or home phones, or even televisions. Skype was the most-downloaded free app chosen by iPad users in 2012.

GUESS WHAT? According to its website, Skype says that, at peak times, there are 40 million users online at the same time.

AMAZING APPS
Here are just a handful of the coolest apps out there.

Action Movie FX: Rated Apple's iPhone App of the Year, this app allows you to add incredible special effects—missile strikes, alien death rays, and more—to your own videos. Made by Bad Robot Interactive LLC.

Figure: You can create music instantly by swiping to lay down electronic synthesizer, bass, and percussion tracks. An Apple app, made by Propellerhead Software.

Angry Birds Space: Rated the Number 1 bestselling app in 116 countries, this out-of-this-world version of the popular game takes the Bad Piggies and the Angry Birds to Mars. For Apple or Android. Made by Rovio Entertainment Ltd.

Paper by FiftyThree: This Apple 2012 Design Award winner lets you capture your ideas as sketches, diagrams, notes, or drawings and share them across the Web, all with just a touch screen. An Apple app, made by FiftyThree Inc.

Cards: Create personalized individual greeting cards with your own text and photos. Made by Apple.

Paper Camera: This app can change a photo image into several different kinds of cartoon or painted versions. It can be used while a person is taking a picture or applied to already-taken photos. It works with videos too. Made by JFDP Labs Limited.

ATTENTION, GAMERS!

Here are a few online games and game sites that will let you test your skills, dexterity, and brainpower.

Neopets: Welcome to the virtual pet world Neopia, where you can create your own Neopet and choose from dozens of games to play. As you play, you earn points so you can buy food and fun things for your Neopet. The choices range from puzzles to arcade-type games to word games and more.

There are dozens of Neopets you can choose from to make your own.

GUESS WHAT? In June 2011, Neopets announced that the website had recorded 1 trillion page views since its launch in 1999.

Poptropica: Named one of 2011's 50 Best Websites by TIME magazine, this virtual world has more than 20 "islands." Kids can visit each one to play games, communicate safely with other players, read comics, and more.

Mahjongg Dimensions and Mahjongg Dark Dimensions: These are just two versions of the many mahjongg games online that test your ability to find matching pairs of tiles as quickly as possible. They're great for hand-eye coordination. From Arkadium.

Free Rice: A game from the United Nations World Food Program, Free Rice challenges players to see how good their vocabulary is. The multiple-choice questions in this game get more difficult as you play. For each question you answer correctly, 10 grains of rice get donated to people in countries in need, including Bangladesh, Uganda, and Nepal.

Chicktionary: Seven googly-eyed hens, each with a different letter on her chest, cluck at you while you try to unscramble the letters and spell as many words of three or more letters as possible. You have to hurry, though—the clock is ticking. This game just hatched an app. From Shockwave. App by Blackdot, Inc.

RECYCLING IN STYLE

E-waste from computers and other electronics is the fastest growing type of solid waste. It is important to dispose of electronics properly or to find ways of recycling them. Fourteen-year-old Taylor Burghard has found a unique way to recycle some computer parts. She designs earrings using letters from the keypads of old computers. She got the idea during a computer-recycling drive at her parents' computer store in Columbia, Missouri, as she was popping the keys out of a used keyboard. The earrings spell out words like "LOVE" or phrases like "G-R-8 M-O-M," and Taylor also makes custom designs.

Check out Taylor's work at *tekchickdesigns.com*.

GREAT SITES FOR KIDS

GENERAL

TIME For Kids timeforkids.com
4Kids.org 4kids.org
Smithsonian Education smithsonianeducation.org/students
Brain Pop brainpop.com
Homework Help Yahoo! Kids kids.yahoo.com/learn
Internet Public Library ipl.org/div/kidspace; ipl.org/div/teen
Bio biography.com
Academy of Achievement achievement.org
CNN Student News cnn.com/studentnews/index.html

ART

The Artist's Toolkit artsconnected.org/toolkit
MuseumKids metmuseum.org/Learn/For-Kids
NGA (National Gallery of Art) Kids nga.gov/kids
The Renaissance Connection renaissanceconnection.org

ENVIRONMENT

EekoWorld pbskids.org/eekoworld
National Institute of Environmental Health Sciences (NIEHS) Kids' Pages kids.niehs.nih.gov
National Wildlife Federation nwf.org/kids
EcoKids ecokids.ca/pub/kids_home.cfm
EPA Environmental Kids Club epa.gov/students

GEOGRAPHY

The CIA World Factbook cia.gov/kids-page
State Facts for Students census.gov/schools/facts
50States.com 50states.com
National Geographic Kids kids.nationalgeographic.com

GOVERNMENT, POLITICS, AND HISTORY

Congress for Kids congressforkids.net
KidsGeo.com kidsgeo.com
Kids.gov kids.usa.gov
Inside the White House whitehouse.gov/about/inside-white-house
Library of Congress loc.gov/families
History.com: This Day in History history.com/this-day-in-history
Women in World History womeninworldhistory.com
America's Story americaslibrary.gov
African American World for Kids pbskids.org/aaworld
NativeWeb nativeweb.org/resources/history

HEALTH

KidsHealth kidshealth.org/kid; kidshealth.org/teen
BAM! Body and Mind (CDC) cdc.gov/bam
Kidnetic.com kidnetic.com

LITERATURE, LANGUAGE, AND COMMUNICATION

FCC Kids Zone fcc.gov/cgb/kidszone
Aaron Shepard's Home Page aaronshep.com/index.html
Sylvan Book Adventure bookadventure.com
ABC's of the Writing Process angelfire.com/wi/writingprocess
RIF Reading Planet rif.org/kids/readingplanet.htm
The Blue Book of Grammar and Punctuation grammarbook.com
Shakespeare for Kids (Folger Library) folger.edu

MUSIC, GAMES, AND ENTERTAINMENT

Zoom: By Kids for Kids pbskids.org/zoom/games/index.html
Dallas Symphony Orchestra (DSO) Kids dsokids.com
AGameADay.com agameaday.com
PBS Kids Games pbskids.org/games/index.html
FunBrain.com funbrain.com/kidscenter.html
Club Penguin clubpenguin.com
San Francisco Symphony (SFS) Kids sfskids.org

NATURE

Animal Corner animalcorner.co.uk
Field Trip Earth fieldtripearth.org
Kids' Planet kidsplanet.org
National Park Service nps.gov/webrangers
San Diego Zoo sandiegozoo.org

SCIENCE, TECHNOLOGY, AND MATHEMATICS

The Exploratorium exploratorium.edu
Funology funology.com
Discovery Kids kids.discovery.com
Coolmath.com coolmath.com
Webmath.com webmath.com
Ask Dr. Math mathforum.org/dr.math
NASA nasa.gov/audience/forstudents/index.html
Weather theweatherchannelkids.com
Wonderville wonderville.ca
Franklin Institute fi.edu/learn
Ology amnh.org/explore/ology

SPORTS

SI Kids sikids.com
Major League Baseball mlb.com
Major League Soccer mlssoccer.com
National Basketball Association nba.com
Women's National Basketball Association wnba.com
National Football League nfl.com
National Hockey League nhl.com
United States Olympic Committee teamusa.org

Computers and Communication

FROM TIME FOR KIDS MAGAZINE

Digging into China

By Stephanie Kraus

After being buried for centuries, 110 new warrior statues have been unearthed in Xi'an, China. The statues are part of a collection of more than 7,000 life-size figures of warriors and horses called the Terracotta Army. The clay sculptures were built in 210 B.C. to guard the tomb of China's first emperor, Qin Shihuangdi.

The Terracotta Army statues were discovered by a group of farmers in 1974. While digging a well, the workers found three pits filled with the lifelike figures, which were made of a type of terra-cotta clay. Experts say that long ago, Emperor Shihuangdi ordered the creation of the clay army, along with a 20-square-mile (52 sq km) tomb in which to house it.

For 36 years, 700,000 laborers crafted this underground city. It contains models of palaces and towers, and was protected from intruders by automatically triggered crossbows. The city lay buried for more than 2,000 years.

Chinese archaeologists clean off a recently unearthed warrior statue.

A Worldwide Attraction

Today, people from around the world visit China to see the terra-cotta warriors. What makes the soldiers so special? Each figure was individually carved, so they have different hairstyles, expressions, and facial features. The details make the soldiers appear true to life. Inside the pit, the statues are arranged by military rank. The higher the rank, the taller the statue. The shortest statue is 5 feet 8 inches tall (165 cm). The tallest is 6 feet 6 inches (198 cm). The lower half of each soldier is made of solid clay, while the upper half is hollow. This makes it easier for the figures to remain upright.

The Terracotta Army

THE GREAT WALL

The discovery of Xi'an's 110 new warriors comes after a new finding about the Great Wall of China. An archaeological survey revealed that the Great Wall of China is more than twice as long as previously thought. The wall was originally measured to be 5,500 miles (8,851 km) but is now measured at 13,170 miles (21,195 km) long. Beijing officials plan to open two new sections of the Great Wall and to expand other areas to make room for more tourists.

NATIONS FROM A TO Z

This sample entry for Monaco explains the kinds of information you will find in this section.

This tells the main languages and the official languages (if any) spoken in a nation.

This is the type of currency, or money, used in the nation.

Life expectancy is the number of years a person can expect to live. It's affected by heredity, a person's health and nutrition, the health care and wealth of a nation, and a person's occupation.

This tells the percentage of people who can read and write.

This is an interesting fact about the country.

MONACO
LOCATION: Europe
CAPITAL: Monaco
AREA: 0.77 sq mi (2 sq km)
POPULATION ESTIMATE (2012): 30,510
GOVERNMENT: Constitutional monarchy
LANGUAGES: French (official), English, Italian, Monégasque
MONEY: Euro (formerly French franc)
LIFE EXPECTANCY: 90
LITERACY RATE: 99%

GUESS WHAT? *There are no airports in Monaco.*

AFGHANISTAN
LOCATION: Asia
CAPITAL: Kabul
AREA: 251,737 sq mi (652,230 sq km)
POPULATION ESTIMATE (2012): 30,419,928
GOVERNMENT: Islamic republic
LANGUAGES: Afghan Persian (Dari) and Pashto (both official), Uzbek, Turkmen
MONEY: Afghani
LIFE EXPECTANCY: 50
LITERACY RATE: 28%

GUESS WHAT? *Kite flying is a national sport in Afghanistan. It was banned under Taliban rule but has become popular again since the end of the Taliban's reign in 2001.*

ALBANIA
LOCATION: Europe
CAPITAL: Tirana
AREA: 11,100 sq mi (28,748 sq km)
POPULATION ESTIMATE (2012): 3,002,859
GOVERNMENT: Parliamentary democracy
LANGUAGES: Albanian (Tosk is the official dialect), Greek, others
MONEY: Lek
LIFE EXPECTANCY: 78
LITERACY RATE: 99%

GUESS WHAT? *Unlike in the United States, shaking your head up and down means no in Albania. Moving your head side to side means yes.*

ALGERIA
LOCATION: Africa
CAPITAL: Algiers
AREA: 919,590 sq mi (2,381,741 sq km)
POPULATION ESTIMATE (2012): 37,367,226
GOVERNMENT: Republic
LANGUAGES: Arabic (official), French, Berber dialects
MONEY: Dinar
LIFE EXPECTANCY: 75
LITERACY RATE: 70%

GUESS WHAT? *Because much of Algeria is dry and desertlike, most people live along the coast of the Mediterranean Sea. More than 90% of people living in Algeria live in only 12% of the country.*

ANDORRA
LOCATION: Europe
CAPITAL: Andorra la Vella
AREA: 181 sq mi (468 sq km)
POPULATION ESTIMATE (2012): 85,082
GOVERNMENT: Parliamentary democracy
LANGUAGES: Catalan (official), French, Castilian, Portuguese
MONEY: Euro (formerly French franc and Spanish peseta)
LIFE EXPECTANCY: 83
LITERACY RATE: 100%

GUESS WHAT? *Andorra is a small country that makes most of its money from tourism. It does not have a regular standing army.*

Countries

ANGOLA

LOCATION: Africa
CAPITAL: Luanda
AREA: 481,350 sq mi
(1,246,700 sq km)
POPULATION ESTIMATE (2012):
18,056,072
GOVERNMENT: Republic
LANGUAGES: Portuguese (official),
Bantu, other African languages
MONEY: Kwanza
LIFE EXPECTANCY: 55
LITERACY RATE: 70%

GUESS WHAT? *Luanda was once known as the Paris of Africa because of its charming architecture and its rich art and culture scene.*

ANTIGUA AND BARBUDA

LOCATION: Caribbean
CAPITAL: Saint John's
AREA: 171 sq mi (443 sq km)
POPULATION ESTIMATE (2012): 89,018
GOVERNMENT: Constitutional
monarchy with a parliamentary
system of government
LANGUAGES: English (official),
local dialects
MONEY: East Caribbean dollar
LIFE EXPECTANCY: 76
LITERACY RATE: 86%

GUESS WHAT? *It is against the law for any nonmilitary personnel to wear camouflage clothing in Antigua and Barbuda.*

ARGENTINA

LOCATION: South America
CAPITAL: Buenos Aires
AREA: 1,073,518 sq mi
(2,780,400 sq km)
POPULATION ESTIMATE (2012):
42,192,494
GOVERNMENT: Republic
LANGUAGES: Spanish (official),
Italian, English, German,
French, native languages
MONEY: Argentine peso
LIFE EXPECTANCY: 77
LITERACY RATE: 98%

GUESS WHAT? *A new species of dinosaur was recently unearthed in Argentina. It is currently being called Bicentenaria Argentina. Scientists believe the dinosaur was a carnivore due to the shape of its teeth and claws.*

ARMENIA

LOCATION: Asia
CAPITAL: Yerevan
AREA: 11,484 sq mi
(29,743 sq km)
POPULATION ESTIMATE (2012):
2,970,495
GOVERNMENT: Republic
LANGUAGES: Armenian (official),
others
MONEY: Dram
LIFE EXPECTANCY: 73
LITERACY RATE: 100%

GUESS WHAT? *There are 38 letters in the Armenian alphabet.*

AUSTRALIA

LOCATION: Oceania, between the
Pacific Ocean and Indian Ocean
CAPITAL: Canberra
AREA: 2,988,902 sq mi
(7,741,220 sq km)
POPULATION ESTIMATE (2012):
22,015,576
GOVERNMENT: Federal
parliamentary democracy
LANGUAGE: English
MONEY: Australian dollar
LIFE EXPECTANCY: 82
LITERACY RATE: 99%

GUESS WHAT? *In 1851, gold deposits were found in Australia, setting off a gold rush. Miners flocked to the country. As a result, the population skyrocketed from 430,000 in 1851 to 1.7 million in 1871.*

AUSTRIA

LOCATION: Europe
CAPITAL: Vienna
AREA: 32,382 sq mi
(83,871 sq km)
POPULATION ESTIMATE (2012):
8,219,743
GOVERNMENT: Federal republic
LANGUAGES: German (official),
Croatian (official in Burgenland),
Turkish, Serbian, others
MONEY: Euro (formerly schilling)
LIFE EXPECTANCY: 80
LITERACY RATE: 98%

GUESS WHAT? *The first Winter Youth Olympic Games were held in Innsbruck, Austria, in 2012. Innsbruck previously hosted the 1964 and 1976 Winter Olympics, making it the first city to host three Olympic events.*

AZERBAIJAN

LOCATION: Asia
CAPITAL: Baku
AREA: 33,400 sq mi (86,600 sq km)
POPULATION ESTIMATE (2012): 9,493,600
GOVERNMENT: Republic
LANGUAGES: Azerbaijani, Lezgi, Russian, Armenian, others
MONEY: Azerbaijani manat
LIFE EXPECTANCY: 71
LITERACY RATE: 100%

GUESS WHAT? *The Azikh Cave in southwestern Azerbaijan served as a shelter for ancient human ancestors during the Stone Age.*

BAHAMAS

LOCATION: Caribbean
CAPITAL: Nassau
AREA: 5,359 sq mi (13,880 sq km)
POPULATION ESTIMATE (2012): 316,182
GOVERNMENT: Constitutional parliamentary democracy
LANGUAGES: English (official), Creole
MONEY: Bahamian dollar
LIFE EXPECTANCY: 71
LITERACY RATE: 96%

GUESS WHAT? *During the late 1600s and early 1700s, many infamous pirates used the Bahamas as a base between voyages. The many islands and inlets of the Bahamas provided excellent hiding places.*

BAHRAIN

LOCATION: Middle East
CAPITAL: Manama
AREA: 293 sq mi (760 sq km)
POPULATION ESTIMATE (2012): 1,248,348
GOVERNMENT: Constitutional monarchy
LANGUAGES: Arabic (official), English, Farsi, Urdu
MONEY: Bahraini dinar
LIFE EXPECTANCY: 78
LITERACY RATE: 95%

GUESS WHAT? *Bahrain was the first of the Gulf states, or countries bordering the Persian Gulf, to discover crude oil and build a refinery.*

BANGLADESH

LOCATION: Asia
CAPITAL: Dhaka
AREA: 55,598 sq mi (143,998 sq km)
POPULATION ESTIMATE (2012): 161,083,804
GOVERNMENT: Parliamentary democracy
LANGUAGES: Bangla (official), English
MONEY: Taka
LIFE EXPECTANCY: 70
LITERACY RATE: 57%

GUESS WHAT? *The majority of the Sundarbans, the largest mangrove forest in the world, is located in Bangladesh. It is home to many endangered animals, including the Bengal tiger—the national animal of Bangladesh.*

BARBADOS

LOCATION: Caribbean
CAPITAL: Bridgetown
AREA: 166 sq mi (430 sq km)
POPULATION ESTIMATE (2012): 287,733
GOVERNMENT: Parliamentary democracy
LANGUAGE: English
MONEY: Barbadian dollar
LIFE EXPECTANCY: 75
LITERACY RATE: 100%

GUESS WHAT? *In Barbados, it is considered good luck if a mongoose crosses in front of you.*

BELARUS

LOCATION: Europe
CAPITAL: Minsk
AREA: 80,154 sq mi (207,600 sq km)
POPULATION ESTIMATE (2012): 9,643,566
GOVERNMENT: Republic in name but actually a dictatorship
LANGUAGES: Belarusian and Russian (both official), others
MONEY: Belarusian ruble
LIFE EXPECTANCY: 71
LITERACY RATE: 100%

GUESS WHAT? *The movement of glaciers in Belarus has helped to create many bodies of water. There are about 11,000 lakes and 20,000 rivers and creeks in the country.*

Countries

BELGIUM

LOCATION: Europe
CAPITAL: Brussels
AREA: 11,787 sq mi (30,528 sq km)
POPULATION ESTIMATE (2012): 10,438,353
GOVERNMENT: Federal parliamentary democracy under a constitutional monarchy
LANGUAGES: Dutch, French, and German (all official)
MONEY: Euro (formerly Belgian franc)
LIFE EXPECTANCY: 80
LITERACY RATE: 99%

GUESS WHAT? *A Neanderthal is an extinct early human. The first Neanderthal fossils were discovered in Engis, Belgium, in 1829.*

BELIZE

LOCATION: Central America
CAPITAL: Belmopan
AREA: 8,867 sq mi (22,966 sq km)
POPULATION ESTIMATE (2012): 327,719
GOVERNMENT: Parliamentary democracy
LANGUAGES: English (official), Spanish, Creole, Mayan dialects, others
MONEY: Belizean dollar
LIFE EXPECTANCY: 68
LITERACY RATE: 77%

GUESS WHAT? *Belize is home to the Cockscomb Basin Wildlife Sanctuary, the world's first jaguar preserve.*

BENIN

LOCATION: Africa
CAPITAL: Porto-Novo
AREA: 43,483 sq mi (112,622 sq km)
POPULATION ESTIMATE (2012): 9,598,787
GOVERNMENT: Republic
LANGUAGES: French (official), Fon, Yoruba, tribal languages
MONEY: CFA franc
LIFE EXPECTANCY: 60
LITERACY RATE: 42%

GUESS WHAT? *Porto-Novo is the name given to the capital by Portuguese traders in Benin. The city also goes by two African names, Hogbonou and Adjatche.*

BHUTAN

LOCATION: Asia
CAPITAL: Thimphu
AREA: 14,824 sq mi (38,394 sq km)
POPULATION ESTIMATE (2012): 716,896
GOVERNMENT: Constitutional monarchy
LANGUAGES: Dzongkha (official), Sharchhopka, Lhotshamkha, others
MONEY: Ngultrum
LIFE EXPECTANCY: 68
LITERACY RATE: 47%

GUESS WHAT? *In 2004, Bhutan became the first country in the world to ban the sale of tobacco.*

BOLIVIA

LOCATION: South America
CAPITALS: La Paz (seat of government), Sucre (legislative capital)
AREA: 424,162 sq mi (1,098,581 sq km)
POPULATION ESTIMATE (2012): 10,290,003
GOVERNMENT: Republic
LANGUAGES: Spanish, Quechua, and Aymara (all official)
MONEY: Boliviano
LIFE EXPECTANCY: 68
LITERACY RATE: 87%

GUESS WHAT? *Bolivia was named after Simón Bolívar, a Venezuelan revolutionary who helped South American countries such as Colombia, Peru, Ecuador, and Bolivia gain independence from Spain.*

BOSNIA AND HERZEGOVINA

LOCATION: Europe
CAPITAL: Sarajevo
AREA: 19,767 sq mi (51,197 sq km)
POPULATION ESTIMATE (2012): 3,879,296
GOVERNMENT: Emerging federal democratic republic
LANGUAGES: Bosnian and Croatian (both official), Serbian
MONEY: Convertible mark
LIFE EXPECTANCY: 79
LITERACY RATE: 98%

GUESS WHAT? *An estimated 60,000 stecci, large, medieval tombstones, are scattered throughout the country. They are decorated with symbols. The oldest stecci are believed to be from the 12th century.*

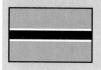

BOTSWANA

LOCATION: Africa
CAPITAL: Gaborone
AREA: 224,607 sq mi
(581,730 sq km)
POPULATION ESTIMATE (2012):
2,098,018
GOVERNMENT: Parliamentary
republic
LANGUAGES: English (official),
Setswana, Kalanga, Sekgalagadi
MONEY: Pula
LIFE EXPECTANCY: 56
LITERACY RATE: 85%

GUESS WHAT? *Jwaneng Mine, in Botswana, is the richest diamond mine in the world.*

BRAZIL

LOCATION: South America
CAPITAL: Brasília
AREA: 3,287,612 sq mi
(8,514,877 sq km)
POPULATION ESTIMATE (2012):
199,321,413
GOVERNMENT: Federal republic
LANGUAGES: Portuguese (official),
Spanish, German, Italian,
Japanese, English, various
Amerindian languages
MONEY: Real
LIFE EXPECTANCY: 73
LITERACY RATE: 89%

GUESS WHAT? *Brazil's soccer team has won the FIFA World Cup five times since the tournament began in 1930. The 2014 FIFA World Cup will be held in Brazil.*

BRUNEI

LOCATION: Asia
CAPITAL: Bandar Seri Begawan
AREA: 2,226 sq mi
(5,765 sq km)
POPULATION ESTIMATE (2012):
408,786
GOVERNMENT: Constitutional
sultanate
LANGUAGES: Malay (official),
English, Chinese
MONEY: Bruneian dollar
LIFE EXPECTANCY: 76
LITERACY RATE: 93%

GUESS WHAT? *Brunei is a single, unified country, but its land is separated into two parts by Malaysia.*

BULGARIA

LOCATION: Europe
CAPITAL: Sofia
AREA: 42,811 sq mi
(110,879 sq km)
POPULATION ESTIMATE (2012):
7,037,935
GOVERNMENT: Parliamentary
democracy
LANGUAGES: Bulgarian (official),
Turkish, Roma, others
MONEY: Lev
LIFE EXPECTANCY: 74
LITERACY RATE: 98%

GUESS WHAT? *Two well-known dishes from Bulgaria are tarator, which is a cold cucumber-and-yogurt soup, and cheverme, an entire lamb roasted on a spit.*

BURKINA FASO

LOCATION: Africa
CAPITAL: Ouagadougou
AREA: 105,870 sq mi
(274,200 sq km)
POPULATION ESTIMATE (2012):
17,275,115
GOVERNMENT: Parliamentary
republic
LANGUAGES: French (official),
native African languages
MONEY: CFA franc
LIFE EXPECTANCY: 54
LITERACY RATE: 22%

GUESS WHAT? *Drums are very important in Burkina Faso. They are used to signal a return from the fields, share news, accompany storytelling and ceremonial dancing, and more.*

BURUNDI

LOCATION: Africa
CAPITAL: Bujumbura
AREA: 10,745 sq mi
(27,830 sq km)
POPULATION ESTIMATE (2012):
10,557,259
GOVERNMENT: Republic
LANGUAGES: Kirundi and French
(both official), Swahili
MONEY: Burundi franc
LIFE EXPECTANCY: 59
LITERACY RATE: 67%

GUESS WHAT? *Burundi is landlocked, which means it does not have access to the ocean or sea. But its southwest border falls on Lake Tanganyika, one of the largest lakes in the world.*

Countries

CAMBODIA

LOCATION: Asia
CAPITAL: Phnom Penh
AREA: 69,900 sq mi
(181,035 sq km)
POPULATION ESTIMATE (2012):
14,952,665
GOVERNMENT: Multiparty
democracy under a
constitutional monarchy
LANGUAGES: Khmer (official),
French, English
MONEY: Riel
LIFE EXPECTANCY: 63
LITERACY RATE: 78%

GUESS WHAT? *Angkor Wat, an enormous 12th-century Hindu temple complex, is on the Cambodian flag. Afghanistan is the only other country to show a building on its flag.*

CAMEROON

LOCATION: Africa
CAPITAL: Yaoundé
AREA: 183,567 sq mi
(475,440 sq km)
POPULATION ESTIMATE (2012):
20,129,878
GOVERNMENT: Republic
LANGUAGES: French and
English (both official),
various African languages
MONEY: CFA franc
LIFE EXPECTANCY: 55
LITERACY RATE: 76%

GUESS WHAT? *Cameroon is home to the largest frogs in the world. Goliath frogs measure up to 12.5 inches (32 cm) in length and weigh up to 7.2 pounds (3.3 kg).*

CANADA

LOCATION: North America
CAPITAL: Ottawa
AREA: 3,855,081 sq mi
(9,984,670 sq km)
POPULATION ESTIMATE (2012):
34,300,083
GOVERNMENT: Parliamentary
democracy, federation, and
constitutional monarchy
LANGUAGES: English and French
(both official)
MONEY: Canadian dollar
LIFE EXPECTANCY: 81
LITERACY RATE: 99%

GUESS WHAT? *Canada is the second-largest country in the world by landmass.*

CAPE VERDE

LOCATION: Africa
CAPITAL: Praia
AREA: 1,557 sq mi (4,033 sq km)
POPULATION ESTIMATE (2012): 523,568
GOVERNMENT: Republic
LANGUAGES: Portuguese, Crioulo
MONEY: Cape Verdean escudo
LIFE EXPECTANCY: 71
LITERACY RATE: 84%

GUESS WHAT? *Morna, a genre of music similar to the blues, is the national music of Cape Verde. It is usually accompanied by a stringed instrument like a violin, viola, or Portuguese guitar.*

CENTRAL AFRICAN REPUBLIC

LOCATION: Africa
CAPITAL: Bangui
AREA: 240,534 sq mi
(622,984 sq km)
POPULATION ESTIMATE (2012):
5,057,208
GOVERNMENT: Republic
LANGUAGES: French (official),
Sangho, other African
languages
MONEY: CFA franc
LIFE EXPECTANCY: 50
LITERACY RATE: 56%

GUESS WHAT? *Endangered African forest elephants can be found in the Central African Republic.*

CHAD

LOCATION: Africa
CAPITAL: N'Djamena
AREA: 495,752 sq mi
(1,284,000 sq km)
POPULATION ESTIMATE (2012):
10,975,648
GOVERNMENT: Republic
LANGUAGES: French and Arabic
(both official), Sara, others
MONEY: CFA franc
LIFE EXPECTANCY: 49
LITERACY RATE: 35%

GUESS WHAT? *After decades of war and conflict, a single movie theater reopened in Chad in 2011. The Normandy cinema had been closed for 20 years.*

CHILE

LOCATION: South America
CAPITAL: Santiago
AREA: 291,933 sq mi
(756,102 sq km)
POPULATION ESTIMATE (2012):
17,067,369
GOVERNMENT: Republic
LANGUAGES: Spanish (official),
Mapudungun, German, English
MONEY: Chilean peso
LIFE EXPECTANCY: 78
LITERACY RATE: 96%

GUESS WHAT? *The world's largest outdoor swimming pool is at Chile's San Alfonso del Mar Resort. It is 3,323 feet (1,013 m) long, 115 feet (35 m) deep, and holds 66 million gallons (250 million L) of water.*

CHINA

LOCATION: Asia
CAPITAL: Beijing
AREA: 3,705,386 sq mi
(9,596,961 sq km)
POPULATION ESTIMATE (2012):
1,343,239,923
GOVERNMENT: Communist state
LANGUAGES: Chinese (Mandarin;
official), Yue (Cantonese), local
dialects
MONEY: Renminbi yuan
LIFE EXPECTANCY: 75
LITERACY RATE: 92%

GUESS WHAT? *The first recorded use of toilet paper occurred in China around 851 A.D.*

COLOMBIA

LOCATION: South America
CAPITAL: Bogotá
AREA: 439,735 sq mi
(1,138,910 sq km)
POPULATION ESTIMATE (2012):
45,239,079
GOVERNMENT: Republic
LANGUAGE: Spanish
MONEY: Colombian peso
LIFE EXPECTANCY: 75
LITERACY RATE: 90%

GUESS WHAT? *Colombia was the first country in South America to form a constitutional government.*

COMOROS

LOCATION: Africa
CAPITAL: Moroni
AREA: 863 sq mi (2,235 sq km)
POPULATION ESTIMATE (2012): 737,284
GOVERNMENT: Republic
LANGUAGES: French and Arabic
(both official), Shikomoro
MONEY: Comoran franc
LIFE EXPECTANCY: 63
LITERACY RATE: 75%

GUESS WHAT? *Comoros is made up of four main islands and several smaller islets. Before the opening of Egypt's Suez Canal in 1869, the islands were a major stopover point for ships traveling from Europe to the Indian Ocean.*

CONGO, DEMOCRATIC REPUBLIC OF THE

LOCATION: Africa
CAPITAL: Kinshasa
AREA: 905,355 sq mi
(2,344,858 sq km)
POPULATION ESTIMATE (2012):
73,599,190
GOVERNMENT: Republic
LANGUAGES: French (official),
Lingala, Kingwana, Kikongo,
Tshiluba
MONEY: Congolese franc
LIFE EXPECTANCY: 56
LITERACY RATE: 67%

GUESS WHAT? *Kinshasa is the third-largest city in Africa. Nearly 10 million people live in the 3,848-square-mile (9,966 sq km) city.*

CONGO, REPUBLIC OF THE

LOCATION: Africa
CAPITAL: Brazzaville
AREA: 132,046 sq mi
(342,000 sq km)
POPULATION ESTIMATE (2012):
4,366,266
GOVERNMENT: Republic
LANGUAGES: French (official),
Lingala, Monokutuba,
Kikongo, others
MONEY: CFA franc
LIFE EXPECTANCY: 55
LITERACY RATE: 84%

GUESS WHAT? *Cassava, a woody shrub with an edible root, is an important crop in the Republic of the Congo.*

COSTA RICA

LOCATION: Central America
CAPITAL: San José
AREA: 19,730 sq mi (51,100 sq km)
POPULATION ESTIMATE (2012): 4,636,348
GOVERNMENT: Democratic republic
LANGUAGES: Spanish (official), English
MONEY: Costa Rican colón
LIFE EXPECTANCY: 78
LITERACY RATE: 95%

GUESS WHAT? *The Costa Rican national anthem is played on most of the country's radio stations every day at 7 a.m.*

COTE D'IVOIRE (IVORY COAST)

LOCATION: Africa
CAPITAL: Yamoussoukro
AREA: 124,502 sq mi (322,463 sq km)
POPULATION ESTIMATE (2012): 21,952,093
GOVERNMENT: Republic
LANGUAGES: French (official), Dioula and many other native dialects
MONEY: CFA franc
LIFE EXPECTANCY: 57
LITERACY RATE: 56%

GUESS WHAT? *Côte d'Ivoire is the world's largest exporter of cocoa beans. Cocoa beans are used to make chocolate.*

CROATIA

LOCATION: Europe
CAPITAL: Zagreb
AREA: 21,851 sq mi (56,594 sq km)
POPULATION ESTIMATE (2012): 4,480,043
GOVERNMENT: Presidential parliamentary democracy
LANGUAGE: Croatian
MONEY: Kuna
LIFE EXPECTANCY: 76
LITERACY RATE: 99%

GUESS WHAT? *The Dalmatian dog breed is named after Croatia's mountainous Dalmatian Coast, which runs along the Adriatic Sea.*

CUBA

LOCATION: Caribbean
CAPITAL: Havana
AREA: 42,803 sq mi (110,860 sq km)
POPULATION ESTIMATE (2012): 11,075,244
GOVERNMENT: Communist state
LANGUAGE: Spanish
MONEY: Cuban peso
LIFE EXPECTANCY: 78
LITERACY RATE: 100%

GUESS WHAT? *In Cuba, there is one doctor for every 150 people. That's the highest ratio of doctors to patients in the world.*

CYPRUS

LOCATION: Middle East
CAPITAL: Nicosia
AREA: 3,572 sq mi (9,251 sq km)
POPULATION ESTIMATE (2012): 1,138,071
GOVERNMENT: Republic
LANGUAGES: Greek and Turkish (both official), English
MONEY: Euro (formerly Cyprus pound)
LIFE EXPECTANCY: 78
LITERACY RATE: 98%

GUESS WHAT? *Archaeologists found a well-preserved cat skeleton in Cyprus that was 9,500 years old. That might be the earliest evidence ever uncovered showing that people kept cats as pets a long, long time ago.*

CZECH REPUBLIC

LOCATION: Europe
CAPITAL: Prague
AREA: 30,451 sq mi (78,867 sq km)
POPULATION ESTIMATE (2012): 10,177,300
GOVERNMENT: Parliamentary democracy
LANGUAGES: Czech, Slovak, others
MONEY: Koruna
LIFE EXPECTANCY: 77
LITERACY RATE: 99%

GUESS WHAT? *The word robot comes from the play R.U.R., by Czech playwright Karel Capek. R.U.R. stands for Rossum's Universal Robots.*

DENMARK

LOCATION: Europe
CAPITAL: Copenhagen
AREA: 16,639 sq mi (43,094 sq km)
POPULATION ESTIMATE (2012): 5,543,453
GOVERNMENT: Constitutional monarchy
LANGUAGES: Danish, Faroese, Greenlandic, German
MONEY: Krone
LIFE EXPECTANCY: 79
LITERACY RATE: 99%

GUESS WHAT? *The popular building toys, Lego bricks, are made in Denmark. In 1939, the first Lego factory had only 10 employees. Today, the company employs about 10,000 people.*

DJIBOUTI

LOCATION: Africa
CAPITAL: Djibouti
AREA: 8,958 sq mi (23,200 sq km)
POPULATION ESTIMATE (2012): 774,389
GOVERNMENT: Republic
LANGUAGES: Arabic and French (both official), Somali, Afar
MONEY: Djiboutian franc
LIFE EXPECTANCY: 62
LITERACY RATE: 68%

GUESS WHAT? *The only U.S. military base in sub-Saharan Africa (which is the portion of the continent to the south of the enormous Sahara desert) is in Djibouti.*

DOMINICA

LOCATION: Caribbean
CAPITAL: Roseau
AREA: 290 sq mi (751 sq km)
POPULATION ESTIMATE (2012): 73,126
GOVERNMENT: Parliamentary democracy
LANGUAGES: English (official), French patois
MONEY: East Caribbean dollar
LIFE EXPECTANCY: 76
LITERACY RATE: 94%

GUESS WHAT? *Dominica is home to about 3,000 Carib Indians, the only pre-Columbian population remaining in the eastern Caribbean. That means that their ancestors lived in the region before the arrival of Christopher Columbus in the New World in 1492.*

DOMINICAN REPUBLIC

LOCATION: Caribbean
CAPITAL: Santo Domingo
AREA: 18,792 sq mi (48,670 sq km)
POPULATION ESTIMATE (2012): 10,088,598
GOVERNMENT: Democratic republic
LANGUAGE: Spanish
MONEY: Dominican peso
LIFE EXPECTANCY: 77
LITERACY RATE: 87%

GUESS WHAT? *The Dominican Republic takes up about two-thirds of the island of Hispaniola. The rest of the island is Haiti.*

EAST TIMOR (TIMOR-LESTE)

LOCATION: Asia
CAPITAL: Dili
AREA: 5,743 sq mi (14,874 sq km)
POPULATION ESTIMATE (2012): 1,143,667
GOVERNMENT: Republic
LANGUAGES: Tetum and Portuguese (both official), Indonesian, English
MONEY: U.S. dollar
LIFE EXPECTANCY: 68
LITERACY RATE: 59%

GUESS WHAT? *East Timor became the first new nation of the 21st century when it was internationally recognized as an independent state on May 20, 2002.*

ECUADOR

LOCATION: South America
CAPITAL: Quito
AREA: 109,484 sq mi (283,561 sq km)
POPULATION ESTIMATE (2012): 15,223,680
GOVERNMENT: Republic
LANGUAGES: Spanish (official), Quechua, other Amerindian languages
MONEY: U.S. dollar
LIFE EXPECTANCY: 76
LITERACY RATE: 93%

GUESS WHAT? *The scaly-eyed gecko, a new species of gecko found in Ecuador, is so tiny it can rest on a pencil eraser.*

Countries

EGYPT

LOCATION: Africa
CAPITAL: Cairo
AREA: 386,660 sq mi
(1,001,450 sq km)
POPULATION ESTIMATE (2012):
83,688,164
GOVERNMENT: Republic
LANGUAGE: Arabic
MONEY: Egyptian pound
LIFE EXPECTANCY: 73
LITERACY RATE: 72%

GUESS WHAT? *The Nile River Valley accounts for less than 4% of the country's area. But that's where almost 99% of the population lives.*

EL SALVADOR

LOCATION: Central America
CAPITAL: San Salvador
AREA: 8,124 sq mi (21,041 sq km)
POPULATION ESTIMATE (2012):
6,090,646
GOVERNMENT: Republic
LANGUAGES: Spanish (official),
Nahua
MONEY: U.S. dollar
LIFE EXPECTANCY: 74
LITERACY RATE: 81%

GUESS WHAT? *Since the end of its civil war in 1992, El Salvador has become a major destination for surfers from all over the world.*

EQUATORIAL GUINEA

LOCATION: Africa
CAPITAL: Malabo
AREA: 10,830 sq mi
(28,051 sq km)
POPULATION ESTIMATE (2012): 685,991
GOVERNMENT: Republic
LANGUAGES: Spanish and French
(both official), Fang, Bubi
MONEY: CFA franc
LIFE EXPECTANCY: 63
LITERACY RATE: 94%

GUESS WHAT? *Djibloho, a new city, is being built in Equatorial Guinea. When finished, it will serve as the nation's new capital.*

ERITREA

LOCATION: Africa
CAPITAL: Asmara
AREA: 45,406 sq mi
(117,600 sq km)
POPULATION ESTIMATE (2012):
6,086,495
GOVERNMENT: Transitional
LANGUAGES: Tigrinya, Arabic, and
English (all official), Tigre,
Kunama, Afar, others
MONEY: Nakfa
LIFE EXPECTANCY: 63
LITERACY RATE: 68%

GUESS WHAT? *Artifacts from what may be the oldest agricultural settlement in Africa were found in present-day Eritrea. The tools, jewelry, and burial chambers give clues as to what life was like 3,000 years ago.*

ESTONIA

LOCATION: Europe
CAPITAL: Tallinn
AREA: 17,463 sq mi
(45,228 sq km)
POPULATION ESTIMATE (2012):
1,274,709
GOVERNMENT: Parliamentary
republic
LANGUAGES: Estonian (official),
Russian
MONEY: Euro (formerly kroon)
LIFE EXPECTANCY: 74
LITERACY RATE: 100%

GUESS WHAT? *In 2005, Estonia became the first country to allow online voting for a national political election.*

ETHIOPIA

LOCATION: Africa
CAPITAL: Addis Ababa
AREA: 426,373 sq mi
(1,104,300 sq km)
POPULATION ESTIMATE (2012):
91,195,675
GOVERNMENT: Federal republic
LANGUAGES: Amarigna, English,
and Arabic (all official),
Oromigna and Tigrigna (both
regional official), others
MONEY: Birr
LIFE EXPECTANCY: 57
LITERACY RATE: 43%

GUESS WHAT? *Many animal species in Ethiopia live naturally only in Ethiopia. They include the Ethiopian wolf, the gelada baboon, the Abyssinian catbird, and the walia ibex.*

FIJI

LOCATION: Oceania
CAPITAL: Suva
AREA: 7,057 sq mi (18,274 sq km)
POPULATION ESTIMATE (2012): 890,057
GOVERNMENT: Republic
LANGUAGES: Fijian and English (both official), Hindustani
MONEY: Fijian dollar
LIFE EXPECTANCY: 72
LITERACY RATE: 94%

GUESS WHAT? *Fiji is made up of about 330 islands. Approximately 110 of them are inhabited. Two islands, Viti Levu and Vanua Levu, make up 85% of the landmass of Fiji.*

FINLAND

LOCATION: Europe
CAPITAL: Helsinki
AREA: 130,559 sq mi (338,145 sq km)
POPULATION ESTIMATE (2012): 5,262,930
GOVERNMENT: Republic
LANGUAGES: Finnish and Swedish (both official), others
MONEY: Euro (formerly markka)
LIFE EXPECTANCY: 79
LITERACY RATE: 100%

GUESS WHAT? *Avantouinti, or ice swimming, is a popular activity in Finland. Often, a chunk of ice is cut off the top of a frozen lake or river, revealing an area that people can swim in. Some Finns believe it is the secret to good health.*

FRANCE

LOCATION: Europe
CAPITAL: Paris
AREA: 248,573 sq mi (643,801 sq km)
POPULATION ESTIMATE (2012): 65,630,692
GOVERNMENT: Republic
LANGUAGE: French
MONEY: Euro (formerly franc)
LIFE EXPECTANCY: 81
LITERACY RATE: 99%

GUESS WHAT? *In most French towns, there is a street named after Victor Hugo, a famous French poet, novelist, and playwright (see page 154).*

GABON

LOCATION: Africa
CAPITAL: Libreville
AREA: 103,346 sq mi (267,667 sq km)
POPULATION ESTIMATE (2012): 1,608,321
GOVERNMENT: Republic
LANGUAGES: French (official), Fang, Myene, Nzebi, Bapounou/Eschira, Bandjabi
MONEY: CFA franc
LIFE EXPECTANCY: 52
LITERACY RATE: 88%

GUESS WHAT? *In 2012, Anthony Obame became the first person from Gabon to win an Olympic medal, when he won the silver medal in tae kwon do at the Summer Games.*

THE GAMBIA

LOCATION: Africa
CAPITAL: Banjul
AREA: 4,361 sq mi (11,295 sq km)
POPULATION ESTIMATE (2012): 1,840,454
GOVERNMENT: Republic
LANGUAGES: English (official), Mandinka, Wolof, Fula, others
MONEY: Dalasi
LIFE EXPECTANCY: 64
LITERACY RATE: 50%

GUESS WHAT? *The Gambia hosts a project every year called Wide Open Walls, in which street artists from around the world spend two weeks painting murals on walls in villages around the country.*

GEORGIA

LOCATION: Asia
CAPITAL: Tbilisi
AREA: 26,911 sq mi (69,700 sq km)
POPULATION ESTIMATE (2012): 4,570,934
GOVERNMENT: Republic
LANGUAGES: Georgian (official), Russian, Armenian, Azeri
MONEY: Lari
LIFE EXPECTANCY: 77
LITERACY RATE: 100%

GUESS WHAT? *Georgia is home to the Krubera Cave (also known as the Voronya Cave), the deepest cave in the world. It has a depth of 1.4 miles (2.2 km).*

GERMANY

LOCATION: Europe
CAPITAL: Berlin
AREA: 137,847 sq mi
(357,022 sq km)
POPULATION ESTIMATE (2012):
81,305,856
GOVERNMENT: Federal republic
LANGUAGE: German
MONEY: Euro (formerly
deutsche mark)
LIFE EXPECTANCY: 80
LITERACY RATE: 99%

GUESS WHAT? *During World War II, bombings destroyed many of Berlin's historic structures.*

GHANA

LOCATION: Africa
CAPITAL: Accra
AREA: 92,098 sq mi
(238,533 sq km)
POPULATION ESTIMATE (2012):
24,652,402
GOVERNMENT: Constitutional
democracy
LANGUAGES: English (official),
Ashanti, Ewe, Fante, Boron,
Dagomba, Dangme, others
MONEY: Cedi
LIFE EXPECTANCY: 61
LITERACY RATE: 72%

GUESS WHAT? *Fufu is a popular dish in Ghana. The meal consists of a sticky ball of pounded cassava, plantains, or yams in a bowl of soup.*

GREECE

LOCATION: Europe
CAPITAL: Athens
AREA: 50,949 sq mi
(131,957 sq km)
POPULATION ESTIMATE (2012):
10,767,827
GOVERNMENT: Parliamentary
republic
LANGUAGE: Greek
MONEY: Euro (formerly drachma)
LIFE EXPECTANCY: 80
LITERACY RATE: 96%

GUESS WHAT? *Many doors, window frames, and church domes in Greece are painted a shade of blue called kyanos. Some ancient Greeks believed that the color helped to keep evil away.*

GRENADA

LOCATION: Caribbean
CAPITAL: Saint George's
AREA: 133 sq mi (344 sq km)
POPULATION ESTIMATE (2012): 109,011
GOVERNMENT: Parliamentary
democracy
LANGUAGES: English (official),
French patois
MONEY: East Caribbean dollar
LIFE EXPECTANCY: 73
LITERACY RATE: 96%

GUESS WHAT? *The national bird of Grenada, the Grenada dove, is currently on the critically endangered list. The bird is found only in Grenada, and scientists estimate that there are fewer than 100 left.*

GUATEMALA

LOCATION: Central America
CAPITAL: Guatemala City
AREA: 42,042 sq mi
(108,889 sq km)
POPULATION ESTIMATE (2012):
14,099,032
GOVERNMENT: Constitutional
democratic republic
LANGUAGES: Spanish, Amerindian
languages
MONEY: Quetzal
LIFE EXPECTANCY: 71
LITERACY RATE: 69%

GUESS WHAT? *Many of the buildings in Antigua, a city in southern Guatemala, were built in the 17th and 18th centuries. They are great examples of Spanish colonial architecture.*

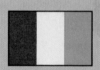

GUINEA

LOCATION: Africa
CAPITAL: Conakry
AREA: 94,926 sq mi
(245,857 sq km)
POPULATION ESTIMATE (2012):
10,884,958
GOVERNMENT: Republic
LANGUAGES: French (official),
native languages
MONEY: Guinean franc
LIFE EXPECTANCY: 59
LITERACY RATE: 41%

GUESS WHAT? *Guinea is one of the world's top bauxite producers. Bauxite is the main source of aluminum, the metal used to make cars, baseball bats, electronics, and more.*

GUINEA-BISSAU

LOCATION: Africa
CAPITAL: Bissau
AREA: 13,948 sq mi
(36,125 sq km)
POPULATION ESTIMATE (2012):
1,628,603
GOVERNMENT: Republic
LANGUAGES: Portuguese (official),
Crioulo, African languages
MONEY: CFA franc
LIFE EXPECTANCY: 49
LITERACY RATE: 54%

GUESS WHAT? *Although the official language of Guinea-Bissau is Portuguese, the majority of the population actually speaks Crioulo, a mixture of Portuguese and a local language.*

GUYANA

LOCATION: South America
CAPITAL: Georgetown
AREA: 83,000 sq mi
(214,969 sq km)
POPULATION ESTIMATE (2012): 741,908
GOVERNMENT: Republic
LANGUAGES: English (official),
Amerindian dialects, Creole,
Caribbean Hindustani, Urdu
MONEY: Guyanese dollar
LIFE EXPECTANCY: 67
LITERACY RATE: 92%

GUESS WHAT? *Guyana is the only English-speaking country in South America.*

HAITI

LOCATION: Caribbean
CAPITAL: Port-au-Prince
AREA: 10,714 sq mi
(27,750 sq km)
POPULATION ESTIMATE (2012):
9,801,664
GOVERNMENT: Republic
LANGUAGES: Creole and French
(both official)
MONEY: Gourde
LIFE EXPECTANCY: 63
LITERACY RATE: 53%

GUESS WHAT? *In the late 1700s, Toussaint Louverture led more than half a million slaves in a revolt that resulted in the country declaring its independence from France in 1804.*

HONDURAS

LOCATION: Central America
CAPITAL: Tegucigalpa
AREA: 43,278 sq mi
(112,090 sq km)
POPULATION ESTIMATE (2012):
8,296,693
GOVERNMENT: Democratic
constitutional republic
LANGUAGES: Spanish (official),
Amerindian dialects
MONEY: Lempira
LIFE EXPECTANCY: 71
LITERACY RATE: 80%

GUESS WHAT? *The ancient Mayan city of Copán, in Honduras, was abandoned around 900 A.D. It features a huge stone stairway and the longest known Mayan inscription, made up of more than 1,800 figures or symbols.*

HUNGARY

LOCATION: Europe
CAPITAL: Budapest
AREA: 35,918 sq mi
(93,028 sq km)
POPULATION ESTIMATE (2012):
9,958,453
GOVERNMENT: Parliamentary
democracy
LANGUAGE: Hungarian
MONEY: Forint
LIFE EXPECTANCY: 75
LITERACY RATE: 99%

GUESS WHAT? *Dohany Street Synagogue, in Budapest, is Europe's largest synagogue. It is 246 feet (75 m) long and 89 feet (27 m) wide, and can seat more than 3,000 people.*

ICELAND

LOCATION: Europe
CAPITAL: Reykjavík
AREA: 39,768 sq mi
(103,000 sq km)
POPULATION ESTIMATE (2012):
313,183
GOVERNMENT: Constitutional
republic
LANGUAGES: Icelandic, English,
Nordic languages, German
MONEY: Icelandic krona
LIFE EXPECTANCY: 81
LITERACY RATE: 99%

GUESS WHAT? *Most of the energy in Iceland comes from renewable sources such as hydroelectric and geothermal power.*

Countries

INDIA

LOCATION: Asia
CAPITAL: New Delhi
AREA: 1,269,219 sq mi
(3,287,263 sq km)
POPULATION ESTIMATE (2012):
1,205,073,612
GOVERNMENT: Federal republic
LANGUAGES: Hindi, Bengali,
Telugu, Marathi, Tamil, Urdu,
Gujarati, Malayalam, Kannada,
Oriya, Punjabi, Assamese,
Kashmiri, Sindhi, and Sanskrit
(all official), English, others
MONEY: Indian rupee
LIFE EXPECTANCY: 67
LITERACY RATE: 61%

GUESS WHAT? *By 2026, India is expected to become the country with the largest population.*

INDONESIA

LOCATION: Asia
CAPITAL: Jakarta
AREA: 735,358 sq mi
(1,904,569 sq km)
POPULATION ESTIMATE (2012):
248,645,008
GOVERNMENT: Republic
LANGUAGES: Bahasa Indonesia
(official), Dutch, English,
many local dialects
MONEY: Rupiah
LIFE EXPECTANCY: 72
LITERACY RATE: 90%

GUESS WHAT? *With 17,508 islands, Indonesia is the world's largest archipelago, or group of islands.*

IRAN

LOCATION: Middle East
CAPITAL: Tehran
AREA: 636,372 sq mi
(1,648,195 sq km)
POPULATION ESTIMATE (2012):
78,868,711
GOVERNMENT: Theocratic republic
LANGUAGES: Persian (official),
Turkic, Kurdish, others
MONEY: Rial
LIFE EXPECTANCY: 70
LITERACY RATE: 77%

GUESS WHAT? *About 60% of the population of Iran is under the age of 30.*

IRAQ

LOCATION: Middle East
CAPITAL: Baghdad
AREA: 169,235 sq mi
(438,317 sq km)
POPULATION ESTIMATE (2012):
31,129,225
GOVERNMENT: Parliamentary
democracy
LANGUAGES: Arabic and Kurdish
(official), Turkmen, Assyrian
MONEY: Iraqi dinar
LIFE EXPECTANCY: 71
LITERACY RATE: 78%

GUESS WHAT? *Many Iraqis celebrate New Year's Day twice: on January 1 and on the first day of Muharram, which is the first month of the Islamic calendar.*

IRELAND

LOCATION: Europe
CAPITAL: Dublin
AREA: 27,132 sq mi
(70,273 sq km)
POPULATION ESTIMATE (2012):
4,722,028
GOVERNMENT: Republic,
parliamentary democracy
LANGUAGES: Irish (Gaelic) and
English (both official)
MONEY: Euro (formerly Irish
pound, or punt)
LIFE EXPECTANCY: 80
LITERACY RATE: 99%

GUESS WHAT? *Irish step dance is popular in Ireland. Dancers keep their upper bodies still while performing fast, complicated footwork.*

ISRAEL

LOCATION: Middle East
CAPITAL: Jerusalem
AREA: 8,019 sq mi (20,770 sq km)
POPULATION ESTIMATE (2012):
7,590,758
GOVERNMENT: Parliamentary
democracy
LANGUAGES: Hebrew (official),
Arabic, English
MONEY: New Israeli shekel
LIFE EXPECTANCY: 81
LITERACY RATE: 97%

GUESS WHAT? *The glue on Israeli postage stamps is certified kosher.*

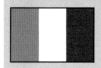

ITALY

LOCATION: Europe
CAPITAL: Rome
AREA: 116,348 sq mi
(301,340 sq km)
POPULATION ESTIMATE (2012):
61,261,254
GOVERNMENT: Republic
LANGUAGES: Italian (official),
German, French, Slovene
MONEY: Euro (formerly lira)
LIFE EXPECTANCY: 82
LITERACY RATE: 98%

GUESS WHAT? *On average, every Italian citizen consumes 0.5 pound (227 g) of bread a day.*

JAMAICA

LOCATION: Caribbean
CAPITAL: Kingston
AREA: 4,244 sq mi
(10,991 sq km)
POPULATION ESTIMATE (2012):
2,889,187
GOVERNMENT: Constitutional
parliamentary democracy
LANGUAGES: English, English patois
MONEY: Jamaican dollar
LIFE EXPECTANCY: 73
LITERACY RATE: 88%

GUESS WHAT? *The Blue Mountains, just north of Kingston, are not actually blue. A mist surrounds the mountain peaks and, when hit by the sun, it appears to have a blue hue.*

JAPAN

LOCATION: Asia
CAPITAL: Tokyo
AREA: 145,914 sq mi
(377,915 sq km)
POPULATION ESTIMATE (2012):
127,368,088
GOVERNMENT: Parliamentary
government with a
constitutional monarchy
LANGUAGE: Japanese
MONEY: Yen
LIFE EXPECTANCY: 84
LITERACY RATE: 99%

GUESS WHAT? *Origami is the traditional Japanese art of paper folding.*

JORDAN

LOCATION: Middle East
CAPITAL: Amman
AREA: 34,495 sq mi
(89,342 sq km)
POPULATION ESTIMATE (2012):
6,508,887
GOVERNMENT: Constitutional
monarchy
LANGUAGE: Arabic (official),
English
MONEY: Jordanian dinar
LIFE EXPECTANCY: 80
LITERACY RATE: 93%

GUESS WHAT? *Petra, in southwestern Jordan, is an ancient city that was carved into the side of a mountain more than 2,000 years ago.*

KAZAKHSTAN

LOCATION: Asia
CAPITAL: Astana
AREA: 1,052,090 sq mi
(2,724,900 sq km)
POPULATION ESTIMATE (2012):
17,522,010
GOVERNMENT: Republic with
authoritarian presidential rule
LANGUAGES: Russian (official),
Kazakh
MONEY: Tenge
LIFE EXPECTANCY: 70
LITERACY RATE: 100%

GUESS WHAT? *New research suggests the Botai people who settled in Kazakhstan 6,000 years ago were the first people to domesticate horses.*

KENYA

LOCATION: Africa
CAPITAL: Nairobi
AREA: 224,081 sq mi
(580,367 sq km)
POPULATION ESTIMATE (2012):
43,013,341
GOVERNMENT: Republic
LANGUAGES: English and
Kiswahili (both official),
others
MONEY: Kenyan shilling
LIFE EXPECTANCY: 63
LITERACY RATE: 87%

GUESS WHAT? *Every year, one million wildebeests migrate 1,800 miles (2,897 km) from the Serengeti Plain in Tanzania, to the Maasai Mara National Reserve, in Kenya.*

KIRIBATI

LOCATION: Oceania
CAPITAL: Tarawa
AREA: 313 sq mi (811 sq km)
POPULATION ESTIMATE (2012): 101,998
GOVERNMENT: Republic
LANGUAGES: English (official), I-Kiribati (Gilbertese)
MONEY: Australian dollar
LIFE EXPECTANCY: 65
LITERACY RATE: Not available

GUESS WHAT? *Kiribati is pronounced keer-uh-bas.*

KOREA, NORTH

LOCATION: Asia
CAPITAL: Pyongyang
AREA: 46,540 sq mi (120,538 sq km)
POPULATION ESTIMATE (2012): 24,589,122
GOVERNMENT: Communist dictatorship
LANGUAGE: Korean
MONEY: North Korean won
LIFE EXPECTANCY: 69
LITERACY RATE: 99%

GUESS WHAT? *Even in North Korea's capital city, Pyongyang, there are many power shortages. When the traffic lights go out, the government has female police officers direct traffic instead.*

KOREA, SOUTH

LOCATION: Asia
CAPITAL: Seoul
AREA: 38,541 sq mi (99,720 sq km)
POPULATION ESTIMATE (2012): 48,860,500
GOVERNMENT: Republic
LANGUAGE: Korean, English
MONEY: South Korean won
LIFE EXPECTANCY: 79
LITERACY RATE: 98%

GUESS WHAT? *South Korea is the world's largest shipbuilding nation.*

KOSOVO

LOCATION: Europe
CAPITAL: Pristina
AREA: 4,203 sq mi (10,887 sq km)
POPULATION ESTIMATE (2012): 1,836,529
GOVERNMENT: Republic
LANGUAGES: Albanian and Serbian (both official), Bosnian, Turkish, Roma
MONEY: Euro (formerly deutsche mark)
LIFE EXPECTANCY: Not available
LITERACY RATE: 92%

GUESS WHAT? *About 90% of Kosovo's population is of Albanian decent.*

KUWAIT

LOCATION: Middle East
CAPITAL: Kuwait City
AREA: 6,880 sq mi (17,818 sq km)
POPULATION ESTIMATE (2012): 2,646,314
GOVERNMENT: Constitutional emirate
LANGUAGES: Arabic (official), English
MONEY: Kuwaiti dinar
LIFE EXPECTANCY: 77
LITERACY RATE: 93%

GUESS WHAT? *Machboos is a popular dish in Kuwait. It is lamb, chicken, or fish served over rice cooked with spices like saffron, cloves, turmeric, and cinnamon. It usually features onions, raisins, and nuts, too.*

KYRGYZSTAN

LOCATION: Asia
CAPITAL: Bishkek
AREA: 77,202 sq mi (199,951 sq km)
POPULATION ESTIMATE (2012): 5,496,737
GOVERNMENT: Republic
LANGUAGES: Kyrgyz and Russian (both official), Uzbek, others
MONEY: Som
LIFE EXPECTANCY: 69
LITERACY RATE: 99%

GUESS WHAT? *Making shyrdaks, or colorful felt carpets, is a popular craft for the nomadic people of Kyrgyzstan.*

LAOS

LOCATION: Asia
CAPITAL: Vientiane
AREA: 91,429 sq mi
(236,800 sq km)
POPULATION ESTIMATE (2012):
6,586,266
GOVERNMENT: Communist state
LANGUAGES: Lao (official), French,
English, others
MONEY: Kip
LIFE EXPECTANCY: 63
LITERACY RATE: 73%

GUESS WHAT? *The Mekong River, stretching from China to Vietnam, is the longest river in Southeast Asia. Most Laotians live along the river. Much of the rest of the country is very mountainous, with ground too steep to live on.*

LATVIA

LOCATION: Europe
CAPITAL: Riga
AREA: 24,938 sq mi
(64,589 sq km)
POPULATION ESTIMATE (2012):
2,191,580
GOVERNMENT: Parliamentary
democracy
LANGUAGES: Latvian, Russian,
Lithuanian, others
MONEY: Lats
LIFE EXPECTANCY: 73
LITERACY RATE: 100%

GUESS WHAT? *People from Latvia are known as Latvians or Letts.*

LEBANON

LOCATION: Middle East
CAPITAL: Beirut
AREA: 4,015 sq mi
(10,400 sq km)
POPULATION ESTIMATE (2012):
4,140,289
GOVERNMENT: Republic
LANGUAGES: Arabic (official),
French, English, Armenian
MONEY: Lebanese pound
LIFE EXPECTANCY: 75
LITERACY RATE: 87%

GUESS WHAT? *A phoenix is a mythical bird that lives a long time, dies in a burst of flames, and is reborn from the ashes. Beirut, which has been destroyed seven times, uses the bird as a symbol for the city.*

LESOTHO

LOCATION: Africa
CAPITAL: Maseru
AREA: 11,720 sq mi
(30,355 sq km)
POPULATION ESTIMATE (2012):
1,930,493
GOVERNMENT: Parliamentary
constitutional monarchy
LANGUAGES: English (official),
Sesotho, Zulu, Xhosa
MONEY: Loti
LIFE EXPECTANCY: 52
LITERACY RATE: 90%

GUESS WHAT? *Lesotho is a mountainous country. It is the only nation that lies entirely above 3,000 feet (914 m) in elevation.*

LIBERIA

LOCATION: Africa
CAPITAL: Monrovia
AREA: 43,000 sq mi
(111,369 sq km)
POPULATION ESTIMATE (2012):
3,887,886
GOVERNMENT: Republic
LANGUAGES: English (official),
ethnic dialects
MONEY: Liberian dollar
LIFE EXPECTANCY: 57
LITERACY RATE: 61%

GUESS WHAT? *Liberia was founded in 1820 by African Americans, many of whom were freed slaves. The word liberia is Latin for "land of the free."*

LIBYA

LOCATION: Africa
CAPITAL: Tripoli
AREA: 679,358 sq mi
(1,759,540 sq km)
POPULATION ESTIMATE (2012):
5,613,380
GOVERNMENT: Transitional
LANGUAGES: Arabic (official),
Italian, English, Berber
MONEY: Libyan dinar
LIFE EXPECTANCY: 78
LITERACY RATE: 89%

GUESS WHAT? *To supply its people with water, Libya has built the Great Man-Made River, a huge system of pipes that draws water from beneath the Sahara desert.*

LIECHTENSTEIN

LOCATION: Europe
CAPITAL: Vaduz
AREA: 62 sq mi (160 sq km)
POPULATION ESTIMATE (2012): 36,713
GOVERNMENT: Constitutional monarchy
LANGUAGES: German (official), Alemannic dialect
MONEY: Swiss franc
LIFE EXPECTANCY: 82
LITERACY RATE: 100%

GUESS WHAT? *Liechtenstein is one of two doubly landlocked countries. It is bordered only by countries that are also landlocked, meaning that they do not have direct access to the ocean or sea.*

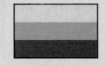

LITHUANIA

LOCATION: Europe
CAPITAL: Vilnius
AREA: 25,212 sq mi (65,300 sq km)
POPULATION ESTIMATE (2012): 3,525,761
GOVERNMENT: Parliamentary democracy
LANGUAGES: Lithuanian (official), Russian, Polish
MONEY: Litas
LIFE EXPECTANCY: 76
LITERACY RATE: 100%

GUESS WHAT? *The first Lithuanian book,* The Simple Words of Catechism, *by Martynas Mazvydas, was published in 1547.*

LUXEMBOURG

LOCATION: Europe
CAPITAL: Luxembourg
AREA: 998 sq mi (2,586 sq km)
POPULATION ESTIMATE (2012): 509,074
GOVERNMENT: Constitutional monarchy
LANGUAGES: Luxembourgish, German, French
MONEY: Euro (formerly Luxembourg franc)
LIFE EXPECTANCY: 80
LITERACY RATE: 100%

GUESS WHAT? *Luxembourg is the only remaining grand duchy. That means it is the only country whose head of state is either a grand duke or duchess. Henri Albert Gabriel Félix Marie Guillaume is the current grand duke.*

MACEDONIA

LOCATION: Europe
CAPITAL: Skopje
AREA: 9,928 sq mi (25,713 sq km)
POPULATION ESTIMATE (2012): 2,082,370
GOVERNMENT: Parliamentary democracy
LANGUAGES: Macedonian and Albanian (both official), Turkish, others
MONEY: Macedonian denar
LIFE EXPECTANCY: 75
LITERACY RATE: 97%

GUESS WHAT? *Ohrid, in southwestern Macedonia, once had 365 churches—one for each day of the year. It is one of the oldest human settlements in Europe.*

MADAGASCAR

LOCATION: Africa
CAPITAL: Antananarivo
AREA: 226,658 sq mi (587,041 sq km)
POPULATION ESTIMATE (2012): 22,005,222
GOVERNMENT: Republic
LANGUAGES: French and Malagasy (both official), English
MONEY: Malagasy ariary
LIFE EXPECTANCY: 64
LITERACY RATE: 65%

GUESS WHAT? *About 80% of the plants and animals found in Madagascar are endemic, meaning they don't exist naturally anywhere else. This includes the fossa, a catlike predator featured in the movie Madagascar.*

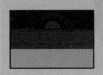

MALAWI

LOCATION: Africa
CAPITAL: Lilongwe
AREA: 45,747 sq mi (118,484 sq km)
POPULATION ESTIMATE (2012): 16,323,044
GOVERNMENT: Multiparty democracy
LANGUAGES: Chichewa (official), Chinyanja, Chiyao, Chitumbuka, others
MONEY: Kwacha
LIFE EXPECTANCY: 52
LITERACY RATE: 75%

GUESS WHAT? *Joyce Banda became Malawi's first female President, in 2012. She is only the second woman to lead a country in Africa.*

MALAYSIA

LOCATION: Asia
CAPITAL: Kuala Lumpur
AREA: 127,355 sq mi (329,847 sq km)
POPULATION ESTIMATE (2012): 29,179,952
GOVERNMENT: Constitutional monarchy
LANGUAGES: Bahasa Malay (official), English, Chinese, Tamil, others
MONEY: Ringgit
LIFE EXPECTANCY: 74
LITERACY RATE: 89%

GUESS WHAT? *Rafflesias, the largest flowers in the world, grow in the forests of Sabah, Malaysia. They can grow to be 3 feet (91 cm) in diameter and weigh up to 15 pounds (7 kg).*

MALDIVES

LOCATION: Asia
CAPITAL: Male
AREA: 115 sq mi (298 sq km)
POPULATION ESTIMATE (2012): 394,451
GOVERNMENT: Republic
LANGUAGES: Dhivehi (official), English
MONEY: Rufiyaa
LIFE EXPECTANCY: 75
LITERACY RATE: 94%

GUESS WHAT? *To draw attention to the threat of climate change, in 2009, officials in the Maldives became the first government cabinet to hold a meeting underwater. The President, Vice President, and 11 cabinet members signed a document urging other countries to cut carbon dioxide emissions.*

MALI

LOCATION: Africa
CAPITAL: Bamako
AREA: 478,841 sq mi (1,240,192 sq km)
POPULATION ESTIMATE (2012): 15,494,466
GOVERNMENT: Republic
LANGUAGES: French (official), Bambara, African languages
MONEY: CFA franc
LIFE EXPECTANCY: 53
LITERACY RATE: 28%

GUESS WHAT? *The Festival au Désert is an annual concert in Mali with performances of traditional Tuareg music. The Tuareg are nomads who live in the Sahara. Due to political unrest, the festival was not held in 2012.*

MALTA

LOCATION: Europe
CAPITAL: Valletta
AREA: 122 sq mi (316 sq km)
POPULATION ESTIMATE (2012): 409,836
GOVERNMENT: Republic
LANGUAGES: Maltese and English (both official)
MONEY: Euro (formerly Maltese lira)
LIFE EXPECTANCY: 80
LITERACY RATE: 93%

GUESS WHAT? *On a child's first birthday, it is tradition for parents to play a game called il-quccija, in which a variety of objects, such as a Bible, pen, wooden spoon, calculator, and coin, are placed in front of the child. Whichever object the child plays with is said to represent the path the child will pursue in life.*

MARSHALL ISLANDS

LOCATION: Oceania
CAPITAL: Majuro
AREA: 70 sq mi (181 sq km)
POPULATION ESTIMATE (2012): 68,480
GOVERNMENT: Constitutional government
LANGUAGES: Marshallese and English (both official)
MONEY: U.S. dollar
LIFE EXPECTANCY: 72
LITERACY RATE: 94%

GUESS WHAT? *The Marshall Islands is home to the world's largest shark sanctuary. Around the islands, commercial fishing of sharks is banned in an area of the Pacific Ocean that is more than four times the size of California.*

MAURITANIA

LOCATION: Africa
CAPITAL: Nouakchott
AREA: 397,953 sq mi (1,030,700 sq km)
POPULATION ESTIMATE (2012): 3,359,185
GOVERNMENT: Military junta
LANGUAGES: Arabic (official), French, Pulaar, Soninke, others
MONEY: Ouguiya
LIFE EXPECTANCY: 62
LITERACY RATE: 58%

GUESS WHAT? *Mauritania, a Saharan desert nation, has some of the world's most abundant fishing areas off its Atlantic coast.*

MAURITIUS

LOCATION: Africa
CAPITAL: Port Louis
AREA: 788 sq mi (2,040 sq km)
POPULATION ESTIMATE (2012): 1,313,095
GOVERNMENT: Parliamentary democracy
LANGUAGES: English (official), Creole, Bhojpuri, French
MONEY: Mauritian rupee
LIFE EXPECTANCY: 75
LITERACY RATE: 89%

GUESS WHAT? *The dodo, an extinct flightless bird, lived only on the island of Mauritius. It was the inspiration for the character of the Dodo in Lewis Carroll's Alice's Adventures in Wonderland.*

MEXICO

LOCATION: North America
CAPITAL: Mexico City
AREA: 758,449 sq mi (1,964,375 sq km)
POPULATION ESTIMATE (2012): 114,975,406
GOVERNMENT: Federal republic
LANGUAGES: Spanish, native languages
MONEY: Peso
LIFE EXPECTANCY: 77
LITERACY RATE: 86%

GUESS WHAT? *Each autumn, millions of monarch butterflies migrate from the United States and Canada to central Mexico. They travel up to 2,000 miles (3,219 km) to get there.*

MICRONESIA, FEDERATED STATES OF

LOCATION: Oceania
CAPITAL: Palikir
AREA: 271 sq mi (702 sq km)
POPULATION ESTIMATE (2012): 106,487
GOVERNMENT: Constitutional government
LANGUAGES: English (official), Chuukese, Kosraean, Pohnpeian, Yapese, Ulithian, others
MONEY: U.S. dollar
LIFE EXPECTANCY: 72
LITERACY RATE: 89%

GUESS WHAT? *Yap, one of Micronesia's four islands, is famous for using stones as money. These large, carved stones, called* rai, *look like wheels.*

MOLDOVA

LOCATION: Europe
CAPITAL: Chisinau
AREA: 13,070 sq mi (33,851 sq km)
POPULATION ESTIMATE (2012): 3,656,843
GOVERNMENT: Republic
LANGUAGES: Moldovan (official), Russian, Gagauz
MONEY: Leu
LIFE EXPECTANCY: 70
LITERACY RATE: 99%

GUESS WHAT? *Throughout its history, Moldova has been involved in border disputes between Russia and Romania.*

MONACO

LOCATION: Europe
CAPITAL: Monaco
AREA: 0.77 sq mi (2 sq km)
POPULATION ESTIMATE (2012): 30,510
GOVERNMENT: Constitutional monarchy
LANGUAGES: French (official), English, Italian, Monégasque
MONEY: Euro (formerly French franc)
LIFE EXPECTANCY: 90
LITERACY RATE: 99%

GUESS WHAT? *There are no airports in Monaco.*

MONGOLIA

LOCATION: Asia
CAPITAL: Ulaanbaatar
AREA: 603,909 sq mi (1,564,116 sq km)
POPULATION ESTIMATE (2012): 3,179,997
GOVERNMENT: Parliamentary republic
LANGUAGES: Khalkha Mongol (official), Turkic, Russian
MONEY: Togrog/tugrik
LIFE EXPECTANCY: 69
LITERACY RATE: 97%

GUESS WHAT? *Mongolia is sometimes called the Land of Blue Sky, because it is sunny nearly all year.*

MONTENEGRO

LOCATION: Europe
CAPITAL: Podgorica
AREA: 5,333 sq mi (13,812 sq km)
POPULATION ESTIMATE (2012): 657,394
GOVERNMENT: Republic
LANGUAGES: Montenegrin (official), Serbian, Bosnian, Albanian, others
MONEY: Euro (formerly deutsche mark)
LIFE EXPECTANCY: Not available
LITERACY RATE: 98%

GUESS WHAT? *The traditional folk dance of Montenegro is the oro. Dancers stand in a circle singing, while others dance in the center. Often it will end with young men in the circle standing on each other's shoulders.*

MOROCCO

LOCATION: Africa
CAPITAL: Rabat
AREA: 172,413 sq mi (446,550 sq km)
POPULATION ESTIMATE (2012): 32,309,239
GOVERNMENT: Constitutional monarchy
LANGUAGES: Arabic (official), French, Berber dialects
MONEY: Dirham
LIFE EXPECTANCY: 76
LITERACY RATE: 56%

GUESS WHAT? *Morocco grows more peppermint than any other nation.*

MOZAMBIQUE

LOCATION: Africa
CAPITAL: Maputo
AREA: 308,642 sq mi (799,380 sq km)
POPULATION ESTIMATE (2012): 23,515,934
GOVERNMENT: Republic
LANGUAGES: Portuguese (official), Emakhuwa, Xichangana, others
MONEY: Metical
LIFE EXPECTANCY: 52
LITERACY RATE: 56%

GUESS WHAT? *Mozambique became independent from Portugal in 1975. A civil war broke out two years later and lasted until 1992.*

MYANMAR (BURMA)

LOCATION: Asia
CAPITAL: Nay Pyi Taw
AREA: 261,228 sq mi (676,578 sq km)
POPULATION ESTIMATE (2012): 54,584,650
GOVERNMENT: Parliamentary government with strong military influence
LANGUAGES: Burmese (official), minority languages
MONEY: Kyat
LIFE EXPECTANCY: 65
LITERACY RATE: 90%

GUESS WHAT? *The Shwezigon Pagoda is a sacred site in Bagan, Myanmar. Every year, pilgrims travel to the temple for a festival.*

NAMIBIA

LOCATION: Africa
CAPITAL: Windhoek
AREA: 318,261 sq mi (824,292 sq km)
POPULATION ESTIMATE (2012): 2,165,828
GOVERNMENT: Republic
LANGUAGES: English (official), Afrikaans, German, native languages
MONEY: Namibian dollar
LIFE EXPECTANCY: 52
LITERACY RATE: 89%

GUESS WHAT? *Hoba, discovered in Namibia in the 1920s, is the largest known meteorite in the world. It is approximately 80,000 years old and weighs more than 50 tons (45 metric tons).*

NAURU

LOCATION: Oceania
CAPITAL: Yaren District (unofficial)
AREA: 8.11 sq mi (21 sq km)
POPULATION ESTIMATE (2012): 9,378
GOVERNMENT: Republic
LANGUAGES: Nauruan (official), English
MONEY: Australian dollar
LIFE EXPECTANCY: 66
LITERACY RATE: Not available

GUESS WHAT? *Nauru is the world's smallest island nation.*

NEPAL

LOCATION: Asia
CAPITAL: Kathmandu
AREA: 56,827 sq mi
(147,181 sq km)
POPULATION ESTIMATE (2012):
29,890,686
GOVERNMENT: Federal democratic
republic
LANGUAGES: Nepali (official),
Maithali, Bhojpuri, Tharu,
Tamang
MONEY: Nepalese rupee
LIFE EXPECTANCY: 67
LITERACY RATE: 60%

GUESS WHAT? *In Nepal, it is considered offensive to touch things with your feet or to point the soles of your feet directly at someone.*

THE NETHERLANDS

LOCATION: Europe
CAPITAL: Amsterdam
AREA: 16,040 sq mi
(41,543 sq km)
POPULATION ESTIMATE (2012):
16,730,632
GOVERNMENT: Constitutional
monarchy
LANGUAGES: Dutch and Frisian
(both official)
MONEY: Euro (formerly guilder)
LIFE EXPECTANCY: 81
LITERACY RATE: 99%

GUESS WHAT? *Dutch people are the tallest in the world. The average height of an adult man in the Netherlands is 6 feet 1 inch (185 cm).*

NEW ZEALAND

LOCATION: Oceania
CAPITAL: Wellington
AREA: 103,363 sq mi
(267,710 sq km)
POPULATION ESTIMATE (2012):
4,327,944
GOVERNMENT: Parliamentary
democracy
LANGUAGES: English, Maori, and
sign language (all official)
MONEY: New Zealand dollar
LIFE EXPECTANCY: 81
LITERACY RATE: 99%

GUESS WHAT? *Before climbing Mount Everest, New Zealander Sir Edmund Hillary trained on Mount Cook (Aoraki in Maori), the country's tallest peak.*

NICARAGUA

LOCATION: Central America
CAPITAL: Managua
AREA: 50,336 sq mi
(130,370 sq km)
POPULATION ESTIMATE (2012):
5,727,707
GOVERNMENT: Republic
LANGUAGE: Spanish (official)
MONEY: Córdoba
LIFE EXPECTANCY: 72
LITERACY RATE: 68%

GUESS WHAT? *Lake Nicaragua is the only freshwater lake in the world that is home to oceanic sharks.*

NIGER

LOCATION: Africa
CAPITAL: Niamey
AREA: 489,189 sq mi
(1,267,000 sq km)
POPULATION ESTIMATE (2012):
16,344,687
GOVERNMENT: Republic
LANGUAGES: French (official),
Hausa, Djerma
MONEY: CFA franc
LIFE EXPECTANCY: 54
LITERACY RATE: 29%

GUESS WHAT? *Researchers estimate that about 200 addax antelopes live in Niger. That's roughly two-thirds of the world's remaining wild addax population.*

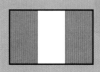

NIGERIA

LOCATION: Africa
CAPITAL: Abuja
AREA: 356,667 sq mi
(923,768 sq km)
POPULATION ESTIMATE (2012):
170,123,740
GOVERNMENT: Federal republic
LANGUAGES: English (official),
Hausa, Yoruba, Igbo, Fulani
and more than 500 other
native languages
MONEY: Naira
LIFE EXPECTANCY: 52
LITERACY RATE: 61%

GUESS WHAT? *Nigeria has the highest rate of twin births in the world.*

NORWAY

LOCATION: Europe
CAPITAL: Oslo
AREA: 125,021 sq mi
(323,802 sq km)
POPULATION ESTIMATE (2012):
4,707,270
GOVERNMENT: Constitutional
monarchy
LANGUAGES: Two official forms
of Norwegian: Bokmal and
Nynorsk
MONEY: Krone
LIFE EXPECTANCY: 80
LITERACY RATE: 100%

GUESS WHAT? *Most Norwegian children start learning to ski when they are very young.*

OMAN

LOCATION: Middle East
CAPITAL: Muscat
AREA: 119,499 sq mi
(309,500 sq km)
POPULATION ESTIMATE (2012):
3,090,150
GOVERNMENT: Monarchy
LANGUAGES: Arabic (official),
English, Baluchi, Urdu,
Indian dialects
MONEY: Omani rial
LIFE EXPECTANCY: 74
LITERACY RATE: 81%

GUESS WHAT? *Oman is known for the breeding of prized Arabian horses.*

PAKISTAN

LOCATION: Asia
CAPITAL: Islamabad
AREA: 307,374 sq mi
(790,095 sq km)
POPULATION ESTIMATE (2012):
190,291,129
GOVERNMENT: Federal republic
LANGUAGES: Urdu (official),
Punjabi, Sindhi, Siraiki,
Pashtu, others
MONEY: Pakistani rupee
LIFE EXPECTANCY: 66
LITERACY RATE: 55%

GUESS WHAT? *Three great mountain ranges meet in Pakistan: the Hindu Kush, the Himalaya, and the Karakoram.*

PALAU

LOCATION: Oceania
CAPITAL: Melekeok
AREA: 177 sq mi (459 sq km)
POPULATION ESTIMATE (2012): 21,032
GOVERNMENT: Constitutional
government
LANGUAGES: Palauan, English,
Sonsoralese, Tobi, Anguar,
Filipino, Chinese
MONEY: U.S. dollar
LIFE EXPECTANCY: 72
LITERACY RATE: 92%

GUESS WHAT? *Jellyfish Lake, located on the rocky island Eil Malk, is home to millions of golden jellyfish. These jellyfish, which do not sting, travel from one side of the lake to the other every day in order to get sunlight.*

PANAMA

LOCATION: Central America
CAPITAL: Panama City
AREA: 29,120 sq mi
(75,420 sq km)
POPULATION ESTIMATE (2012):
3,510,045
GOVERNMENT: Constitutional
democracy
LANGUAGES: Spanish (official),
English
MONEY: Balboa, U.S. dollar
LIFE EXPECTANCY: 78
LITERACY RATE: 92%

GUESS WHAT? *There are more than 10,000 plant species and 1,500 animal species in Panama.*

PAPUA NEW GUINEA

LOCATION: Oceania
CAPITAL: Port Moresby
AREA: 178,703 sq mi
(462,840 sq km)
POPULATION ESTIMATE (2012):
6,310,129
GOVERNMENT: Constitutional
parliamentary democracy
LANGUAGES: Tok Pisin, English,
and Hiri Motu(all official),
about 860 native languages
MONEY: Kina
LIFE EXPECTANCY: 66
LITERACY RATE: 57%

GUESS WHAT? *More languages are spoken in Papua New Guinea than anywhere else.*

Countries

PARAGUAY

LOCATION: South America
CAPITAL: Asunción
AREA: 157,047 sq mi
(406,752 sq km)
POPULATION ESTIMATE (2012):
6,541,591
GOVERNMENT: Constitutional
republic
LANGUAGES: Spanish and Guaraní
(both official)
MONEY: Guaraní
LIFE EXPECTANCY: 76
LITERACY RATE: 94%

GUESS WHAT? *One of the world's largest hydroelectric dams, the Itaipú, is on the border of Paraguay and Brazil.*

PERU

LOCATION: South America
CAPITAL: Lima
AREA: 496,225 sq mi
(1,285,216 sq km)
POPULATION ESTIMATE (2012):
29,549,517
GOVERNMENT: Constitutional
republic
LANGUAGES: Spanish and Quechua
(both official), Aymara, others
MONEY: Nuevo sol
LIFE EXPECTANCY: 73
LITERACY RATE: 93%

GUESS WHAT? *Peru was the last colony in South America to gain independence from Spain.*

PHILIPPINES

LOCATION: Asia
CAPITAL: Manila
AREA: 115,830 sq mi
(300,000 sq km)
POPULATION ESTIMATE (2012):
103,775,002
GOVERNMENT: Republic
LANGUAGES: Filipino (based on
Tagalog) and English (both
official), regional languages
MONEY: Philippine peso
LIFE EXPECTANCY: 72
LITERACY RATE: 93%

GUESS WHAT? *About 350 to 400 million texts are sent every day by cell phone users in the Philippines. That's more than are sent in the United States and Europe combined.*

POLAND

LOCATION: Europe
CAPITAL: Warsaw
AREA: 120,728 sq mi
(312,685 sq km)
POPULATION ESTIMATE (2012):
38,415,284
GOVERNMENT: Republic
LANGUAGE: Polish
MONEY: Zloty
LIFE EXPECTANCY: 76
LITERACY RATE: 100%

GUESS WHAT? *In 1543, Polish astronomer Nicolaus Copernicus proposed the theory that the sun, not the Earth, was the center of the universe.*

PORTUGAL

LOCATION: Europe
CAPITAL: Lisbon
AREA: 35,556 sq mi
(92,090 sq km)
POPULATION ESTIMATE (2012):
10,781,459
GOVERNMENT: Republic,
parliamentary democracy
LANGUAGES: Portuguese and
Mirandese (both official)
MONEY: Euro (formerly escudo)
LIFE EXPECTANCY: 79
LITERACY RATE: 95%

GUESS WHAT? *At 10.7 miles (17.2 km), the Vasco da Gama Bridge over the Tagus River, in Lisbon, is the longest bridge in Europe.*

QATAR

LOCATION: Middle East
CAPITAL: Doha
AREA: 4,473 sq mi (11,586 sq km)
POPULATION ESTIMATE (2012):
1,951,591
GOVERNMENT: Traditional
monarchy (emirate)
LANGUAGES: Arabic (official),
English
MONEY: Qatari rial
LIFE EXPECTANCY: 78
LITERACY RATE: 96%

GUESS WHAT? *Qatar is one of the richest countries in the world.*

ROMANIA

LOCATION: Europe
CAPITAL: Bucharest
AREA: 92,043 sq mi
(238,391 sq km)
POPULATION ESTIMATE (2012):
21,848,504
GOVERNMENT: Republic
LANGUAGES: Romanian (official),
Hungarian, Romany
MONEY: Leu
LIFE EXPECTANCY: 74
LITERACY RATE: 98%

GUESS WHAT? *Bram Stoker based his novel* Dracula *on Vlad Tepes, a cruel 15th-century Wallachian prince. Wallachia merged with Moldavia in 1859 and became Romania in 1862.*

RUSSIA

LOCATION: Europe and Asia
CAPITAL: Moscow
AREA: 6,601,668 sq mi
(17,098,242 sq km)
POPULATION ESTIMATE (2012):
142,517,670
GOVERNMENT: Federation
LANGUAGES: Russian, others
MONEY: Ruble
LIFE EXPECTANCY: 66
LITERACY RATE: 100%

GUESS WHAT? *On April 12, 1961, Russian cosmonaut Yuri Gagarin became the first person to travel to space.*

RWANDA

LOCATION: Africa
CAPITAL: Kigali
AREA: 10,169 sq mi
(26,338 sq km)
POPULATION ESTIMATE (2012):
11,689,696
GOVERNMENT: Republic
LANGUAGES: Kinyarwanda,
French, and English
(all official)
MONEY: Rwandan franc
LIFE EXPECTANCY: 58
LITERACY RATE: 71%

GUESS WHAT? *Imigongo is a popular art form in Rwanda. Works of art, usually featuring spirals or geometric designs, are crafted using cow dung and other organic materials.*

SAINT KITTS AND NEVIS

LOCATION: Caribbean
CAPITAL: Basseterre
AREA: 101 sq mi (261 sq km)
POPULATION ESTIMATE (2012): 50,726
GOVERNMENT: Parliamentary
democracy
LANGUAGE: English
MONEY: East Caribbean dollar
LIFE EXPECTANCY: 75
LITERACY RATE: 98%

GUESS WHAT? *The island of Nevis held a vote in 1998 on the subject of separating from Saint Kitts. Nevis did not get the two-thirds majority it needed to split from Saint Kitts, and many still campaign for independence.*

SAINT LUCIA

LOCATION: Caribbean
CAPITAL: Castries
AREA: 238 sq mi (616 sq km)
POPULATION ESTIMATE (2012): 162,178
GOVERNMENT: Parliamentary
democracy
LANGUAGES: English (official),
French patois
MONEY: East Caribbean dollar
LIFE EXPECTANCY: 77
LITERACY RATE: 90%

GUESS WHAT? *Saint Lucia is known for the Pitons—Gros Piton and Petit Piton—which are twin peaks that dominate the island's landscape.*

SAINT VINCENT AND THE GRENADINES

LOCATION: Caribbean
CAPITAL: Kingstown
AREA: 150 sq mi
(389 sq km)
POPULATION ESTIMATE (2012):
103,537
GOVERNMENT: Parliamentary
democracy
LANGUAGES: English, French
patois
MONEY: East Caribbean dollar
LIFE EXPECTANCY: 74
LITERACY RATE: 96%

GUESS WHAT? *Located on the island of Saint Vincent, King's Hill Forest Reserve is one of the oldest forest reserves in the world.*

countries

SAMOA

LOCATION: Oceania
CAPITAL: Apia
AREA: 1,093 sq mi (2,831 sq km)
POPULATION ESTIMATE (2012): 194,320
GOVERNMENT: Parliamentary democracy
LANGUAGES: Samoan (official), English
MONEY: Tala
LIFE EXPECTANCY: 73
LITERACY RATE: 100%

GUESS WHAT? *Tattooing is important in Samoan culture. Traditional tattoos, or pe'a, cover men's bodies from their mid-back to their knees. The patterns of women's tattoos, known as malu, are lighter and use less ink than the men's.*

SAN MARINO

LOCATION: Europe
CAPITAL: San Marino
AREA: 24 sq mi (61 sq km)
POPULATION ESTIMATE (2012): 32,140
GOVERNMENT: Republic
LANGUAGE: Italian
MONEY: Euro (formerly Italian lira)
LIFE EXPECTANCY: 83
LITERACY RATE: 96%

GUESS WHAT? *San Marino is only 24 square miles (61 sq km) and is completely surrounded by Italy. Its capital city is perched atop Mount Titano.*

SAO TOME AND PRINCIPE

LOCATION: Africa
CAPITAL: São Tomé
AREA: 372 sq mi (964 sq km)
POPULATION ESTIMATE (2012): 183,176
GOVERNMENT: Republic
LANGUAGE: Portuguese (official)
MONEY: Dobra
LIFE EXPECTANCY: 63
LITERACY RATE: 85%

GUESS WHAT? *The world's smallest ibis birds, the dwarf olive ibis, and the world's largest sunbird, the giant sunbird, can be found in São Tomé and Princípe.*

SAUDI ARABIA

LOCATION: Middle East
CAPITAL: Riyadh
AREA: 830,000 sq mi (2,149,690 sq km)
POPULATION ESTIMATE (2012): 26,534,504
GOVERNMENT: Monarchy
LANGUAGE: Arabic
MONEY: Saudi riyal
LIFE EXPECTANCY: 74
LITERACY RATE: 87%

GUESS WHAT? *Some people in Saudi Arabia use a miswak to clean their teeth rather than a standard toothbrush. Made from a twig from the arak tree, these natural toothbrushes have been used throughout history.*

SENEGAL

LOCATION: Africa
CAPITAL: Dakar
AREA: 75,955 sq mi (196,722 sq km)
POPULATION ESTIMATE (2012): 12,969,606
GOVERNMENT: Republic
LANGUAGES: French (official), Wolof, Pulaar, Jola, Mandinka
MONEY: CFA franc
LIFE EXPECTANCY: 60
LITERACY RATE: 39%

GUESS WHAT? *A 2012 flood in Dakar washed away sand and revealed artifacts, including shell jewelry, pottery, and tools dating back thousands of years.*

SERBIA

LOCATION: Europe
CAPITAL: Belgrade
AREA: 29,913 sq mi (77,474 sq km)
POPULATION ESTIMATE (2012): 7,276,604
GOVERNMENT: Republic
LANGUAGES: Serbian (official), Hungarian, others
MONEY: Serbian dinar
LIFE EXPECTANCY: 75
LITERACY RATE: 98%

GUESS WHAT? *Serbia is one of the biggest exporters of raspberries in the world. About one-third of the world's raspberries come from this small, landlocked nation.*

SEYCHELLES

LOCATION: Africa
CAPITAL: Victoria
AREA: 176 sq mi (455 sq km)
POPULATION ESTIMATE (2012): 90,024
GOVERNMENT: Republic
LANGUAGES: English (official), Creole, other
MONEY: Seychelles rupee
LIFE EXPECTANCY: 74
LITERACY RATE: 92%

GUESS WHAT? *Almost half of the land in the Seychelles is set aside by law to be used for national parks and nature reserves.*

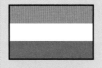

SIERRA LEONE

LOCATION: Africa
CAPITAL: Freetown
AREA: 27,699 sq mi (71,740 sq km)
POPULATION ESTIMATE (2012): 5,485,998
GOVERNMENT: Constitutional democracy
LANGUAGES: English (official), Mende, Temne, Krio
MONEY: Leone
LIFE EXPECTANCY: 56
LITERACY RATE: 57%

GUESS WHAT? *Sierra Leone is one of the youngest democracies in the world. It held its first democratic election in 2007.*

SINGAPORE

LOCATION: Asia
CAPITAL: Singapore
AREA: 269 sq mi (697 sq km)
POPULATION ESTIMATE (2012): 5,353,494
GOVERNMENT: Parliamentary republic
LANGUAGES: Chinese (Mandarin), English, Malay, Hokkien, Cantonese, others
MONEY: Singapore dollar
LIFE EXPECTANCY: 84
LITERACY RATE: 93%

GUESS WHAT? *The world's largest bat, known as the flying fox, lives on Pulau Ubin, an island off of mainland Singapore. The flying fox can have a wingspan of up to 5 feet (152 cm).*

SLOVAKIA

LOCATION: Europe
CAPITAL: Bratislava
AREA: 18,933 sq mi (49,035 sq km)
POPULATION ESTIMATE (2012): 5,483,088
GOVERNMENT: Parliamentary democracy
LANGUAGES: Slovak (official), Hungarian, Roma, Ukranian
MONEY: Euro (formerly koruna)
LIFE EXPECTANCY: 76
LITERACY RATE: 100%

GUESS WHAT? *The oldest known artifact found in Slovakia is the Moravian Venus, a small sculpture of a woman that was cut from a mammoth tusk. According to scientists, it was carved around 22,860 B.C.*

SLOVENIA

LOCATION: Europe
CAPITAL: Ljubljana
AREA: 7,827 sq mi (20,273 sq km)
POPULATION ESTIMATE (2012): 1,996,617
GOVERNMENT: Parliamentary republic
LANGUAGES: Slovenian (official), Serbo-Croatian
MONEY: Euro (formerly Slovenian tolar)
LIFE EXPECTANCY: 77
LITERACY RATE: 100%

GUESS WHAT? *Until 1991, Hostel Celica was a military prison in Slovenia. More than 80 artists from around the world transformed it into a youth hostel that has been open since 2003.*

SOLOMON ISLANDS

LOCATION: Oceania
CAPITAL: Honiara
AREA: 111,157 sq mi (28,896 sq km)
POPULATION ESTIMATE (2012): 584,578
GOVERNMENT: Parliamentary democracy
LANGUAGES: English (official), Melanesian pidgin, more than 120 local languages
MONEY: Solomon Islands dollar
LIFE EXPECTANCY: 74
LITERACY RATE: Not available

GUESS WHAT? *Guadalcanal, one of the 992 islands that make up the Solomon Islands, served as a battleground for fierce fighting between the United States and Japan during World War II.*

Countries

SOMALIA

LOCATION: Africa
CAPITAL: Mogadishu
AREA: 246,199 sq mi
(637,657 sq km)
POPULATION ESTIMATE (2012):
10,085,638
GOVERNMENT: Transitional,
parliamentary federal
government
LANGUAGES: Somali and Arabic
(both official), English, Italian
MONEY: Somali shilling
LIFE EXPECTANCY: 51
LITERACY RATE: 38%

GUESS WHAT? *Somalia's national women's basketball team competed in the 2011 Arab Games. It was the first time they played on an international level since 1987.*

SOUTH AFRICA

LOCATION: Africa
CAPITALS: Pretoria (administrative),
Cape Town (legislative),
Bloemfontein (judicial)
AREA: 471,008 sq mi
(1,219,090 sq km)
POPULATION ESTIMATE (2012):
48,810,427
GOVERNMENT: Republic
LANGUAGES: Zulu, Xhosa, Afrikaans,
Sepedi, English, Setswana,
Sesotho, Tsonga, others
MONEY: Rand
LIFE EXPECTANCY: 49
LITERACY RATE: 86%

GUESS WHAT? *The Vredefort Dome, in South Africa, was formed about 2 billion years ago, when a meteorite hit Earth. It is the world's oldest meteorite scar.*

SPAIN

LOCATION: Europe
CAPITAL: Madrid
AREA: 195,124 sq mi
(505,370 sq km)
POPULATION ESTIMATE (2012):
47,042,984
GOVERNMENT: Parliamentary
monarchy
LANGUAGES: Castilian Spanish
(official), Catalan, Galician,
Basque
MONEY: Euro (formerly peseta)
LIFE EXPECTANCY: 81
LITERACY RATE: 98%

GUESS WHAT? *The Prado Museum, in Madrid, is one of the world's most visited museums. Known for its collection of European art, it has many works by the Spanish artist Francisco de Goya.*

SRI LANKA

LOCATION: Asia
CAPITAL: Colombo
AREA: 25,332 sq mi
(65,610 sq km)
POPULATION ESTIMATE (2012):
21,481,334
GOVERNMENT: Republic
LANGUAGES: Sinhala (official),
Tamil, English
MONEY: Sri Lankan rupee
LIFE EXPECTANCY: 76
LITERACY RATE: 91%

GUESS WHAT? *The Sri Lankan elephant is the largest of all Asian elephants. Considered sacred, they are often featured in Buddhist festivals and parades.*

SUDAN

LOCATION: Africa
CAPITAL: Khartoum
AREA: 718,723 sq mi
(1,861,484 sq km)
POPULATION ESTIMATE (2012):
34,206,710
GOVERNMENT: Federal republic
LANGUAGES: Arabic and English
(both official), Nubian,
Ta Bedawie, Fur
MONEY: Sudanese pound
LIFE EXPECTANCY: 63
LITERACY RATE: 61%

GUESS WHAT? *Egypt isn't the only country in Africa with huge pyramids. Sudan's pyramids, built from 592 B.C. to 320 A.D., house the remains of the royalty of the ancient kingdom of Kush.*

SUDAN, SOUTH

LOCATION: Africa
CAPITAL: Juba
AREA: 284,777 sq mi
(644,329 sq km)
POPULATION ESTIMATE (2012):
10,625,176
GOVERNMENT: Republic
LANGUAGES: Arabic and English
(both official), others
MONEY: South Sudanese pound
LIFE EXPECTANCY: Not available
LITERACY RATE: 27%

GUESS WHAT? *South Sudan's national anthem, "South Sudan Oyee [Hurray]," was written by a group of students from the University of Juba. Their lyrics were chosen during a competition held in 2010.*

SURINAME

LOCATION: South America
CAPITAL: Paramaribo
AREA: 63,251 sq mi (163,820 sq km)
POPULATION ESTIMATE (2012): 560,157
GOVERNMENT: Constitutional democracy
LANGUAGES: Dutch (official), English, Surinamese, Caribbean Hindustani, Javanese
MONEY: Surinamese dollar
LIFE EXPECTANCY: 71
LITERACY RATE: 90%

GUESS WHAT? *Suriname achieved total independence from the Netherlands on November 25, 1975.*

SWAZILAND

LOCATION: Africa
CAPITAL: Mbabane
AREA: 6,704 sq mi (17,364 sq km)
POPULATION ESTIMATE (2012): 1,386,914
GOVERNMENT: Monarchy
LANGUAGES: Swati and English (both official)
MONEY: Lilangeni
LIFE EXPECTANCY: 49
LITERACY RATE: 82%

GUESS WHAT? *At the end of every summer, some Swazi women and girls participate in the Umhlanga, or "reed dance," an eight-day festival filled with parades, dancing, and feasts.*

SWEDEN

LOCATION: Europe
CAPITAL: Stockholm
AREA: 173,860 sq mi (450,295 sq km)
POPULATION ESTIMATE (2012): 9,103,788
GOVERNMENT: Constitutional monarchy
LANGUAGE: Swedish
MONEY: Krona
LIFE EXPECTANCY: 81
LITERACY RATE: 99%

GUESS WHAT? *Sweden is one of the most generous nations in the world. According to the Organization for Economic Co-operation and Development, the country gave nearly 36 billion kronor ($5.5 billion) to third-world countries in 2011.*

SWITZERLAND

LOCATION: Europe
CAPITAL: Bern
AREA: 15,937 sq mi (41,277 sq km)
POPULATION ESTIMATE (2012): 7,925,517
GOVERNMENT: Confederation (similar to a federal republic)
LANGUAGES: German, French, Italian, and Romansh (all official), others
MONEY: Swiss franc
LIFE EXPECTANCY: 81
LITERACY RATE: 99%

GUESS WHAT? *People in Switzerland are never more than 15 miles (24 km) from a lake or river.*

SYRIA

LOCATION: Middle East
CAPITAL: Damascus
AREA: 71,498 sq mi (185,180 sq km)
POPULATION ESTIMATE (2012): 22,530,746
GOVERNMENT: Republic under an authoritarian regime
LANGUAGES: Arabic (official), Kurdish, Armenian, Aramaic, Circassian
MONEY: Syrian pound
LIFE EXPECTANCY: 75
LITERACY RATE: 80%

GUESS WHAT? *Damascus is one of the oldest cities in the world.*

TAIWAN

LOCATION: Asia
CAPITAL: Taipei
AREA: 13,892 sq mi (35,980 sq km)
POPULATION ESTIMATE (2012): 23,234,936
GOVERNMENT: Multiparty democracy
LANGUAGES: Chinese (Mandarin), Taiwanese, Hakka dialects
MONEY: New Taiwan dollar
LIFE EXPECTANCY: 78
LITERACY RATE: 96%

GUESS WHAT? *Taiwan has the lowest poverty rate in the world. In 2010, only 1.16% of its population was below the poverty line, which is the level of income needed to be able to afford basic needs.*

Countries

TAJIKISTAN

LOCATION: Asia
CAPITAL: Dushanbe
AREA: 55,251 sq mi (143,100 sq km)
POPULATION ESTIMATE (2012): 7,768,385
GOVERNMENT: Republic
LANGUAGES: Tajik (official), Russian
MONEY: Somoni
LIFE EXPECTANCY: 66
LITERACY RATE: 100%

GUESS WHAT? *More than 90% of Tajikistan's territory is mountainous.*

TANZANIA

LOCATION: Africa
CAPITALS: Dar es Salaam (commercial), Dodoma (political)
AREA: 365,755 sq mi (947,300 sq km)
POPULATION ESTIMATE (2012): 46,912,768
GOVERNMENT: Republic
LANGUAGES: Swahili and English (both official), Arabic, others
MONEY: Tanzanian shilling
LIFE EXPECTANCY: 53
LITERACY RATE: 69%

GUESS WHAT? *Tanzanian hip-hop is called* bongoflava. *The name comes from the Swahili word for "brains,"* ubongo.

THAILAND

LOCATION: Asia
CAPITAL: Bangkok
AREA: 198,117 sq mi (513,120 sq km)
POPULATION ESTIMATE (2012): 67,091,089
GOVERNMENT: Constitutional monarchy
LANGUAGES: Thai (Siamese), English, regional dialects
MONEY: Baht
LIFE EXPECTANCY: 74
LITERACY RATE: 93%

GUESS WHAT? *The world's largest gold Buddha sits in Wat Traimit, a temple located in Bangkok. The gleaming statue is 9.8 feet (3 m) tall and weighs 5.5 tons (5 metric tons).*

TOGO

LOCATION: Africa
CAPITAL: Lomé
AREA: 21,925 sq mi (56,785 sq km)
POPULATION ESTIMATE (2012): 6,961,049
GOVERNMENT: Republic, under transition to multiparty democratic rule
LANGUAGES: French (official), Ewe, Mina, Kabye, Dagomba
MONEY: CFA franc
LIFE EXPECTANCY: 63
LITERACY RATE: 61%

GUESS WHAT? *In the Ewe language, the word* Togo *means "house of sea," though only a small part of the country touches the ocean.*

TONGA

LOCATION: Oceania
CAPITAL: Nuku'alofa
AREA: 288 sq mi (747 sq km)
POPULATION ESTIMATE (2012): 106,146
GOVERNMENT: Constitutional monarchy
LANGUAGES: Tongan and English (both official)
MONEY: Pa'anga
LIFE EXPECTANCY: 75
LITERACY RATE: 99%

GUESS WHAT? *In Tonga, it is illegal to be shirtless in public unless you are at a resort.*

TRINIDAD AND TOBAGO

LOCATION: Caribbean
CAPITAL: Port-of-Spain
AREA: 1,980 sq mi (5,128 sq km)
POPULATION ESTIMATE (2012): 1,226,383
GOVERNMENT: Parliamentary democracy
LANGUAGES: English (official), Caribbean Hindustani, French, Spanish, Chinese
MONEY: Trinidad and Tobago dollar
LIFE EXPECTANCY: 72
LITERACY RATE: 99%

GUESS WHAT? *Trinidad and Tobago is made up of two islands. Tobago makes up only about 6% of the country's total area. Throughout history, it has been invaded or claimed by England, Spain, France, Latvia, the Netherlands, and others.*

TUNISIA

LOCATION: Africa
CAPITAL: Tunis
AREA: 63,170 sq mi
(163,610 sq km)
POPULATION ESTIMATE (2012):
10,732,900
GOVERNMENT: Republic
LANGUAGES: Arabic (official),
French, Berber
MONEY: Tunisian dinar
LIFE EXPECTANCY: 75
LITERACY RATE: 74%

GUESS WHAT? *Scenes from many Hollywood films, including Raiders of the Lost Ark and Star Wars, have been filmed in Tunisia.*

TURKEY

LOCATION: Europe and Asia
CAPITAL: Ankara
AREA: 302,535 sq mi
(783,562 sq km)
POPULATION ESTIMATE (2012):
79,749,461
GOVERNMENT: Republican
parliamentary democracy
LANGUAGES: Turkish (official),
Kurdish, others
MONEY: New Turkish lira
LIFE EXPECTANCY: 73
LITERACY RATE: 87%

GUESS WHAT? *Istanbul, the largest city in Turkey, is the only city in the world that straddles two continents—Europe and Asia.*

TURKMENISTAN

LOCATION: Asia
CAPITAL: Ashgabat
AREA: 188,455 sq mi
(488,100 sq km)
POPULATION ESTIMATE (2012):
5,054,828
GOVERNMENT: Republic with
authoritarian presidential
rule
LANGUAGES: Turkmen (official),
Russian, Uzbek, others
MONEY: Manat
LIFE EXPECTANCY: 69
LITERACY RATE: 99%

GUESS WHAT? *The rocks in Turkmenistan's Koytendag State Nature Reserve are embedded with dinosaur footprints.*

TUVALU

LOCATION: Oceania
CAPITAL: Funafuti
AREA: 10 sq mi (26 sq km)
POPULATION ESTIMATE (2012): 10,619
GOVERNMENT: Parliamentary
democracy
LANGUAGES: Tuvaluan and English
(both official), Samoan, Kiribati
MONEY: Australian dollar,
Tuvaluan dollar
LIFE EXPECTANCY: 65
LITERACY RATE: Not available

GUESS WHAT? *Although it is surrounded by water, there are no rivers, lakes, or streams in Tuvalu. People rely on rain for their drinking water. A water-treatment facility can also remove salt from salt water.*

UGANDA

LOCATION: Africa
CAPITAL: Kampala
AREA: 93,065 sq mi
(241,038 sq km)
POPULATION ESTIMATE (2012):
33,640,833
GOVERNMENT: Republic
LANGUAGES: English (official),
Luganda, other Niger-Congo
languages, Nilo-Saharan
languages, Swahili, Arabic
MONEY: Ugandan shilling
LIFE EXPECTANCY: 53
LITERACY RATE: 67%

GUESS WHAT? *Uganda's national bird is the crested crane. The colors of the country's flag echo the bird's black, yellow, and red feathers.*

UKRAINE

LOCATION: Europe
CAPITAL: Kiev
AREA: 233,032 sq mi
(603,550 sq km)
POPULATION ESTIMATE (2012):
44,854,065
GOVERNMENT: Republic
LANGUAGES: Ukrainian,
Russian, others
MONEY: Hryvnia
LIFE EXPECTANCY: 69
LITERACY RATE: 100%

GUESS WHAT? *The world's largest and heaviest aircraft, the Antonov An-225 Mriya, was designed in Ukraine, in 1988, and is still manufactured in Kiev.*

Countries

UNITED ARAB EMIRATES

LOCATION: Middle East
CAPITAL: Abu Dhabi
AREA: 32,278 sq mi (83,600 sq km)
POPULATION ESTIMATE (2012): 5,314,317
GOVERNMENT: Federation
LANGUAGES: Arabic (official), Persian, English, Hindi, Urdu
MONEY: U.A.E. dirham
LIFE EXPECTANCY: 77
LITERACY RATE: 78%

GUESS WHAT? *The Mall of the Emirates, in Dubai, features an indoor ski slope. The slope is more than 1,300 feet (396 m) tall. It uses 6,000 tons (5,443 metric tons) of snow.*

UNITED KINGDOM

LOCATION: Europe
CAPITAL: London
AREA: 94,058 sq mi (243,610 sq km)
POPULATION ESTIMATE (2012): 63,047,162
GOVERNMENT: Constitutional monarchy
LANGUAGES: English, Scots, Scottish Gaelic, Welsh, Irish
MONEY: British pound
LIFE EXPECTANCY: 80
LITERACY RATE: 99%

GUESS WHAT? *London was the first city to have an underground metro system. More than a million passengers ride the trains every year.*

UNITED STATES

LOCATION: North America
CAPITAL: Washington, D.C.
AREA: 3,794,100 sq mi (9,826,675 sq km)
POPULATION ESTIMATE (2012): 313,847,465
GOVERNMENT: Constitution-based federal republic
LANGUAGES: English, Spanish (spoken by a sizable minority)
MONEY: U.S. dollar
LIFE EXPECTANCY: 78
LITERACY RATE: 99%

GUESS WHAT? *The average U.S. kid uses about 730 crayons by age 10.*

URUGUAY

LOCATION: South America
CAPITAL: Montevideo
AREA: 67,960 sq mi (176,015 sq km)
POPULATION ESTIMATE (2012): 3,316,328
GOVERNMENT: Constitutional republic
LANGUAGES: Spanish (official), Portuñol, Brazilero
MONEY: Uruguayan peso
LIFE EXPECTANCY: 76
LITERACY RATE: 98%

GUESS WHAT? *Uruguay has one of the highest literacy rates and one of the lowest poverty rates in South America.*

UZBEKISTAN

LOCATION: Asia
CAPITAL: Tashkent
AREA: 172,741 sq mi (447,400 sq km)
POPULATION ESTIMATE (2012): 28,394,180
GOVERNMENT: Republic with authoritarian presidential rule
LANGUAGES: Uzbek (official), Russian, Tajik, others
MONEY: Uzbekistani som
LIFE EXPECTANCY: 73
LITERACY RATE: 99%

GUESS WHAT? *Al-Khwarizmi, who introduced the use of Arabic numbers, was born in Uzbekistan. He is sometimes called the father of algebra.*

VANUATU

LOCATION: Oceania
CAPITAL: Port-Vila
AREA: 4,706 sq mi (12,189 sq km)
POPULATION ESTIMATE (2012): 256,155
GOVERNMENT: Parliamentary republic
LANGUAGES: Most people speak one of more than 100 local languages; Bislama, English
MONEY: Vatu
LIFE EXPECTANCY: 65
LITERACY RATE: 74%

GUESS WHAT? *Vanuatu is an archipelago (see page 109). It consists of about 82 islands, known as the New Hebrides. Most are inhabited and feature mountains, tropical rain forests, and active volcanoes.*

VATICAN CITY (HOLY SEE)

LOCATION: Europe
CAPITAL: Vatican City
AREA: 0.17 sq mi (0.44 sq km)
POPULATION ESTIMATE (2012): 836
GOVERNMENT: Ecclesiastical
LANGUAGES: Italian, Latin, French
MONEY: Euro
LIFE EXPECTANCY: Not available
LITERACY RATE: 100%

GUESS WHAT? *A walled-in area within the city of Rome, Italy, Vatican City is the smallest nation-state in the world. It is only about seven-tenths the size of the National Mall in Washington, D.C.*

VENEZUELA

LOCATION: South America
CAPITAL: Caracas
AREA: 352,143 sq mi (912,050 sq km)
POPULATION ESTIMATE (2012): 28,047,938
GOVERNMENT: Federal republic
LANGUAGES: Spanish (official), native languages
MONEY: Bolívar
LIFE EXPECTANCY: 74
LITERACY RATE: 93%

GUESS WHAT? *Venezuela has the largest oil reserves in the Western Hemisphere and the second largest in the world.*

VIETNAM

LOCATION: Asia
CAPITAL: Hanoi
AREA: 127,881 sq mi (331,210 sq km)
POPULATION ESTIMATE (2012): 91,519,289
GOVERNMENT: Communist state
LANGUAGES: Vietnamese (official), French, English, Khmer, Chinese
MONEY: Dong
LIFE EXPECTANCY: 72
LITERACY RATE: 94%

GUESS WHAT? *About 40% of all Vietnamese people—more than 30 million individuals—share the same family name, Nguyen.*

YEMEN

LOCATION: Middle East
CAPITAL: Sanaa
AREA: 203,850 sq mi (527,968 sq km)
POPULATION ESTIMATE (2012): 24,771,809
GOVERNMENT: Republic
LANGUAGE: Arabic
MONEY: Yemeni rial
LIFE EXPECTANCY: 64
LITERACY RATE: 64%

GUESS WHAT? *Yemen is home to Tawakkol Karman, the first Arab woman to win the Nobel Peace Prize. She won the award in 2011 for working hard for women's rights and promoting peace.*

ZAMBIA

LOCATION: Africa
CAPITAL: Lusaka
AREA: 290,587 sq mi (752,618 sq km)
POPULATION ESTIMATE (2012): 13,817,479
GOVERNMENT: Republic
LANGUAGES: Bemba, Nyanja, Tonga, Lozi, Lunda, Kaonde, Luvale, and English (all official), others
MONEY: Kwacha
LIFE EXPECTANCY: 53
LITERACY RATE: 81%

GUESS WHAT? *Zambia got its name from the Zambezi River, which is an important source of energy, fish, and water for crops. Zambezi comes from the local word* yambezhi, *which translates to "heart of all."*

ZIMBABWE

LOCATION: Africa
CAPITAL: Harare
AREA: 150,872 sq mi (390,757 sq km)
POPULATION ESTIMATE (2012): 12,619,600
GOVERNMENT: Parliamentary democracy
LANGUAGES: English (official), Shona, Ndebele (Sindebele)
MONEY: Zimbabwean dollar
LIFE EXPECTANCY: 52
LITERACY RATE: 91%

GUESS WHAT? *Zimbabwe is known for its Balancing Rocks, unusual stone formations that look like pillars and stacks of blocks. They were created over many, many years as the surrounding rock was worn down by the wind and rain.*

INCREDIBLE PLACES AROUND THE WORLD

Eiffel Tower, France

Empire State Building, United States

Hollywood Walk of Fame, United States

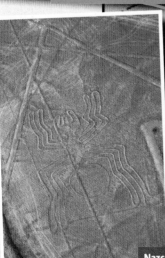
Nazca lines, Peru

TOP 5 Most-Photographed Places

Researchers studied 35 million Flickr photos. They discovered the places that people most visited and photographed. Here are the five most-photographed city sites.

1. Empire State Building, New York, New York
2. Trafalgar Square, London, England
3. Union Square, San Francisco, California
4. Eiffel Tower, Paris, France
5. Hollywood Walk of Fame, Los Angeles, California

Source: FLICKR

Niterói Contemporary Art Museum, Brazil

Temple of Abu Simbel, Egypt

St. Basil's Cathedral, Russia

Potala Palace, China (Tibet)

Shwedagon Pagoda, Myanmar (Burma)

Itsukushima Shrine, Japan

a Falls, Zambia and Zimbabwe

Sydney Opera House, Australia

Countries

95

RENEWABLE SOURCES OF ENERGY

Renewable energy sources are created continually by nature. They are sources of energy that can be used over and over again. Renewable sources include biomass, geothermal energy, hydrogen, sunlight, wind, and hydropower.

BIOMASS is an energy source found in plants and animals. It includes such natural products as wood, corn, sugarcane, manure, and plant and animal fats. It can also be found in organic trash. Biomass energy can be used in three ways.

⇨ When burned, it creates steam that can be converted into electricity or captured to heat homes.

⇨ Sources such as manure and organic trash give off a gas called **methane,** which can be used as fuel.

⇨ Crops and plant and animal fats can be made into **ethanol** and **biodiesel,** two fuels used in vehicles.

Some biomass facilities burn wood chips and other scraps from lumberyards.

GEOTHERMAL ENERGY uses the heat that rises from Earth's core, which is located 3,000 to 4,000 miles (4,800 to 6,400 km) under the planet's surface. The most common way of harnessing geothermal energy involves capturing steam that comes from deep in the Earth and emerges in hot springs, fumaroles (vents in the Earth's surface that give off steam), **volcanoes,** and geysers (fountainlike bursts of hot water). This steam, heat, or hot water can be trapped in pipes that lead directly to electrical power plants and even to homes.

HYDROGEN is the most common element in the universe. It is everywhere, but it doesn't exist on its own. Instead, hydrogen atoms bind with the atoms of other elements to form such compounds as water (hydrogen and oxygen), methane (hydrogen and carbon), and ammonia (hydrogen and nitrogen). Up-to-date technology is being used to separate hydrogen molecules and turn the hydrogen gas into a liquid that can be used in fuel cells. These fuel cells can power vehicles and electrical generators.

SUNLIGHT can be converted into heat and electricity.

⇨ Solar cells absorb the heat from the sun and convert it into energy. They are used in calculators, watches, and some highway signs.

⇨ Solar power plants collect the sun's heat on huge **solar panels,** which then heat water to produce steam. The steam, in turn, powers electrical generators. A similar system is used on a smaller scale in solar-powered homes.

GUESS WHAT? Renewable energy sources do not rely on fossil fuels, but that doesn't mean that they are completely eco-friendly. Hydropower dams and reservoirs can have environmental impacts, such as the disruption of plant and animal life.

HYDROPOWER is energy generated by the movement of water. Water pressure can turn the shafts of powerful electrical generators, making electricity. Waterfalls and fast-running rivers are major sources of hydropower because their natural flow creates pressure. Another way to harness hydropower is the storage method, in which dams are used to trap water in large reservoirs. When power is needed, the dams are opened and the water flows out. The water pressure created is then converted into energy.

WIND has been used as an energy source for centuries. For example, windmills were once used to help grind grain. Today, wind towers much taller than those windmills—usually about 20 stories high—are used to capture the power of wind. The wind turns giant blades connected to a long shaft that moves up and down to power electrical generators. Scientists and engineers are constantly working to improve the shape and placement of windmills; some windmills are being placed offshore to capture strong ocean breezes.

Energy

HOW CAN A STOVE POWER YOUR PHONE?

A company called BioLite has created a cool, new type of cooking stove. It works with a wood fire to cook food and is able to harness some of the heat energy from the fire and convert it into electric power. This kind of invention could be used to provide efficient electricity to people who lose power after natural disasters or who live in the developing world and are not hooked up to a power grid.

NONRENEWABLE SOURCES OF ENERGY

Most of the energy we use comes from burning fossil fuels. Fossil fuels are found in many places on Earth, usually deep under the Earth's surface. They were formed millions of years ago, when prehistoric plants and animals died and what was left over turned into gooey petroleum, hard coal, or natural gas. Once these natural resources are used up, they are gone forever. Uranium, a metallic chemical element, is another nonrenewable source, but it is not a fossil fuel. Uranium is converted into fuel and used in nuclear power plants.

COAL is a hard rock made of carbon. It started out as decaying plant matter that was covered with many layers of dirt. Over the course of millions of years, the pressure of all this dirt, as well as Earth's heat, transformed the matter into coal. Because coal takes so long to form, it cannot be manufactured.

GUESS WHAT? Since the 1880s, coal has been the top electricity-producing fuel in the United States. But in 2012, natural gas tied with coal for the top spot.

PETROLEUM is found deep within the Earth and has to be drilled and piped to the surface. It is made of decaying plant and animal remains that were trapped or covered with mud. Like coal, it was formed from pressure and heat over millions of years. Petroleum can be refined into oil, gasoline, and diesel fuel, which are used to power engines in vehicles, machines in factories, and furnaces in homes.

GUESS WHAT? Many household products, such as deodorant, crayons, bubble gum, CDs and DVDs, sunglasses, shower curtains, and footballs, contain petroleum.

GUESS WHAT? People in the United States use some of the coal that is unearthed here, but companies also export coal to other countries. In 2011, the U.S. exported more coal to the Netherlands than to any other country.

NATURAL GAS was formed in the same way and over the same amount of time as coal and petroleum, except that it is the odorless by-product of decaying matter. Bubbles of gas are trapped underground and can be piped to the surface. Natural gas is used as a source of home heating as well as for cooking.

TOP 5 Crude-Oil-Producing States

The liquid petroleum that is pumped to the surface is known as crude oil. In 2011, the United States imported about 60% of the crude oil it used from other countries. The rest came from within the United States. Here are the top oil-producing states.

1. Texas
2. North Dakota
3. Alaska
4. California
5. Oklahoma

Source: U.S. Energy Information Administration, 2012

NUCLEAR ENERGY was developed in the 20th century. It relies on the heat given off when an atom is split during a process known as **nuclear fission.** In nuclear fission, the nucleus of a uranium-235 atom is hit with an atomic particle called a neutron. The uranium atom splits and gives off a lot of heat, which is used to boil water. The steam from this water powers electrical generators. Nuclear power does not cause the kind of air pollution that other fossil fuels emit, but the waste created during nuclear fission can be harmful to people and the environment. It is extremely dangerous and must be stored for thousands of years away from people.

UNITED STATES ENERGY USE

More energy is used for industrial purposes than by people in their homes.

COMMERCIAL SPACES 19%
Offices, schools, stores, malls, hotels, hospitals, and other buildings

INDUSTRY 31%
Including manufacturing, agriculture, mining, and construction

RESIDENTIAL 22%
Houses and apartments

TRANSPORTATION 28%
Cars, trucks, buses, trains, motorcycles, subways, aircraft, and boats

Energy

YOU HAVE THE POWER!

For the past several years, scientists around the planet have been experimenting with ways to harness the energy created by the ordinary movements of people. Walking and pedaling a bicycle—two simple, everyday activities—produce kinetic energy, and emerging technologies are now able to convert that energy into electricity. Human movements are not being used as an energy source on a large scale, but here are a few cool places around the world that are harnessing the power of the people.

> **Kinetic energy** is the energy of motion. Moving people or objects have kinetic energy. Heat, light, sound, and electrical energy are types of kinetic energy.

LET'S STEP ON IT!

Thanks to the creation of a variety of piezoelectric (pee-*ay*-zo-ih-*lek*-trik) floor tiles, human footsteps are powering up everything from a Dutch dance club to subway ticket gates in Tokyo, Japan. Crystals in the floor tiles react to the pressure of people's feet on the tiles. The pressure gets converted into electricity. In Toulouse, France, foot traffic generates enough electricity to power the streetlights. For several years, a club in Rotterdam, the Netherlands, featured a dance floor that converted the dancers' motions into the electricity that kept the room's lighting system going. Piezoelectricity has been researched since the late 1880s, but the idea to use people's footsteps to generate electricity is relatively new and holds great promise for the future.

Twelve PaveGen rubber tiles, which are similar to piezoelectric tiles, were installed on a walkway at the London subway station that connected visitors to the 2012 Olympic Park. Over the course of the Olympic Games, the tiles recorded nearly 1 million footsteps, which created enough electricity to keep the walkway well lit.

Energy-generating tiles at the 2012 London Olympics

Young women walk over a piezoelectric sheet in Tokyo. The sheet generates electricity to power a holiday display.

 GUESS WHAT? PaveGen tiles are largely made from recycled materials, including old Nike sneakers!

A crowd demonstrates how simple it is to power the lights—just by dancing.

EXERCISE TO KEEP THE LIGHTS ON!

In 2010, to increase guests' awareness about the world's energy needs, the award-winning green Crowne Plaza Copenhagen Towers, in Denmark, installed two exercise bikes that produced electricity. Guests who pedaled long enough to produce 10 watt-hours or more of electricity received a free meal for their efforts. (It takes 100 watt-hours of electricity to power one 100-watt lightbulb for an hour.) Producing 10 watt-hours of electricity took most guests less than 15 minutes, so the amount of effort required by guests was minimal.

But hotels aren't the only places experimenting with energy-harvesting stationary bikes. At some health clubs around the country, members can not only burn calories as they pedal but they can help keep the power on in the gym. The pedaling motion turns a generator that produces electricity used by the building.

The board on the right shows how many watts of electricity this fitness instructor has created during an exercise class.

Energy

MULTITASKING IN MOTION

A Belgian manufacturer has come up with the We-Bike circular table, which comes with seats and pedals for three people. The idea is to give people the chance to get a little exercise while at work, waiting for a plane, or even in a restaurant, and at the same time, generate enough electricity to power up mobile devices. Other versions of the table can fit together into long, straight lines or curved formations.

The We-Bike is made with sustainable materials.

How Does the Garden Grow?

By Bryan Walsh

Just because something is green doesn't mean it is good for the environment! Take the average American lawn or garden—each one drinks up water at alarming rates. It is especially bad in the western United States, where more than half of the water used by homeowners is poured into landscaping. Chemical fertilizers and pesticides can damage the land as well. But xeriscaping (*zeer*-ih-skay-ping), which means "dry landscaping," is becoming more and more popular. "We're getting the message that homeowners aren't interested in environmentally irresponsible things," says Joel Lerner, founder of the landscaping firm Environmental Design in Maryland.

Replacing grass with less-thirsty plants and laying down mulch and walkways are a few ways to use less water on a lawn.

Growing Green

Talk to your parents about having a healthy yard and garden. Here are some tips to make your yard more beautiful and better for the environment.

Say No to Mow

Grass is a thirsty plant, so think about ways to limit your lawn to areas that really need it. Some kinds of grass don't need as much water. Stone or brick walkways are a good way to cover ground.

Mulch Away

Mulching—spreading material like wood chips or stone around plants—helps keep the water from evaporating into the air. This is a very important part of dry landscaping.

Dig It

Try adding 3 to 5 inches (8 to 13 cm) of compost—organic material that is made up of natural waste such as dead leaves or banana peels—to the top of your soil. Then work this into the soil, and get ready for things to grow.

Just a Drip

Even trimmed-down gardens need water, especially as they just start to sprout. But they rarely need as much as people think. Use a drip emitter, a special tool that puts the plug on wasted water.

Compost

GUESS WHAT? About 30% of the water that families use is to water lawns, wash cars, and clean outdoor areas. But most people water their lawns too often and too much. Try to cut down. If you step on grass and it bounces back, the grass does not need water.

102

BIOMES

The landmasses on Earth can be grouped into large regions called biomes. The animal and plant life of each biome reflects the climate, temperature, and geographical features that exist there. Here are the six major biomes.

Fennec fox

Zebras

Deserts can be hot or cold. They receive very little rain. The Sahara is a hot, dry desert. Cactuses, fennec foxes, camels, and scorpions are some plants and animals found there. The Gobi Desert, in northern Asia, and the Antarctic are cold deserts. Shrubs, sagebrush, gazelles, and hawks are some examples of plants and animals found in cold deserts.

There are several types of **grassland,** including the savannas of South America, the prairies of North America, and the steppes of central Asia. Grass is the main type of plant because there isn't enough rain to support many shrubs or trees. Grassland animals include zebras, elephants, giraffes, buffalo, ostriches, meerkats, and coyotes.

Macaws

Deer

Tropical rain forests are hot, humid, and rainy. More kinds of trees exist in rain forests than anywhere else in the world. Rain forests in Africa, Asia, and South America have different species of animals and insects, but include monkeys, jaguars, toucans, colorful butterflies, ants, and camouflaged stick insects.

In **temperate forests**, also known as deciduous forests, there are four seasons and a moderate amount of rain. Many hardwood trees, such as maple and oak, grow in temperate forests. Other plant life includes mushrooms, moss, and lichen. Deer, foxes, squirrels, frogs, rabbits, eagles, cardinals, and black bears are also found in temperate forests.

Gray wolf

Polar bears

Winter in the **taiga** is long, snowy, and cold. The summers are short and wet. Many evergreen, or coniferous, trees live there. The rocky soil of the taiga is covered with twigs and evergreen needles. Elk, grizzly bears, moose, lynx, wolverines, rabbits, sparrows, and reindeer are some examples of taiga wildlife.

It is very cold year-round in the **tundra,** and there is hardly any rain or snow. The soil is permanently frozen, preventing trees or most plant life, aside from moss, lichen, and grasses, from growing. During the short, cool summers, some flowering plants flourish. Tundra animals include polar bears, foxes, seals, wolves, owls, falcons, and salmon.

Environment

THE DANGERS OF FOSSIL FUELS

About 82% of the energy used in the United States today is supplied by fossil fuels (see page 98). Unearthing these fuels and using them to create electricity has negative effects on humans, wildlife, and the environment. For example, burning fossil fuels contributes to global warming, causes acid rain, and makes water dirty and air unhealthy. Mining coal damages the land, destroys water supplies, and harms the health of miners.

ACID RAIN

Many pollutants, including sulfur dioxide (SO_2) and nitrogen dioxide (NO_2), are released into the air when fossil fuels such as coal and petroleum are burned. Acid rain is formed when water vapor in the air combines with SO_2 and NO_2 to form sulfuric and nitric acids. Acid rain falls to the ground, damaging trees and other plants. It poisons streams, rivers, and lakes. Fish and other aquatic animals fall ill or die in the poisoned water. Acid rain eats away at stone, destroying buildings and monuments.

THE GREENHOUSE EFFECT

Earth's atmosphere is made up of layers of gases that surround the planet and protect it from extreme heat and cold. Burning fossil fuels releases carbon dioxide (CO_2), methane, and other gases that trap the heat of the sun in the atmosphere, just as the walls of a greenhouse trap heat and moisture inside. In this way, gases like CO_2 and methane help keep the temperature of the planet warm enough for living things. But scientists believe that humans are producing far more CO_2 and methane than the atmosphere needs, causing global warming.

GUESS WHAT? Without gases like CO_2 and methane in the atmosphere, the Earth would have an average temperature of 0°F (-18°C).

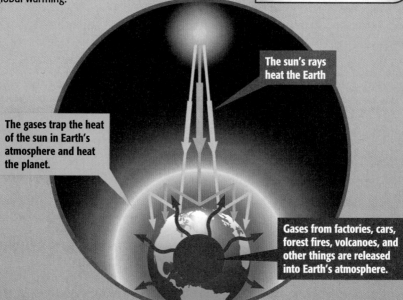

The sun's rays heat the Earth

The gases trap the heat of the sun in Earth's atmosphere and heat the planet.

Gases from factories, cars, forest fires, volcanoes, and other things are released into Earth's atmosphere.

GUESS WHAT? For every gallon of gasoline used, about 19 pounds (9 kg) of carbon dioxide are produced. That may not seem like a lot, but in 2011, Americans used about 367 million gallons (1.4 billion L) of gasoline per day—that's almost 7 billion pounds (3.2 billion kg) of carbon dioxide.

MAKING A MESS OF THE ENVIRONMENT

Earth is always changing. Volcanoes, earthquakes, floods, erosion, and other natural occurrences constantly alter the planet. Humans also leave their mark on the environment. Industrial development, overfarming, deforestation, and generating trash are just a few of the ways that people can damage the world around them. Here are some forms of pollution that threaten the health of the planet.

SMOG

The word *smog* is a combination of the words *smoke* and *fog.* Car and truck exhaust, the burning of wood, factory emissions, and certain chemical processes release particles into the air. These particles contain pollutants, which can get trapped in the air close to the ground. The resulting smog can be especially harmful to the elderly and people with asthma or other breathing problems.

OIL SPILLS

Oil poisons, blinds, suffocates, and kills sea creatures. It also harms the birds and land animals that come into contact with polluted water or food sources.

> **GUESS WHAT?** One of the world's worst oil spills was the Deepwater Horizon spill that began on April 20, 2010. An estimated 210 million gallons (795 million L) of oil were released into the Gulf of Mexico.

CHEMICAL CONTAMINATION

Chemical contamination of the Earth comes in different forms, the most common being agricultural pesticides (used to kill insects), herbicides (which kill weeds), and fertilizers (used to enrich the soil), as well as the chemical waste products of factories—especially those that work with metals and plastics. These contaminants can hurt people and wildlife.

TRASH

More than 250 million tons (227 million metric tons) of garbage are produced in the United States every year. That's more than 4.3 pounds (2 kg) of waste per person each day. All of this garbage poses a serious threat to wildlife. Inorganic items like plastics, metal, Styrofoam, and glass do not decompose quickly. They may take months, years, or even centuries to break down. If not properly disposed of, inorganic trash can end up clogging waterways and damaging habitats, or it may be mistaken for food by animals.

Environment

105

KIDS COMMITTED TO ENVIRONMENTAL ACTION

There are a lot of ways one person's efforts can have a positive impact on the environment. Here are four determined kids and what they've already done at a young age to help our planet. They're all featured in author and filmmaker Lynne Cherry's documentary series, *Young Voices for the Planet.*

SIBERIAN CITIZEN SCIENTIST

Thirteen-year-old Anya Suslova lives along the Lena River, in Siberia, an area of the Arctic where the Earth is warming the most. She helped Max Holmes, an Arctic researcher from the Woods Hole Research Center, collect samples during the Arctic winter, when Holmes was back in the United States. Every two weeks, Anya went out on her father's boat and dug holes in the ice to reach the water below. Using bottles she received from Holmes, Anya collected the water samples and shipped them to him for analysis. What the samples reveal about changes in the river will help Holmes with his research on global warming.

Anya Suslova

PLANTER FOR THE PLANET

Felix Finkbeiner

Felix Finkbeiner was only 9 years old when he founded Plant for the Planet. While doing research for a homework assignment on the climate crisis, Felix came across information about Wangari Maathai, a Kenyan environmentalist who founded a movement that has planted more than 50 million trees in Africa. Felix decided that his fellow students in Germany could also plant trees. As the result of one school assignment, Felix founded a nonprofit organization that, in just a few years, has been responsible for planting more than 12 billion trees around the world!

ARTIST FOR THE ENVIRONMENT

After the 2010 oil spill in the Gulf of Mexico, 11-year-old Olivia Bouler, an artist and animal lover from New York, became an activist with a paintbrush. She created and sold 500 paintings of birds and raised more than $200,000, which she donated to the National Audubon Society for its rescue and cleanup efforts to help birds affected by the spill.

Olivia Bouler

CAMPAIGNER FOR CLIMATE CHANGE

Alec Loorz meets with Al Gore.

The Academy Award–winning documentary film about climate change, *An Inconvenient Truth,* based on former Vice President Al Gore's book of the same name, inspired then-12-year-old Alec Loorz to make his own multimedia presentation about climate change to share with other young people. He also founded the nonprofit organization Kids vs. Global Warming to educate kids about how they can get involved and help the environment. Alec has met Al Gore, who invited him to become an officially trained presenter for his climate-change program. Alex eagerly accepted! Alex has now given the presentation more than 100 times, to thousands of people.

SCIENCE TOYS FROM TRASH

Engineer Arvind Gupta found his calling when he began teaching science to children living in villages in India. His initial idea was simply to make learning science fun for kids. Now he helps run the Children's Science Center in Pune, India, where he and his colleagues have designed more than 800 educational science toys—all from recycled trash! On their Toys from Trash website, they have posted free visual instructions on how kids can make the toys themselves. Some science toys include balancing toys, magnetic toys, **simple motors,** and bottle jets. India is still considered a developing country, and there are not a lot of options for science toys for kids.

GUESS WHAT? One of the most popular toys Gupta and his colleagues created is called Matchstick Mecanno. Using small, rubber bicycle valve tubes and matchsticks, kids can create simple shapes, such as triangles, or build more complex 3-D constructions.

TIME FOR KIDS GAME

WORLDLY WORDS

Hidden in this grid are 15 terms about the environment. Can you find them all?

GRASSLAND   RAIN FOREST   OZONE   POLLUTION   TAIGA
RECYCLE   SMOG   WILDLIFE   REUSE   ECOSYSTEM
GLACIER   DESERT   TUNDRA   TREES   EARTH

G	R	A	S	S	L	A	N	D	Z	E	B
L	K	R	E	C	Y	C	L	E	A	L	O
A	E	A	R	T	H	D	P	S	M	O	G
C	M	I	A	J	U	O	Z	E	C	Z	W
I	A	N	G	T	U	N	D	R	A	O	I
E	R	F	E	X	N	H	O	T	J	N	L
R	P	O	L	L	U	T	I	O	N	E	D
K	O	R	V	I	R	E	U	S	E	S	L
T	R	E	E	S	V	A	P	Y	F	A	I
I	F	S	D	O	E	U	S	D	G	X	F
X	R	T	A	I	G	A	M	H	U	Y	E
E	C	O	S	Y	S	T	E	M	V	O	G

Environment

ANSWERS ON PAGE 244

THE SEVEN CONTINENTS

NORTH AMERICA
(including Central America and the Caribbean)
How big is it? 9,449,460 square miles (24,474,000 sq km)
Highest point Mount McKinley, 20,322 feet (6,194 m)
Lowest point Death Valley, 282 feet (86 m) below sea level

ASIA
(including the Middle East)
How big is it? 17,212,000 square miles (44,579,000 sq km)
Highest point Mount Everest, 29,035 feet (8,850 m)
Lowest point Dead Sea, 1,286 feet (392 m) below sea level

EUROPE
How big is it? 3,837,000 square miles (9,938,000 sq km)
Highest point Mount Elbrus, 18,481 feet (5,642 m)
Lowest point Caspian Sea, 92 feet (28 m) below sea level

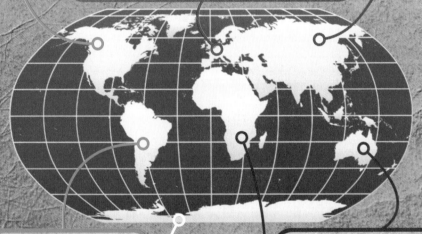

SOUTH AMERICA
How big is it? 6,879,000 square miles (17,819,000 sq km)
Highest point Mount Aconcagua, 22,834 feet (6,960 m)
Lowest point Valdes Peninsula, 131 feet (40 m) below sea level

AUSTRALIA/OCEANIA
How big is it? 3,132,000 square miles (8,112,000 sq km)
Highest point Mount Wilhelm, 14,794 feet (4,509 m)
Lowest point Lake Eyre, 52 feet (16 m) below sea level

ANTARCTICA
How big is it? 5,100,000 square miles (13,209,000 sq km)
Highest point Vinson Massif, 16,066 feet (4,897 m)
Lowest point Bentley Subglacial Trench, 8,383 feet (2,555 m) below sea level

AFRICA
How big is it? 11,608,000 square miles (30,065,000 sq km)
Highest point Mount Kilimanjaro, 19,340 feet (5,895 m)
Lowest point Lake Assal, 512 feet (156 m) below sea level

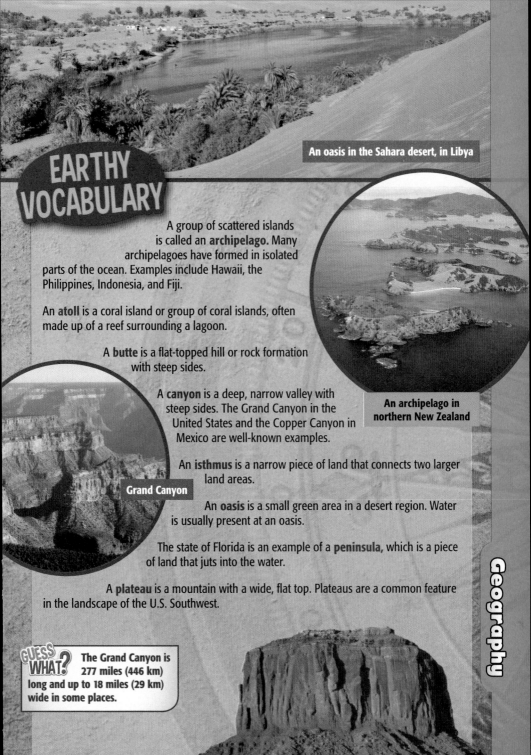

EARTHY VOCABULARY

An oasis in the Sahara desert, in Libya

A group of scattered islands is called an **archipelago.** Many archipelagoes have formed in isolated parts of the ocean. Examples include Hawaii, the Philippines, Indonesia, and Fiji.

An **atoll** is a coral island or group of coral islands, often made up of a reef surrounding a lagoon.

A **butte** is a flat-topped hill or rock formation with steep sides.

A **canyon** is a deep, narrow valley with steep sides. The Grand Canyon in the United States and the Copper Canyon in Mexico are well-known examples.

An archipelago in northern New Zealand

An **isthmus** is a narrow piece of land that connects two larger land areas.

Grand Canyon

An **oasis** is a small green area in a desert region. Water is usually present at an oasis.

The state of Florida is an example of a **peninsula,** which is a piece of land that juts into the water.

A **plateau** is a mountain with a wide, flat top. Plateaus are a common feature in the landscape of the U.S. Southwest.

GUESS WHAT? The Grand Canyon is 277 miles (446 km) long and up to 18 miles (29 km) wide in some places.

Merrick Butte is located in Monument Valley on the Arizona–Utah border.

Geography

THE FIVE OCEANS

More than 70% of the surface of Earth is water. Here are the five oceans that cover much of the planet.

ARCTIC OCEAN

Area: 5,427,000 square miles (14,056,000 sq km)

Average depth: 3,953 feet (1,205 m)

Chunks of ice float in the Arctic Ocean.

ATLANTIC OCEAN

Area: 29,637,900 square miles (76,762,000 sq km)

Average depth: 12,880 feet (3,926 m)

Waves from the Atlantic Ocean crash onto the shore in Portugal.

INDIAN OCEAN

Area: 26,469,500 square miles (68,556,000 sq km)

Average depth: 13,002 feet (3,963 m)

A sea turtle swims over a coral reef in the Indian Ocean.

PACIFIC OCEAN

Area: 60,060,700 square miles (155,557,000 sq km)

Average depth: 15,215 feet (4,638 m)

A humpback whale pokes its head above water in the Pacific Ocean.

GUESS WHAT? The Pacific Ocean covers about one-third of Earth's surface.

SOUTHERN OCEAN

Area: 7,848,300 square miles (20,327,000 sq km)

Average depth: 13,100–16,400 feet (4,000–5,000 m)*

*Official depths of the Southern Ocean are in dispute.

A large ship travels through ice in the Southern Ocean.

WATERY WORDS

A **bay** is a section of an ocean or lake that fills an indentation in the coastline. Large bays are usually called gulfs. Examples include San Francisco Bay and the Gulf of Mexico.

A **canal** is a man-made waterway. The Suez and Panama Canals are two well-known examples built to provide shorter passageways for people and goods. Venice, Italy, is famous for its canals.

At the mouth of a river, water will often branch out into a triangle-shaped area called a **delta**. Known for their diverse wildlife, **estuaries** form in deltas. They are partially separated bodies of water where the salt water from the ocean mixes with freshwater from the river. Rivers with deltas include the Nile and the Mississippi. Chesapeake Bay (in Maryland and Virginia) and Puget Sound (in Washington) are estuaries.

A **fjord** is a narrow inlet of sea that is bordered by steep cliffs. There are many fjords along the coastline of Norway.

A **geyser** is a naturally occurring hot spring that sometimes sprays water and steam above the ground.

Geyser

Reefs are found just under the surface of a body of water. They are made up of coral, rock, or sand.

A **sea** is an inland body of water. It is often filled with salt water and is sometimes connected to the ocean. Examples include the Aegean Sea off of Greece and the Dead Sea between Israel and Jordan.

A **strait**, sometimes called a channel, is a narrow strip of water connecting two larger bodies of water. The Bering Strait is between Alaska and Russia. The English Channel separates Great Britain and France.

Coral reef

BUT CAN YOU DRINK IT?

Only about 2.5% of the water on Earth is freshwater. The rest is salt water. Only a small amount of the world's freshwater is safe and available for use by people. Water is a valuable natural resource—remember to use it wisely. Take shorter showers and don't leave water running when you are not using it.

GUESS WHAT? The Dead Sea is very salty. The high salt content of the water makes the water much more dense than the water in most other seas. The high density of the water makes it extremely easy for people to float in the water.

Dead Sea

DISPUTED LANDS

On a map, the borders between countries seem immovable. But on the ground, it's not always clear where one country begins and another one ends. Border disputes have been the cause of many wars throughout history and continue to be sources of conflict to the present day.

KASHMIR'S LINE OF CONTROL

To the north and west of India and to the north and east of neighboring Pakistan sits the hotly disputed region called Kashmir. After India's independence from Britain in 1947, the country was divided into two nations: India and Pakistan. India's population is mostly Hindu, whereas Pakistan's is largely Muslim. Each of the new nations wanted control of the region of Kashmir. From 1947 to 1948, they fought their

Most families living in Kashmir are Muslims.

first war over it. With the United Nations' help, the countries agreed to a ceasefire along a line that gave control of one-third of Kashmir to Pakistan and two-thirds to India. In 1972, that line became known as the Line of Control. That line still exists today.

Pakistan insists that since the majority of Kashmiri citizens are Muslim, it should have control over the entire region. As for the Kashmiri people, since 1989, they have been fighting for independence from both India and Pakistan.

GUESS WHAT? In the Kashmir Valley of Kashmir, 95% of the people are Muslims, while in the Jammu region 66% are Hindu. Both these regions are in Indian Kashmir.

SOUTH OSSETIA'S FIGHT FOR INDEPENDENCE

After the Russian revolution in 1917, when the Soviet Union was formed, the Soviet region of Georgia was given two republics. One was South Ossetia. As a republic, South Ossetia had some independence from Georgia, but the South Ossetians wanted to be completely self-governing. After decades of violent flare-ups between South Ossetia and Georgia, South Ossetia declared its independence in 1990. But Georgia refused to recognize it. The next year, the Soviet Union collapsed. Georgia, Russia, and other regions became separate countries, while South Ossetia remained a part of Georgia.

South Ossetia still wants to be independent. And it has a large and powerful ally in Russia. In 2008, Georgia launched an air and ground assault on South Ossetia. Russia came to South Ossetia's defense, sending in troops

Even while it fights for complete independence, South Ossetia still holds presidential elections.

and attacking Georgia by air. Russia was so successful, it began to take over parts of Georgia. It pulled back only after the international community put pressure on it. Russia declared South Ossetia to be a fully independent nation, but most other countries do not recognize it because of the conflict that led up to this declaration.

GUESS WHAT? Most South Ossetians have Russian, not Georgian, passports.

WHAT'S IN A NAME?

In 2010, Topeka, Kansas, temporarily changed its name to Google, Kansas, in the hopes of getting the company to relocate there. Here are some other places that have been renamed, along with the reason for the name change.

Name (type of place)	Previous Name	Year Changed	Reason(s) for Change
Beijing, China (city)	Peking, China	1949	Peking is how the name is written using the Latin alphabet. Beijing is closer to the Chinese pronunciation. The name was officially changed to Beijing (a name it had held during the Ming Dynasty centuries ago) when China came under communist rule.
Truth or Consequences, New Mexico (town)	Hot Springs, New Mexico	1950	A radio quiz show called *Truth or Consequences* promised to hold a broadcast in the first town that named itself after the program. The show now broadcasts from the town once a year.
Tanzania (country)	Tanganyika and Zanzibar	1964	Two states in East Africa under British rule gained independence and joined their land—and names—to form a new country.
Guyana (country)	British Guiana	1966	The South American country became independent from British rule.
Myanmar (country)	Burma	1989	When the military took control of the country, they changed the name. Myanmar is the name recognized by the United Nations, but not by all countries, because they do not recognize the right of the military to rule by force.
St. Petersburg, Russia (city)	Leningrad, Russia	1991	Originally named St. Petersburg by Tsar Peter the Great in 1703, the city became Petrograd in 1914 and then Leningrad in 1924. It became St. Petersburg again in 1991, after the collapse of the Soviet Union. The city's residents voted to restore the name.
Czech Republic and Slovakia (two countries)	Czechoslovakia	1993	The people of this European country voted for a peaceful separation.
Mumbai, India (city)	Bombay, India	1995	Bombay was thought to be a leftover name from when Great Britain ruled India. Mumbai comes from two words that mean "mother" in Marathi, the language of the ethnic party in power who insisted on the name change.
Sleepy Hollow, New York (village)	North Tarrytown, New York	1996	The citizens wanted to honor the famous Washington Irving short story "The Legend of Sleepy Hollow," which was set there.

Geography

St. Petersburg, Russia

GOVERNMENT

TYPES OF GOVERNMENT

There are many different kinds of government in the world. The United States is a **federal republic.** In a federal republic, key officials are elected to run a central government that shares power with a number of smaller, locally elected governments. In the United States, the President, Vice President, and members of Congress are the main part of the central government, which is based in Washington, D.C. Each of the 50 states elects its own governor and other officials. These officials make decisions about issues that are particular to their state or to regions within that state. The United States is also a **democracy.** The people elect the government officials. Other examples of federal republics include Austria, Germany, Pakistan, Mexico, Brazil, and Nigeria.

Here are just a few of the other kinds of government.

Absolute monarchy: The monarch—a king or queen—rules the country without any checks or balances or opposition. The monarch inherits the kingdom and is not elected. Countries with absolute monarchies include Oman, Saudi Arabia, and Swaziland.

Constitutional monarchy: The monarch is the head of state within guidelines and with restrictions as spelled out in a country's constitution. Often the main business of government is handled by an elected Prime Minister and a Parliament. Examples of constitutional monarchies include the United Kingdom, Denmark, Norway, and Thailand.

Theocracy: This type of government recognizes religion as the supreme authority and appoints religious leaders to rule the people according to religious laws. Iran is an Islamic theocracy. The country has a President but the highest-ranking authority is a religious leader and politician called the Supreme Leader.

Iran's Supreme Leader, Ayatollah Ali Khamenei (left), and President Mahmoud Ahmadinejad (right)

Communist: A communist government controls and owns all of a country's land and many businesses. It controls many things about the everyday life of its citizens. China and Cuba are two communist countries.

GUESS WHAT? Queen Elizabeth II of the United Kingdom has ruled for more than 60 years. But the longest-reigning living monarch in 2012 was King Bhumibol Adulyadej of Thailand, also known as Rama IX. He has been on the throne since 1950.

THE BILL OF RIGHTS

At first, some states refused to sign the U.S. Constitution. To make the representatives of these states more comfortable, James Madison and Thomas Jefferson wrote a group of 10 amendments, or changes, to the Constitution. This group of amendments is known as the Bill of Rights.

Amendment I provides for freedom of religion, speech, and the press. It also guarantees the right to assemble peacefully and to petition the government.

Amendment II guarantees citizens the right to own and use firearms to defend their country.

Amendment III states that in peacetime a soldier cannot stay in a citizen's home without the owner's consent.

Rules of Government

By Brenda Iasevoli

On September 17, 1787, 39 men signed one of history's most important documents: the U.S. Constitution. It describes how our government works. It is the shortest and oldest constitution in the world.

"It's the rules of the game," says Rick Stengel, managing editor of TIME magazine. For three years, he was president of the National Constitution Center, in Philadelphia, Pennsylvania. "Just as the rules of baseball tell us how to play the game, everything we do in America is shaped by the principles of the Constitution."

The Constitution's writers knew it would have to change with the times. There have been 27 amendments to the Constitution. The first 10 are known as the Bill of Rights. These include freedom of speech and of religion.

A 2004 law established September 17 as Constitution Day. But studies show that too few Americans know enough about the document. Stengel suggests we all read the Constitution. "Our country is based on a set of ideas," he says. "You need to know those ideas and how they were created. That binds you even more as a citizen to the country."

We the People of the United States, in order to form a more perfect union, establish justice, insure domestic tranquility, provide for the common defense, promote the general welfare, and secure the blessings of liberty to ourselves and our posterity, do ordain and establish this Constitution for the United States of America.

Because of his hard work at the Constitutional Convention, James Madison is sometimes called the Father of the Constitution.

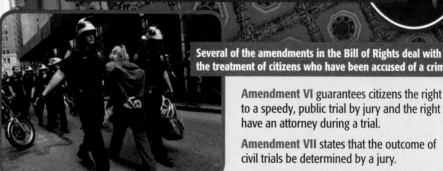

Several of the amendments in the Bill of Rights deal with the treatment of citizens who have been accused of a crime.

Amendment IV protects citizens, their belongings, and their homes from being searched without a reasonable cause and prior legal consent.

Amendment V says, among other things, people cannot be tried twice for the same crime or forced to testify against themselves. Citizens can't have their possessions or property taken away without a trial, and private property can't be taken by the government for public use without fair payment to the owner.

Amendment VI guarantees citizens the right to a speedy, public trial by jury and the right to have an attorney during a trial.

Amendment VII states that the outcome of civil trials be determined by a jury.

Amendment VIII ensures that reasonable amounts be set for fines and bail, which is a sum of money provided by a prisoner so that he or she may leave prison while awaiting trial. This amendment also prohibits cruel and unusual punishment for convicted criminals.

Amendment IX declares that citizens have rights other than those stated in the Constitution.

Amendment X guarantees that any powers not assigned to the federal government as provided in the Constitution belong to the states and the people.

Government

THREE BRANCHES

The U.S. government is divided into three branches: the legislative, executive, and judicial branches. The purpose of this structure is to provide a separation of powers among three equally important branches. The three branches of government have different responsibilities, but they work together to keep any one branch from becoming too powerful. For example, the legislative branch creates laws, but the judicial branch can strike down a law if it conflicts with the spirit of the Constitution.

THE LEGISLATIVE BRANCH

The LEGISLATIVE branch makes the laws. It is made up of a bicameral, or two-chambered, legislature. The two chambers are the Senate and the House of Representatives. To become a law, a bill must be approved by both chambers. Both chambers have the power to hold hearings to gather information on the bills they are considering.

The political party with the most members in either chamber is called the majority party. The other is called the minority party.

Senators and representatives meet in the Capitol building, in Washington, D.C.

THE SENATE

This chamber includes 100 senators, two for each state. Senators are elected to six-year terms, with one-third of the Senate being elected every even-numbered year. The Vice President (or president pro tempore, in the Vice President's absence) presides over the sessions. The Senate has the following special powers and responsibilities:

Ratify, or approve, treaties made by the President. This requires a two-thirds vote of all senators.

Accept or reject (by majority vote of all senators) the President's appointments of Supreme Court Justices and federal judges, ambassadors, Cabinet secretaries, and other high-level executive-branch officials.

Hold trials of officials impeached by the House of Representatives and convict or acquit them. A two-thirds vote of all senators is needed for conviction.

In December 2012, Patrick Leahy became president pro tempore of the Senate.

SO YOU WANT TO BE A SENATOR?

In order to run for a seat in the Senate, a candidate must be

☑ at least 30 years of age

☑ a U.S. citizen for nine years

☑ a resident of the state he or she wants to represent

MYSTERY PERSON

I was born February 1, 1878, in Tennessee, but later moved to Arkansas. After my husband, Thaddeus, died, I was appointed to fill his seat in the United States Senate. On January 12, 1932, I became the first woman to be elected to the Senate.

Who Am I?

ANSWER ON PAGE 244

THE HOUSE OF REPRESENTATIVES

This chamber includes 435 representatives. The larger a state's population, the more representatives it has. Representatives are elected to two-year terms. The Speaker of the House presides over the sessions. The House of Representatives has the following special powers and responsibilities:

- Create bills that allow the government to collect taxes.

- Create bills that empower the government to spend money.

- Elect the President in the event that no candidate receives a majority of electoral votes.

- Vote to impeach the President, Vice President, or other elected official. This means to formally charge a public official with wrongdoing.

John Boehner is the Speaker of the House.

HOW MANY FROM EACH STATE?

STATE	NUMBER OF REPRESENTATIVES	STATE	NUMBER OF REPRESENTATIVES	STATE	NUMBER OF REPRESENTATIVES
Alabama	7	Kentucky	6	North Dakota	1
Alaska	1	Louisiana	7	Ohio	18
Arizona	8	Maine	2	Oklahoma	5
Arkansas	4	Maryland	8	Oregon	5
California	53	Massachusetts	10	Pennsylvania	19
Colorado	7	Michigan	15	Rhode Island	2
Connecticut	5	Minnesota	8	South Carolina	6
Delaware	1	Mississippi	4	South Dakota	1
Florida	25	Missouri	9	Tennessee	9
Georgia	13	Montana	1	Texas	32
Hawaii	2	Nebraska	3	Utah	3
Idaho	2	Nevada	3	Vermont	1
Illinois	19	New Hampshire	2	Virginia	11
Indiana	9	New Jersey	13	Washington	9
Iowa	5	New Mexico	3	West Virginia	3
Kansas	4	New York	29	Wisconsin	8
		North Carolina	13	Wyoming	1

Representative Nancy Pelosi takes part in a committee meeting about small businesses.

SO YOU WANT TO BE A REPRESENTATIVE?

In order to run for a seat in the House of Representatives, a candidate must be

- ✓ at least 25 years of age

- ✓ a U.S. citizen for seven years

- ✓ a resident of the state he or she wants to represent

Government

THE EXECUTIVE BRANCH

The EXECUTIVE branch carries out the laws made by the legislative branch. This branch is made up of the President, the Vice President, and the Cabinet.

THE PRESIDENT

The President has the following powers and responsibilities:

- Carry out the laws of the land.
- Appoint U.S. ambassadors, Supreme Court Justices, federal judges, and Cabinet secretaries (who then must be approved by the Senate).
- Give the annual State of the Union address to Congress.
- Receive foreign ambassadors, thus recognizing their governments.
- Propose treaties with other nations.
- Serve as Commander in Chief of the armed forces; send troops overseas. (He needs congressional approval to declare war.)
- Call both houses of Congress to meet in a special session.
- Approve or veto bills passed by Congress.
- Grant pardons for federal crimes.

> The President serves a term of four years, with a maximum of two terms. A President must be a native-born U.S. citizen, at least 35 years old, and must have lived in the United States for at least 14 years.

President Obama meets with a group of Girl Scouts in the White House.

VETO POWER

To keep Congress in check, the President has the power to veto, or refuse to approve, bills that have been written and okayed by both houses of Congress. In return, if two-thirds of the lawmakers in the house that wrote the original bill can agree, then the bill can be considered for passage without the President's signature.

THE VICE PRESIDENT

The Vice President presides over the Senate but casts a vote only in the event of a tie. If the President dies, resigns, or is removed from office, the Vice President assumes the office of President. The Vice President must also be a native-born U.S. citizen and meet the same age and residential qualifications as the President.

Vice President Joe Biden

THE CABINET

Since 1789, Presidents have designated certain responsibilities to members of their Cabinet, called secretaries, who oversee separate executive departments. Today the President's Cabinet consists of the Vice President plus 15 secretaries. Here are the Cabinet departments in the order of their creation.

DEPARTMENT	WEBSITE
State	state.gov
Treasury	treasury.gov
Interior	doi.gov
Agriculture	usda.gov
Justice (Attorney General)	usdoj.gov
Commerce	commerce.gov
Labor	dol.gov
Defense	defenselink.mil
Housing and Urban Development	hud.gov
Transportation	dot.gov
Energy	energy.gov
Education	ed.gov
Health and Human Services	hhs.gov
Veterans Affairs	va.gov
Homeland Security	dhs.gov

U.S. Attorney General Eric Holder heads the Department of Justice.

CABINET-LEVEL POSITIONS

In addition to the Cabinet, there are several other Cabinet-level positions in the executive branch, including the White House chief of staff, the administrator of the Environmental Protection Agency, the director of the Office of Management and Budget, the United States trade representative, the United States ambassador to the United Nations, the chairman of the Council of Economic Advisers, and the administrator of the Small Business Administration.

Health and Human Services Secretary Kathleen Sebelius speaks with President Obama.

GUESS WHAT? In 2002, Congress passed the Homeland Security Act, which brought parts of 22 different agencies together into one department. The Department of Homeland Security was the last Cabinet department to be established.

THE JUDICIAL BRANCH

The JUDICIAL branch determines whether the laws created by the legislature and enforced by the executive branch are constitutional. The judicial branch is made up of the Supreme Court and the courts of law found all over the country.

THE SUPREME COURT

Stephen Breyer

Samuel Alito Jr.

Sonia Sotomayor

Elena Kagan

Clarence Thomas

Chief Justice John Roberts

Ruth Bader Ginsburg

Antonin Scalia

Anthony Kennedy

The U.S. Supreme Court and federal courts interpret the way an established law must be carried out. The Supreme Court also has the power to declare a law unconstitutional.

Supreme Court Justices and federal judges are appointed by the President and confirmed by the Senate. They serve for life or until they decide to resign or retire. The Supreme Court consists of eight Associate Justices and a Chief Justice. All decisions are made by a majority vote of the Justices.

RECENT SUPREME COURT DECISIONS

Brown v. Entertainment Merchants Association (2011)
A 2005 law in California banned the sale of some violent video and computer games to children under the age of 18. The drafters of the law believed that the violent games led to aggressive behavior in some children who played them. The Supreme Court decided that the law was unconstitutional because the content of the games is protected under the First Amendment, which guarantees the right to free speech.

United States v. Antoine Jones (2012)
In 2004, agents from the Federal Bureau of Investigation (FBI) placed a GPS device on a suspect's car. They did not have a search warrant, which is a court order allowing police officers to search a person or a place in order to find evidence that can be used in a court case. The Justices decided that the FBI agent's actions violated the suspect's Fourth Amendment rights, which protect citizens from having their belongings and homes searched without a reasonable cause and legal consent.

Miller v. Alabama (2012)
In this case, the Supreme Court ruled that a mandatory sentence of life in prison without the possibility of parole, or early release, may not be applied to juvenile offenders. Justice Elena Kagan explained that this sort of a sentence for people under the age of 18 was prohibited by the Eighth Amendment, which says that prisoners cannot be subject to cruel and unusual punishments.

FROM TIME FOR KIDS MAGAZINE

A Landmark Decision

By Julien Hawthorne

In June 2012, more than 1,000 people gathered outside the U.S. Supreme Court in Washington, D.C., to hear the Court's decision about President Barack Obama's health care law. The Patient Protection and Affordable Care Act (PPACA) states that all Americans must have health insurance or else pay a penalty. Lawyers representing 26 states and others challenged that law. They said that the law forced people to buy something that they did not want, and that was unconstitutional. But on June 28, 2012, the Supreme Court ruled that PPACA did not violate the Constitution. States and individuals must abide by the health care law by 2014.

Citizens voiced their opinions outside the Supreme Court.

Two Parts of the Law

The law has two important parts that impact people and the government. The first part of the law is called the "individual mandate." The individual mandate requires every U.S. citizen to buy health insurance. People who choose not to have health insurance have to pay a penalty. This is the part of the law that the Court said is constitutional because the penalty is a tax. Under the Constitution, Congress has the right to enforce and collect taxes.

The second part of the law deals with a government program called Medicaid. Medicaid provides health care to people who need financial help or have certain disabilities. Along with the federal government, states pay part of the cost of Medicaid for their residents. Under PPACA, the federal government would stop giving Medicaid money to states that did not agree to expand Medicaid to cover more people. The Court said this part of the law was unconstitutional. Congress can expand Medicaid, but it cannot punish states for not expanding coverage.

A Big Decision

The health care law has both supporters and critics. Supporters say the law will help make health insurance affordable for everyone. Critics say the law will cost insurance companies money and will raise health care costs.

The Supreme Court ruling is considered a win for President Obama. "The highest Court in the land has now spoken," Obama said in a speech at the White House. "Whatever the politics, today's decision was a victory for people all over this country whose lives will be more secure because of this law."

Government

MYSTERY PERSON

I was a lawyer and a civil rights activist who was born in Baltimore, Maryland, in 1908. I argued *Brown v. Board of Education* in front of the nation's top court in 1954. In deciding the case, the court declared racial segregation in public schools to be illegal. I was the first African American to be appointed to the U.S. Supreme Court.

Who Am I?

ANSWER ON PAGE 245

121

5000–3500 B.C. Sumer, located in what is now Iraq, becomes the earliest known civilization. Among other innovations, Sumerians develop a written alphabet.

3500–2600 B.C. People settle in the Indus River Valley, in what is now India and Pakistan.

2600 B.C. Minoan civilization begins on the island of Crete, in the Mediterranean Sea.

CIRCA 2560 B.C. The Egyptian king Khufu finishes building the Great Pyramid at Giza. The Great Sphinx is completed soon after by Khufu's son Khaefre.

2000 B.C. Babylonians develop a system of mathematics.
 • The kingdom of Kush, in Africa, becomes a major center of trade and learning.

1792 B.C. Hammurabi becomes the ruler of Babylonia. He creates the first set of laws, now known as Hammurabi's Code.

CIRCA 1600–1050 B.C. The Shang Dynasty is the first Chinese dynasty to leave written records.

1200 B.C. The Trojan War is fought between the Greeks and the Trojans.

814 B.C. The city of Carthage, located in what is now Tunisia, is founded by the Phoenicians.

753 B.C. According to legend, Rome is founded by Romulus.

563 B.C. Siddhartha Gautama, who becomes the Buddha, or Enlightened One, is born. He will become the founder of the Buddhist religion.

551 B.C. Chinese philosopher Confucius is born. His teachings on honesty, humanity, and how people should treat one another are the foundations of Confucianism.

510 B.C. Democracy is established in Athens, Greece.

438 B.C. Construction of the Parthenon on the Acropolis (the highest hill in Athens) is completed.

431 B.C. The Peloponnesian War breaks out between Sparta and Athens. In 404 B.C., Sparta finally wins the war and takes over Athens.

334 B.C. Alexander the Great invades Persia. He eventually conquers lands from Greece to India. He even crosses into North Africa.

100 B.C. The great city of Teotihuacán flourishes in Mexico.

58 B.C. Julius Caesar leaves Rome for Gaul (France) and spends nine years conquering much of central Europe. He is murdered in 44 B.C.

27 B.C. Octavian becomes the first Roman emperor, ushering in a long period of peace. He is also known by the title Augustus.

Hammurabi's Code

Confucius

WORLD HISTORY

CIRCA 1 A.D. Jesus Christ is born. He is crucified by the Romans around 30 A.D.

66 Jews rebel against Roman rule. The revolution is put down by the Romans, who destroy Jerusalem (in present-day Israel) in 70 A.D. and force many Jews into slavery.

79 Mount Vesuvius erupts, destroying the city of Pompeii (in present-day Italy).

122 Construction on Hadrian's Wall begins. It spans northern England and offers protection from the tribes to the north.

CIRCA 250 The classic period of Mayan civilization begins. It lasts until about 900. The Maya erect impressive stone buildings and temples in areas that are now part of Mexico and Central America.

330 Constantine the Great chooses Byzantium as the capital of the Roman Empire, and the city becomes known as Constantinople.

476 The Roman Empire collapses.

622 Muhammad, the founder of Islam, flees from Mecca to Medina in what is now Saudi Arabia. This journey is called the Hegira. After the death of Muhammad in 632, Muslims conquer much of North Africa and the Middle East. In 711, Muslims also conquer Spain.

800 Charlemagne is crowned the first Holy Roman Emperor by Pope Leo III.

960 The Song Dynasty begins in China. This dynasty is known for its advances in art, poetry, and philosophy.

CIRCA 1000–1300 During the classic period of their culture, Anasazi people build homes and other structures in the sides of cliffs in what is now the southwestern United States.

1066 At the Battle of Hastings, the Norman king William the Conqueror invades England and defeats English king Harold II.

1095 Pope Urban II delivers a speech urging Christians to capture the Holy Land from the Muslims. The fighting between 1096 and 1291 is known as the Crusades.

CIRCA 1200 The Inca Empire begins, and elaborate stone structures are eventually built in Cuzco and Machu Picchu, Peru. The Incas flourish until Francisco Pizarro, a Spaniard, conquers them in 1533.

1206 A Mongolian warrior named Temujin is proclaimed Genghis Khan. He expands his empire so that it includes most of Asia.

1215 A group of barons in England force King John to sign the Magna Carta, a document limiting the power of the king.

Magna Carta

1271–1295 Marco Polo, a Venetian merchant, travels throughout Asia. His book, *Il Milione* (*The Million*), is a major European source of information about Asia.

1273 The Habsburg Dynasty begins in Eastern Europe. It remains a powerful force in the region until World War I.

1325 Aztecs begin building Tenochtitlán on the site of modern Mexico City.

1337 The Hundred Years' War starts between the English and French. France finally wins in 1453.

1347 The Black Death, or bubonic plague, breaks out in Europe. It spreads quickly, killing more than one-third of Europe's population.

1368 The Ming Dynasty is founded in China by Buddhist monk Zhu Yuanzhang (or Chu Yuan-Chang).

1434 Portuguese explorer Gil Eannes sails past Cape Bojador, in western Africa, which was thought to be the end of the world.

El Castillo, a Mayan temple located in Chichen Itza, Mexico

1453 Constantinople falls to the Ottoman Turks, ending the Byzantine Empire.

1455 Johannes Gutenberg invents the printing press. The Gutenberg Bible is the first book printed on the press.

1478 The Spanish Inquisition begins.

1487–1488 Bartholomeu Dias of Portugal leads the first European expedition around the Cape of Good Hope, at the southern tip of Africa, opening up a sea route to Asia.

1492 Christopher Columbus leaves Spain, hoping to sail to the East Indies. Instead, he and his crew land in the Bahamas and visit Cuba, Hispaniola (which is now Haiti and the Dominican Republic), and other small islands.

1497–1499 Portuguese explorer Vasco da Gama leads the first European expedition to India by sea via the Cape of Good Hope.

1517 Martin Luther protests the abuses of the Catholic Church, which leads to a religious split and the rise of the Protestant faith.

1519 While exploring Mexico, Spanish adventurer Hernán Cortés conquers the Aztec Empire.

1519–1522 Portuguese explorer Ferdinand Magellan's expedition circumnavigates, or sails around, the globe.

1532–1533 Spanish explorer Francisco Pizarro conquers the Inca Empire in South America.

1543 Polish astronomer Copernicus shares his theory that the sun, not the Earth, is the center of the universe.

1547 Ivan the Terrible becomes the first czar, or ruler, of Russia.

1588 The English defeat the Spanish Armada, or fleet of warships, when Spain attempts to invade England.

1618 The Thirty Years' War breaks out between Protestants and Catholics in Europe.

1620 English Pilgrims aboard the *Mayflower* land at Plymouth Rock.

1632 Italian astronomer Galileo, the first person to use a telescope to look into space, confirms Copernicus's theory that Earth revolves around the sun.

1642 The English Civil War, sometimes called the Puritan Revolution, begins in Britain.

1688 The Glorious Revolution, or Bloodless Revolution, takes place in England. James II is removed from the throne, and William and Mary become the heads of the country.

1721 Peter the Great becomes czar of Russia.

1789 An angry mob storms the Bastille, a prison in Paris, setting off the French Revolution.

1819 Simón Bolívar crosses the Andes to launch a surprise attack against the Spanish, liberating New Granada (now Colombia, Venezuela, Panama, and Ecuador) from Spain.

1824 Mexico becomes independent from Spain.

Simón Bolívar

MYSTERY PERSON

I was born in 1254 in Venice, Italy. I was a merchant and an explorer. I traveled the Silk Road east from Italy to China. Nearly 200 years later, my journey inspired Christopher Columbus to find a western route to China.

Who Am I?

ANSWER ON PAGE 245

Columbian Exposition

1845 A blight ruins the potato crop in Ireland. More than 1 million Irish starve to death, and another million leave for the United States to escape the Irish potato famine.

1848 This is known as the year of revolutions in Europe, as there is upheaval in France, Italy, Germany, Hungary, and elsewhere.

1859 Charles Darwin publishes *On the Origin of Species.*

1871 A group of independent states unifies, creating the German Empire.

1876 Alexander Graham Bell invents the telephone.

1884 Representatives of 14 European countries meet at the Berlin West Africa Conference and divide Africa into areas of control.

1892 The diesel engine is invented by Parisian Rudolf Diesel.

1893 New Zealand becomes the first country to give women the right to vote.
• The Columbian Exposition, also known as the Chicago World's Fair, is held.

1894 The Sino-Japanese War breaks out between China and Japan, who are fighting for control of Korea. An 1895 treaty declares Korea independent.

1898 The Spanish-American War begins.

1899 During the Boxer Rebellion, the Chinese fight against Christian and foreign influences in their country. American, Japanese, and European forces help stop the fighting by 1901.

1904 Japan declares war on Russia, beginning the Russo-Japanese War. The countries clash over influence in Manchuria and Korea. Japan wins the conflict and becomes a world power.

1909 Robert Peary is credited as the first to reach the North Pole, although recent evidence suggests he might have been as far as 30 to 60 miles (48 to 97 km) away.

1911 Roald Amundsen, the first man to travel the Northwest Passage, reaches the South Pole.

1914 Austro-Hungarian archduke Franz Ferdinand is assassinated, setting off the chain of events that starts World War I.

1917 The United States enters World War I.
• Led by socialist Vladimir Lenin, the Russian Revolution begins. The czarist government is overthrown and, in 1922, the Soviet Union is formed.

1918 A flu epidemic spreads quickly around the world, killing more than 20 million people.

1919 The Treaty of Versailles ends World War I.

1927 Philo Farnsworth invents the television.

1928 Alexander Fleming discovers penicillin accidentally after leaving a dish of staphylococcus bacteria uncovered and finding mold.

1929 The U.S. stock market collapses, beginning the Great Depression.

1933 Adolf Hitler becomes chancellor of Germany.
• Frequency modulation, or FM, radio is developed by Edwin Armstrong.

1936 The Spanish Civil War breaks out.

1939 World War II begins when Germany invades Poland. Britain responds by declaring war on Germany. The United States declares neutrality.

Philo Farnsworth

History

1941 The Japanese launch a surprise attack on the United States, bombing U.S. ships docked in Hawaii's Pearl Harbor. In response, the United States declares war on Japan, and both Germany and Italy declare war on the United States.

1945 Germany surrenders on May 7, ending the war in Europe. In August, the United States drops two atomic bombs on the Japanese cities Hiroshima and Nagasaki. Japan surrenders, ending World War II.

1947 India and Pakistan become free of British colonial rule.

1948 Israel becomes a nation.

1949 Following China's civil war, Mao Zedong sets up the Communist People's Republic of China.
• South Africa enacts apartheid laws, which make discrimination against nonwhite people part of public policy.

1950 North Korean communist forces invade South Korea, beginning the Korean War. U.S. forces support South Korea. China backs North Korea. The war ends three years later.
• Frank McNamara develops the first credit card, the Diners Club.

1952 The hydrogen bomb is developed by Edward Teller and a team at a laboratory in Los Alamos, New Mexico.

1953 Edmund Hillary and Tenzing Norgay climb to the top of Mount Everest.

1955 Jonas Salk's polio vaccine is introduced.

1961 A group of Cuban exiles, supported by the United States, invades Cuba at the Bay of Pigs. The invasion fails, and U.S.-Cuban relations worsen.

1962 The Cuban Missile Crisis, a conflict between the United States, the Soviet Union, and Cuba, brings the world to the brink of nuclear war.

1963 U.S. President John F. Kennedy is assassinated on November 22, 1963. Vice President Lyndon B. Johnson is inaugurated.

1965 The United States begins officially sending troops to Vietnam to aid South Vietnam in its civil war with North Vietnam.

1967 The Six-Day War breaks out between Israel and neighboring Arab nations Egypt, Syria, and Jordan. Israel seizes the Golan Heights, the Gaza Strip, the Sinai Peninsula, and part of the west bank of the Jordan River.

1973 The Paris Peace Accords end the Vietnam War. North Vietnam later violates the terms of the treaty and, in 1975, takes control of Saigon, the capital of South Vietnam.
• Egypt and Syria launch a surprise attack on Israel, beginning the Yom Kippur War.

1978 U.S. President Jimmy Carter, Israeli President Menachem Begin, and Egyptian President Anwar Sadat sign the Camp David Accords in an attempt to achieve peace in the Middle East.

1979 Religious leader Ayatollah Khomeini declares Iran to be an Islamic republic.

1989 The Chinese army crushes a demonstration in Tiananmen Square in Beijing, killing hundreds, possibly thousands, of students and protestors.
• The Berlin Wall is torn down, and the city of Berlin, Germany, is reunified.

The Six-Day War

Mao Zedong

1990 Apartheid ends in South Africa. Four years later, Nelson Mandela is elected President in the country's first free, multiracial elections.
• The Persian Gulf War begins when Iraq invades Kuwait.

1991 The Soviet Union dissolves.
• Croatia, Slovenia, and Macedonia declare independence from Yugoslavia. The next year, Bosnia and Herzegovina also declares independence, but war breaks out and does not end until 1995.
• Tim Berners-Lee develops the World Wide Web.

1994 Tensions between the Hutu majority and the Tutsi minority in Rwanda, Africa, lead to a genocide, or systematic killing of a racial or ethnic group. About 800,000 Tutsis are killed.

1999 Honda releases the two-door Insight, the first hybrid car marketed to the masses in the United States. A year later, the Toyota Prius, the first hybrid four-door sedan, is released.

2001 After the September 11 terrorist attacks in New York City and Washington, D.C., the United States declares an international War on Terror, attacking the Taliban government in Afghanistan and searching for Osama bin Laden and al-Qaeda.

2003 With the aid of Britain and other allies, the United States invades Iraq. Though the government falls quickly, resistance and fighting continue. In 2006, Saddam Hussein is executed for crimes against humanity.
• War in the Darfur region of Sudan begins, leading to a humanitarian crisis.

2004 A powerful tsunami kills nearly 300,000 people in Indonesia, Sri Lanka, India, Thailand, and other Asian countries.

2006 Ellen Johnson-Sirleaf becomes President of Liberia. She is Africa's first elected female leader.

2008 A global economic crisis leads to loss of jobs and homes, and to a downturn in trade.

2010 A devastating earthquake hits Haiti.

Honda Insight

• An oil rig in the Gulf of Mexico explodes, causing one of the largest oil spills in history.

2011 Protests erupt in the Middle East and North Africa, toppling leaders in Tunisia and Egypt. There is instability throughout the region.
• A massive earthquake strikes Japan, triggering a powerful tsunami.
• After intense fighting in Libya, rebels gain control of most of the country. Libyan President Muammar Gaddafi is killed. The National Transitional Council (NTC) struggles to form a stable government.
• The world population officially exceeds 7 billion on October 31. It continues to rise.

2012 In Syria, demonstrators demand the resignation of President Bashar al-Assad and the overthrow of the government. The government deploys its army to quash the uprising and kills thousands.

2013 A meteor enters Earth's atmosphere and explodes over Russia.

2010 oil rig explosion

History

127

U.S. HISTORY

1524 Italian explorer Giovanni da Verrazano is the first European to reach New York Harbor.

1540 In search of gold, Spanish explorer Francisco Vásquez de Coronado travels north from Mexico. One of his lieutenants is the first European to spot the Grand Canyon.

1541 Spaniard Hernando de Soto crosses the Mississippi River.

1579 Sir Francis Drake of England explores California's coastline.

1607 English settlers found Jamestown in Virginia. The colony's leader, John Smith, is captured by Native Americans. According to legend, he is saved by Pocahontas.

1609–1611 Henry Hudson visits the Chesapeake Bay, Delaware Bay, and New York Bay and becomes the first European to sail up the Hudson River.

1620 Pilgrims land at Plymouth, Massachusetts.

1626 Dutchman Peter Minuit buys the island of Manhattan from the Canarsie tribe.

1692 In Massachusetts, accusations of witchcraft lead to the Salem witch trials and the executions of 20 people.

1770 Tensions between British soldiers and colonists erupt in the Boston Massacre, when British troops kill five men.

1773 Colonists protest a tax on tea by dressing up as Native Americans, boarding ships, and dumping tea into Boston Harbor. Known as the Boston Tea Party, the protest angers the British, who pass other harsh taxes.

1775 Paul Revere warns the colonists that the British are coming. The Battle of Lexington and Concord is the first fight of the American Revolution. The British surrender at Yorktown, Virginia, in 1781.

1776 Drafted by Thomas Jefferson, the Declaration of Independence is signed, and the United States is formed.

1787 The U.S. Constitution is written and submitted to the states for ratification. By the end of the year, Delaware, Pennsylvania, and New Jersey have accepted it.

1789 George Washington becomes the first President of the United States.

1791 The Bill of Rights, written mostly by James Madison, becomes part of the Constitution.

1803 President Thomas Jefferson buys the Louisiana Territory from France, adding 885,000 square miles (2,292,139 sq km) to the United States.

1804–1806 Meriwether Lewis and William Clark explore the Louisiana territory. They reach the Pacific Ocean in 1805.

1812 The War of 1812 breaks out between the United States and Britain because of trade and border disputes, as well as disagreements about freedom of the seas. The Treaty of Ghent ends the war in 1814.

1823 President James Monroe issues the Monroe Doctrine, warning that the Americas are not open for colonization.

1836 Texas declares independence from Mexico. In response, the Mexican army attacks and kills the 189 Texans defending the Alamo.

Sir Francis Drake

MYSTERY PERSON

I was born a member of the Shoshone tribe. I was an interpreter for Meriwether Lewis and William Clark. Starting in 1805, we explored the Wild West. Since 2000, my portrait has been on the U.S. dollar coin.

Who Am I?

ANSWER ON PAGE 245

Transcontinental railroad

1865 General Robert E. Lee of the Confederacy surrenders to Union General Ulysses S. Grant at Appomattox Court House, in Virginia, ending the Civil War.
• President Lincoln is assassinated at Ford's Theater by John Wilkes Booth, and Andrew Johnson becomes President.
• The 13th Amendment, which puts an end to slavery, is ratified.

1869 The transcontinental railroad is completed.

1890 The Battle of Wounded Knee is the last major defeat for Native American tribes.

1898 The Spanish-American War is fought. At the end of the war, Cuba is independent, and Puerto Rico, Guam, and the Philippines become territories of the United States.

1903 Wilbur and Orville Wright complete their first airplane flight at Kitty Hawk, North Carolina.

1908 Henry Ford, founder of the Ford Motor Company, builds the Model T and sells it for $825, making automobiles much more affordable than ever before.

1917 The United States enters World War I.

1920 With the passage of the 19th Amendment, women get the right to vote.

1929 The U.S. stock market crashes, and the Great Depression begins.

1941 In a surprise attack, Japan bombs the U.S. fleet at Pearl Harbor, in Hawaii. The United States declares war on Japan. Germany and Italy declare war on the United States.

1838 In what is known as the Trail of Tears, the U.S. government forces 16,000 Cherokees to leave their land in Georgia and relocate to a reservation in Oklahoma. Roughly a quarter of the Cherokees die.

1846 The Mexican-American War begins. At the end of the fighting, in 1848, Mexico gives California and New Mexico (which also includes present-day Arizona, Utah, and Nevada) to the United States. In return, the United States agrees to pay Mexico $15 million.

1848 John Sutter strikes gold in California, kicking off the California gold rush.

1860 Tensions between the North and the South over slavery, taxes, and representation reach a boiling point, and South Carolina secedes from the United States.

1861 Mississippi, Florida, Alabama, Georgia, Louisiana, and Texas secede from the Union, and the Confederate government is formed. The first shots of the American Civil War are fired by Confederate soldiers at Fort Sumter, in South Carolina's Charleston Harbor. Virginia, Arkansas, Tennessee, and North Carolina also secede from the Union.

1862 The Homestead Act promises 160 acres of land to anyone who remains on the land for five years. This law encourages settlers to move west.

1863 President Abraham Lincoln issues the Emancipation Proclamation, which frees all slaves in the Confederate states. The Battle of Gettysburg is fought. It is the bloodiest battle of the Civil War.

Pearl Harbor

History

1945 Germany surrenders on May 7, ending the war in Europe. In August, the U.S. aircraft *Enola Gay* drops an atomic bomb on Hiroshima, Japan. Three days later, a U.S. plane drops an atomic bomb on the city of Nagasaki. The effects are devastating. Six days later, Japan surrenders, ending World War II.

1946 The first bank-issued credit card is developed by John Biggins for the Flatbush National Bank of Brooklyn, in New York City.

1950 North Korean communist forces invade South Korea. U.S. forces enter the Korean War to defend South Korea. Despite three years of bitter fighting, little land changes hands.

1954 In *Brown v. Board of Education of Topeka, Kansas,* the U.S. Supreme Court declares that segregated schools are unconstitutional.

1955 Rosa Parks is arrested for refusing to give up her bus seat to a white person, leading to a boycott of the entire bus system in Montgomery, Alabama.

1962 The United States discovers that the Soviet Union has installed missiles on the island of Cuba that are capable of reaching the United States. Known as the Cuban Missile Crisis, this event brings the United States and the Soviet Union to the brink of nuclear war. After two weeks of extremely tense negotiations, the crisis comes peacefully to an end.

1963 Martin Luther King Jr. delivers his famous "I Have a Dream" speech to a crowd of more than 250,000 people in Washington, D.C.
• President John F. Kennedy is assassinated.

President Richard Nixon

1965 Civil rights advocate and black militant leader Malcolm X is killed.
• A race riot in the Watts section of Los Angeles, California, is one of the worst in history.
• President Lyndon B. Johnson authorizes air raids over North Vietnam.

1968 James Earl Ray shoots and kills Martin Luther King Jr. in Memphis, Tennessee. Riots break out across the country.

1973 The Vietnam War ends when peace accords are signed. Two years later, North Vietnam takes over Saigon (now Ho Chi Minh City), the capital of South Vietnam.

1974 Due to his involvement in the Watergate scandal, President Richard Nixon resigns. Gerald Ford becomes President.

1979 Islamic militants storm the U.S. embassy in Tehran, Iran, and 52 Americans are held hostage for 444 days.

Students in a newly integrated classroom in Washington, D.C., in 1954

1991 After Iraq invades Kuwait, the United States begins bombing raids. The first Persian Gulf War ends quickly as Iraqi forces are driven from Kuwait.

1999 President Bill Clinton is acquitted of impeachment charges.

2000 The election race between Democrat Al Gore and Republican George W. Bush is very close, and there are allegations of voter fraud. The U.S. Supreme Court determines the outcome, and Bush is declared the winner.

2001 On September 11, two passenger planes are hijacked and flown into the World Trade Center, in New York City, causing the buildings to collapse. Another plane is flown into the Pentagon, near Washington, D.C. A fourth hijacked plane is crashed into a field in Pennsylvania by the passengers on board before it can reach its target. The United States and Britain respond by attacking the Taliban government in Afghanistan for harboring Osama bin Laden, the alleged mastermind of the attacks. The U.S. government declares the War on Terror.

2003 Along with its allies—Britain and other countries—the United States goes to war in Iraq. Saddam Hussein's government falls quickly, but resistance and fighting continue.

2005 Hurricane Katrina hits the Gulf Coast, destroying parts of Mississippi and Louisiana, and areas along the coast of the southeastern United States. About 80% of New Orleans, Louisiana, is flooded.

2008 A global economic crisis causes a sharp rise in unemployment. Many U.S. homeowners lose their homes.

2009 Barack Obama becomes America's first African-American President.

2010 A controversial federal law is enacted to overhaul the U.S. health-care system and extend health insurance to the 32 million Americans who did not have it before.
• An oil rig in the Gulf of Mexico explodes, causing one of the largest oil spills in history.

2011 The U.S. Secretary of Defense announces that the war in Iraq is officially over and that all remaining U.S. troops will leave Iraq by the end of 2011. During the conflict, nearly 4,500 U.S. troops lost their lives in Iraq, and about 30,000 were wounded.

TOP 5 Veteran Wars

These are the wars served by the most U.S. forces.

1. World War II (1941–45)
16,112,566 U.S. service members

2. Vietnam War (1964–75)
8,744,000 U.S. service members

3. Korean War (1950–53)
5,720,000 U.S. service members

4. World War I (1917–18)
4,734,991 U.S. service members

5. Gulf War (1990–91)
2,225,000 U.S. service members

Source: U.S. Department of Veterans Affairs

President George W. Bush (left) and Al Gore

History

FROM TIME FOR KIDS MAGAZINE

Life-Saving Inventions

By Stephanie Kraus

Ashok Gadgil invented a clean, fuel-efficient stove that saves homes more than $300 a year.

On May 2, 2012, Ashok Gadgil became the recipient of the $100,000 Lemelson-MIT Award for Global Innovation. Each year, the honor is given to an inventor who has improved the lives of people in developing countries. Gadgil's inventions have helped more than 100 million people around the world.

Gadgil is a professor and physicist at the University of California, Berkeley. When he's not teaching, he works to find solutions to global problems such as energy efficiency and water safety. "I chose [to focus on problems] where my knowledge of science could help," Gadgil told TFK.

Man on a Mission

Gadgil's global quest to help people began in the 1980s, when he came up with a program to make energy-efficient lightbulbs more affordable for people in developing countries.

Then, in the 1990s, Gadgil designed his first life-saving invention, UV Waterworks. The device uses ultraviolet light to kill deadly disease-carrying germs in drinking water. It costs just one cent to clean 1.3 gallons (5 L) of water (or about 21 cups). Gadgil was inspired to find an inexpensive solution to the clean-water crisis after more than 10,000 people in his home country of India died from an outbreak of Bengal cholera in 1993. The infection is spread through contaminated food and drinking water.

So far, the invention has provided safe drinking water to more than 5 million people in India, Liberia, Nigeria, the Philippines, and Ghana.

Energy-Saving Stove

The long and violent war in Darfur, Sudan, has caused many people to leave the country. A person who flees to a foreign country to escape danger is called a refugee. More than 80% of the Darfur refugees are females.

Families in refugee camps are given food aid. But they still have to cook the meals. In order to do so, refugee women leave the camps three to five times a week, walking up to seven hours a day to find enough wood to fuel their stoves. This can be dangerous because of street violence in the area. To avoid danger, some women spend much of their money—which they make by selling the food they need to feed their families—buying firewood from vendors.

Cooking over an open flame causes smoke, which can be hazardous to one's health and to the environment, too. Gadgil visited the area many times with his students and his colleagues to work with the refugee women on designing a clean, fuel-efficient stove. The Berkeley-Darfur Stove he created uses less than half the fuel of other cooking methods. That means the women don't have to leave the camps to find firewood as often. An estimated 125,000 women and their families have been helped. Gadgil is currently developing a version of the stove for Ethiopia.

"Be optimistic when you try a hard problem," Gadgil says. "It's when you solve a large problem that you can have a big impact on the world."

COOLEST INVENTIONS OF 2012

BY TIME FOR KIDS STAFF

A high-tech submarine that can travel 7 miles (11km) below the surface of the sea. A toy pet that responds to your gestures and voice. Gloves that can translate sign language into speech. Every day, inventors find ways to improve our lives and transform our world. Read on to learn about some of the coolest inventions of 2012. Which would you most like to own? Which do you think will have the most positive impact on the world? Which do you wish you had invented?

A 3-D PRINTER

The Replicator 2 is a desktop-size 3-D printer that can create an actual object—or, if you want, hundreds of copies of it. Just download or create a design, hit print, and watch as ultrathin plastic layers melt together to create the object you want. The printer is fast and easy to use. For $2,199, it can instantly turn anyone's home into a mini-factory.

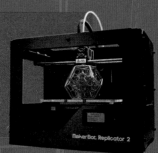

DEEPSEA CHALLENGER SUBMARINE

In March, the Deepsea Challenger reached the ocean's deepest point, about 7 miles (11 km) below the surface of the western Pacific. Weighing 12 tons (11,000 kg) and measuring 24 feet long (7 m), it can withstand about as much pressure as the equivalent of three SUVs sitting on your toe. The sub, designed by filmmaker James Cameron, cost $8 million to create. It has digital 3-D cameras to document the deep.

BAXTER

Baxter is a new breed of industrial robot. Rodney Brooks, who helped invent the Roomba vacuum cleaner, built Baxter for light, repetitive tasks like packing and sorting. At $22,000, Baxter is cheap compared with other robots that perform the same types of tasks. This gives small businesses greater access to electronic help. Baxter is also easy to use, so people can put it right to work.

INDOOR CLOUDS

Dutch artist Berndnaut Smilde has developed a way to create a small, perfect white cloud in the middle of a room. For the cloud to take shape, the temperature, humidity, and lighting all have to be perfectly planned. Once everything is ready, Smilde summons the cloud out of the air using a fog machine. Although the cloud lasts only for moments, the memory of its beauty stays with you.

Inventions and Technology

WINGSUIT RACING

In October 2012, flying humans wearing batlike suits competed in the first-ever **Wingsuit Flying World Championship** in China. Currently, just 20 people are qualified to compete, and the suits cost up to $2,000. The participants dropped, glided, and parachuted about 0.75 miles (1.2 km) in about 30 seconds. South African Julian Boulle finished in 23.41 seconds, setting a world record.

CLOSE-UP VIEWS

A college student and an Army Ranger have come up with technology to help protect first responders like firefighters and police. **Bounce** creates a full picture of an emergency situation such as a burning building. This baseball-size sphere is tossed into the area. Six cameras snap pictures. Its sensors detect air quality, temperature, and other hazards. It beams the data to mobile devices.

TECHPET

The toy company Bandai has created a lovable new virtual pet. Download the **TechPet** app and connect an iPhone to the robotic doggy frame. Your phone's screen turns into the cartoon face of a dog that is eager to be taken care of. Using the phone's camera and microphone, this smart puppy can recognize simple hand gestures and respond to spoken commands.

GOOGLE GLASS

Just by looking up and to the right, a **Google Glass** user can take and share photos, video-chat, and use the Internet. The frame contains a computer, a camera, a battery, a microphone and sensors that respond to voice commands, and touch controls in an earpiece. The device has a 0.5-inch (1 cm) display and weighs about the same as sunglasses. Google Glass should be on sale by late 2013 or early 2014.

THE DO-IT-YOURSELF MACHINE KIT

Marcin Jakubowski built a tractor in six days. Then he told the world how to do it: He posted the designs, the budget, and a how-to video online. Now Jakubowski, founder of Open Source Ecology, is making free **instruction kits** for low-cost versions of 50 important machines. If anyone anywhere can build them, he says, "we can unleash massive amounts of human potential."

MADE FOR EXPLORATION

As the U.S. prepares for new deep-space missions, NASA has created a space suit that is up for new challenges. The **Z-1 space suit** has joints that are more flexible. The material has radiation protection for long stays in space. A hatch on the back allows the suit to dock with a spacecraft or rover. That way, the astronaut can crawl through without letting dust in or air out.

TALK TO THE GLOVE

Four Ukrainian students created **Enable Talk** gloves to help people with a speech or hearing impairment communicate with people who don't know sign language. The $75 gloves have sensors that recognize sign language and translate it into text that can be read out loud on a smartphone. So if you sign the word *hello* while wearing the gloves, your phone will then say "hello" out loud.

A SLIPPERY SLIDE

Five college students and their professor have come up with a way to make a surface that nothing will stick to. **Liquiglide** can be used to get ketchup out of bottles, get ice off of airplane wings, and do many things in between. The product is made from safe-to-eat plant materials. The slippery coating can work with glass, ceramic, metal, or plastic.

SCREWDRIVER IN MOTION

Using the sensors found in smartphones and Nintendo Wii controllers, Black & Decker's cordless **Max Gyro** is being called the world's first motion-activated screwdriver. The $40 tool uses tiny technology to sense wrist motions. It turns these movements into changes in the drill's speed and direction.

MYSTERY PERSON

I was a chemist, engineer, and inventor who was born in Sweden in 1833. I was especially interested in explosives. In 1867, I invented dynamite. It was used to build canals, tunnels, and railroads. Before I died, I asked that most of my money be used for annual international awards. The prizes are named after me.

Who Am I?

ANSWER ON PAGE 245

Inventions and Technology

135

LANGUAGE

LOTS OF LANGUAGES

❯ There are 6,909 languages spoken in the world. Of these, 473 are almost extinct, which means that only a few people still speak them.

❯ Taki-Taki, a language spoken in Suriname, has only 340 words. This is the smallest number of words in a written language.

❯ In Papua New Guinea, 860 different languages are spoken.

❯ The consonant sounds that are most common in the world's languages are *p, t, k, m,* and *n.*

❯ English has at least 250,000 words. That may be the largest number of words in any language.

❯ The language with the most speakers is **Mandarin Chinese.** More than 845 million people speak Mandarin.

The Chinese language is made up of characters.

TOP 10 Languages Spoken in the United States

A recent census reported that there were 280,950,438 people age 5 or older in the United States. Of them, 55,444,485 people spoke a language other than English at home. Here's the breakdown.

1. Spanish	34,547,077
2. Chinese	2,464,572
3. French	1,984,824
4. Tagalog	1,480,429
5. Vietnamese	1,207,004
6. German	1,104,354
7. Korean	1,062,337
8. Russian	851,174
9. Italian	798,801
10. Portuguese	687,126

Source: United States Census Bureau

SUPER SPELLER

Snigdha Nandipati, a 14-year-old girl from San Diego, California, won the 85th Scripps National Spelling Bee on May 31, 2012. She beat 277 other great spellers and won by spelling the word *guetapens* correctly. *Guetapens* means "ambush" or "trap." For her amazing spelling skills, Snigdha won $30,000, plus $5,000 in scholarship money, a $2,500 savings bond, $2,600 in reference works from the Encyclopedia Britannica, and an online language course. A coin collector and fan of Sherlock Holmes stories, she hopes to be a neurosurgeon or a psychiatrist one day.

Spelling bee winner Snigdha Nandipati's brother rushed onto the stage to congratulate her after her big win.

MOST COMMON WORDS

Here are the 50 words used most often in English. Can you come up with a sentence that doesn't use any of them?

the	you	are	this	had			
of	that	as	from	not			
and	it	with	I	but	we	which	will
a	he	his	have	what	there	their	each
to	for	they	or	all	can	said	about
in	was	at	by	were	an	if	how
is	on	be	one	when	your	do	up

LETTERS AND STATES

There are only seven letters that do not begin state names: *b, e, j, q, x, y,* and *z.*

Q is the only letter that does not occur in any of the U.S. state names.

Maine is the only U.S. state whose name is only one syllable.

There is only one state name that ends in a *k*. Can you name it?

_____

ANSWER ON PAGE 245

GUESS WHAT? There aren't any words in English that rhyme with *dangerous, discombobulate, marathon, month, ninth, orange, pint, purple, silver,* or *wolf.*

NEW YEAR, NEW WORDS

Every year, the editors of the *Merriam-Webster Dictionary* add new words and phrases to the dictionary. Here are a few of the 2012 additions.

AHA MOMENT: a moment of sudden realization, inspiration, insight, recognition, or comprehension

BUCKET LIST: a list of things that a person has not done but wants to do before dying

CLOUD COMPUTING: the practice of storing regularly used computer data on servers that are accessed through the Internet

EARWORM: a song or melody that is stuck in a person's head

ENERGY DRINK: a usually carbonated beverage that typically contains caffeine and other ingredients intended to boost a person's energy level

GAME CHANGER: a factor that changes an existing situation or activity in a major way

MASH-UP: something created by combining elements from two or more sources. This technique is often used in movie trailers, viral videos, music, and books.

Language

PLAYING WITH WORDS

There are many ways to have fun with words. You might try creating an anagram, saying sentences with lots of alliteration, or making a pun.

To make an **ANAGRAM**, you rearrange all of the letters from one word or phrase to form another word or other words. For example, the letters in the word *care* can be rearranged to make *race.* The letters in the word *pets* can be reordered to be *step.* And the letters that make up *dormitory* can be used to spell *dirty room.* Here are some neat anagrams.

Secure . . . rescue
The eyes . . . they see
The Morse code . . . here come dots
The countryside . . . no city dust here
Garbage man . . . bag manager
Debit card . . . bad credit
Eleven plus two . . . Twelve plus one
Write down all of the letters in your name, and see what you can come up with.

Rearrange the letters in my name and you might get Hairball Conman . . . or Ball Chain Manor . . . or A Lamb Ranch Lion.

When writers use **ALLITERATION**, they use more than two words in a row that begin with the same consonant.
The silly snakes slithered toward Steven.
Lazy lizards like lounging on the lawn.
Naomi nibbled noodles noisily.
Peter prefers peaches and pickles to pears and pancakes.

A **PALINDROME** is a word or sentence that is the same when read forward and backward. Some word examples are *mom, dad, pop, eye, nun, civic,* and *kayak.* Here are a few longer examples:

Delia failed.
He did, eh?
Madam, I'm adam.
Nate bit a Tibetan.
Never odd or even

Nurses run.
Pupils slip up.
Race car
Step on no pets.
Too bad I hid a boot.

Was it a rat I saw?

A **HOMOPHONE** is each of two words that sound the same but have different meanings: *new* and *knew, rows* and *rose, ate* and *eight, sea* and *see,* and *there, their,* and *they're.*

Can you see the sea?

GUESS WHAT? An idiom is an expression that means something other than exactly what the words say. For example, "That was a piece of cake," "It's raining cats and dogs," and "He kicked the bucket."

THAT'S PUNNY!

A **PUN** is a joke that makes use of a word that has several possible meanings or uses two words that sound a lot alike. Here are a few examples.

Why did the pony go to the doctor? Because she was a little horse
What is a gossip? Someone with a great sense of rumor
Did you hear about the guy whose whole left side was cut off? He's all right now.
What do you call a chicken crossing the road? Poultry in motion
What is the purpose of reindeer? It makes the grass grow, sweetie.
What do you call a train that sneezes? Achoo-choo train

TIME FOR KIDS GAME

THE WISDOM OF WORDS

Use the chart below to match a letter to each symbol. Fill in the blanks to reveal a quotation by the writer Toni Morrison.

—TONI MORRISON

ANSWERS ON PAGE 245

Language

ATLANTIC OCEAN

BLACK SEA

MEDITERRANEAN SEA

RED SEA

ASIA

EUROPE

Equator

GEORGIA
ARMENIA
TURKEY
SYRIA
IRAQ
SAUDI ARABIA
YEMEN
JORDAN
ISRAEL
LEBANON
CYPRUS
Crete
GREECE
ALBANIA
MACEDONIA
KOSOVO
MONTENEGRO
SERBIA
BOSNIA AND HERZEGOVINA
BULGARIA
ITALY
Sicily
MALTA
Sardinia
Corsica
PORTUGAL
SPAIN
Majorca
Madeira Islands
Canary Islands

DJIBOUTI
Djibouti
Mogadishu
SOMALIA
Hargeysa
Harer
ERITREA
Asmara
Port Sudan
Addis Ababa
ETHIOPIA
Gore
KENYA
UGANDA
Kampala
RWANDA
Juba
SOUTH SUDAN
SUDAN
Khartoum
Nile R.
Congo R.
CENTRAL AFRICAN REPUBLIC
Bangui
CHAD
N'Djamena
CAMEROON
Yaoundé
Douala
Libreville
EQUATORIAL GUINEA
Malabo
SAO TOME
NIGERIA
Kano
Zinder
Abuja
Ibadan
Lagos
Benue R.
Niger R.
NIGER
Agadez
BENIN
Porto-Novo
TOGO
Lomé
GHANA
Accra
Abidjan
COTE D'IVOIRE
Yamoussoukro
Gaoua
BURKINA FASO
Ouagadougou
Niamey
MALI
Timbuktu
Bamako
GUINEA
Conakry
Freetown
SIERRA LEONE
Monrovia
LIBERIA
GUINEA-BISSAU
Bissau
THE GAMBIA
Banjul
Dakar
SENEGAL
Nouakchott
MAURITANIA
WESTERN SAHARA
(Occupied by Morocco)
Laayoune
MOROCCO
Rabat
Casablanca
Marrakech
Fès
Erfoud
Tangier
Oran
ALGERIA
Algiers
Constantine
TUNISIA
Tunis
Tripoli
LIBYA
Banghazi
Al Jawf
EGYPT
Cairo
Alexandria
Suez
Luxor
Aswan

S A H A R A

140

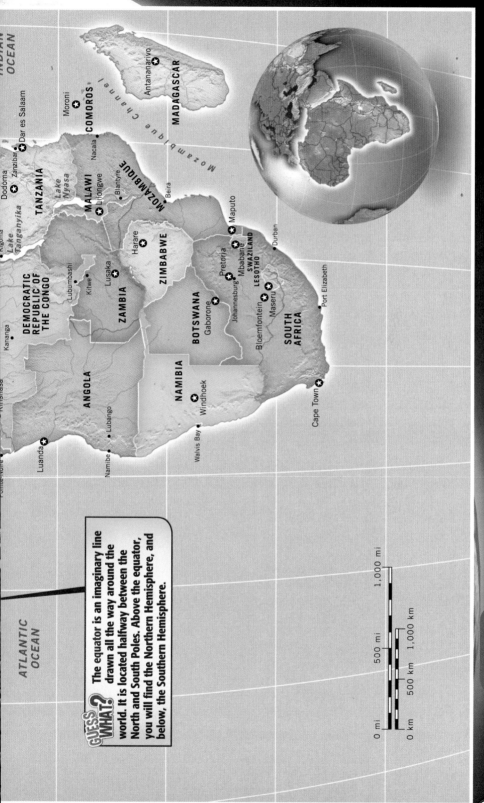

INDIAN
OCEAN

MADAGASCAR

Antananarivo

Mozambique Channel

Moroni

COMOROS

Dar es Salaam

Zanzibar

TANZANIA

Dodoma

Lake
Nyasa

MALAWI

Nacala

Lilongwe

Blantyre

MOZAMBIQUE

Beira

Lake
Tanganyika

Ngoma

DEMOCRATIC
REPUBLIC OF
THE CONGO

Harare

ZIMBABWE

Maputo

Maputo

Lubumbashi

Kitwe

Lusaka

ZAMBIA

Pretoria

Mbabane

Durban

SWAZILAND

Kananga

Johannesburg

LESOTHO

Kinshasa

BOTSWANA

Gaborone

Maseru

Bloemfontein

Port Elizabeth

ANGOLA

NAMIBIA

Windhoek

SOUTH
AFRICA

Pointe-Noire

Luanda

Namibe

Lubango

Walvis Bay

Cape Town

ATLANTIC
OCEAN

GUESS WHAT? The equator is an imaginary line drawn all the way around the world. It is located halfway between the North and South Poles. Above the equator, you will find the Northern Hemisphere, and below, the Southern Hemisphere.

0 mi   500 mi   1,000 mi

0 km   500 km   1,000 km

Maps

141

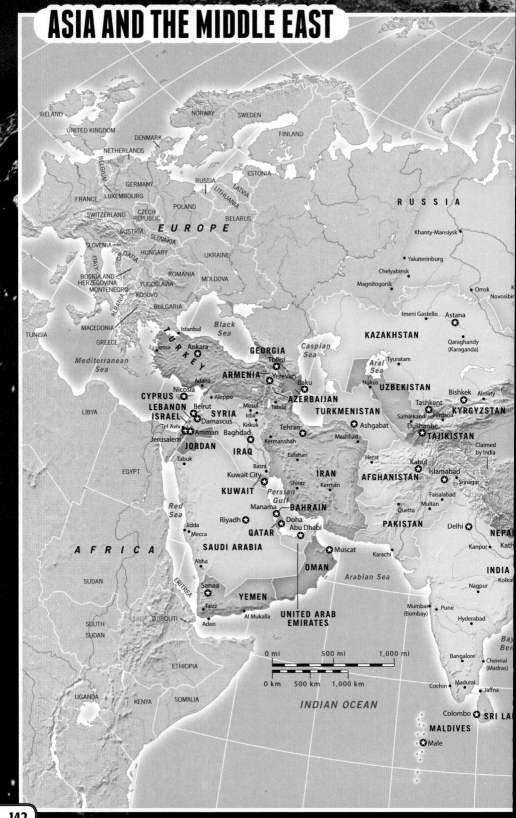

IRELAND

UNITED KINGDOM

NETHERLANDS

DENMARK

BELGIUM

GERMANY

FRANCE   LUXEMBOURG

SWITZERLAND

CZECH
REPUBLIC

AUSTRIA

SLOVENIA

SLOVAKIA

CROATIA

ITALY

BOSNIA AND
HERZEGOVINA
MONTENEGRO

KOSOVO

ALBANIA

MACEDONIA

TUNISIA

GREECE

HUNGARY

ROMANIA

YUGOSLAVIA

BULGARIA

NORWAY   SWEDEN

FINLAND

ESTONIA

RUSSIA

LITHUANIA

LATVIA

POLAND

BELARUS

UKRAINE

MOLDOVA

E U R O P E

R U S S I A

Khanty-Mansiysk

Yakaterinburg

Chelyabinsk

Magnitogorsk

Omsk   K
Novosibir

Imeni Gastello   Astana

KAZAKHSTAN

Qaraghandy
(Karaganda)

Mediterranean
Sea

Istanbul

Black
Sea

Caspian
Sea

Tyuratam

Aral
Sea

Nukus

Izmir

Ankara

T U R K E Y

GEORGIA
Tbilisi

Baku

UZBEKISTAN

Bishkek   Almaty

Adana

ARMENIA   Yerevan

Tashkent

LIBYA

Nicosia

CYPRUS

Aleppo

Mosul

Tabriz

AZERBAIJAN

Samarkand   Fergana

KYRGYZSTAN

LEBANON   Beirut
ISRAEL

Irbil

SYRIA

TURKMENISTAN

Dushanbe

Tel Aviv

Damascus

Kirkuk

Tehran

Ashgabat

TAJIKISTAN

Jerusalem

Amman   Baghdad

Kermanshah

Mashhad

Claimed
by India

JORDAN   IRAQ

Esfahan

Herat

Kabul

Islamabad

Tabuk

Basra

IRAN

AFGHANISTAN

Srinagar

EGYPT

Kuwait City

Shiraz

Kerman

Faisalabad

KUWAIT

Persian
Gulf

Quetta

Multan

Red
Sea

Manama

BAHRAIN

PAKISTAN

Delhi

NEPA

Jidda

Riyadh

Doha

Abu Dhabi

QATAR

Kanpur   Kath

Mecca

SAUDI ARABIA

Muscat

Karachi

INDIA

Abha

OMAN

Arabian Sea

Nagpur

AFRICA

SUDAN

Sanaa

YEMEN

Mumbai
(Bombay)

Pune

Hyderabad

SOUTH
SUDAN

ERITREA

Taizz

Aden

Al Mukalla

UNITED ARAB
EMIRATES

Bay
Ber

DJIBOUTI

ETHIOPIA

UGANDA

KENYA

SOMALIA

INDIAN OCEAN

Bangalore

Chennai
(Madras)

Cochin

Madurai

Jaffna

Colombo   SRI LA

MALDIVES

Male

| 0 mi | 500 mi | 1,000 mi |
| 0 km | 500 km | 1,000 km |

Kolk

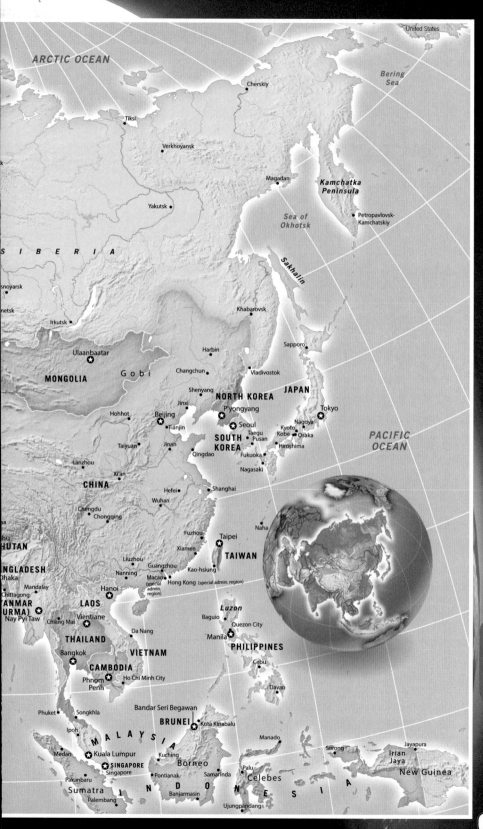

ARCTIC OCEAN

United States

Bering
Sea

Cherskiy

Tiksi

Verkhoyansk

Magadan

*Kamchatka
Peninsula*

Yakutsk

*Sea of
Okhotsk*

Petropavlovsk-
Kamchatskiy

S I B E R I A

snoyarsk

Sakhalin

netsk

Khabarovsk

Irkutsk

Harbin

Sapporo

Ulaanbaatar

G o b i

Changchun

Vladivostok

MONGOLIA

Shenyang

JAPAN

Hohhot

Jinxi

NORTH KOREA

Beijing

P'yongyang

Tokyo

Tianjin

Seoul

Nagoya

Kyoto
Kobe
Osaka

Taiyuan

Jinan

**SOUTH
KOREA**

Taegu
Pusan

Hiroshima

Qingdao

Fukuoka

Lanzhou

**PACIFIC
OCEAN**

Xi'an

Nagasaki

CHINA

Hefei

Shanghai

Wuhan

Chengdu

Chongqing

Naha

sa

HUTAN

Fuzhou

Taipei

NGLADESH

Xiamen

TAIWAN

haka

Liuzhou

Mandalay

Nanning

Guangzhou

Kao-hsiung

Chittagong

Macao
(special
admin.
region)

Hong Kong (special admin. region)

ANMAR
URMA)

Hanoi

LAOS

Luzon

Nay Pyi Taw

Vientiane

Baguio

Chiang Mai

Da Nang

Quezon City

THAILAND

Manila

PHILIPPINES

Bangkok

VIETNAM

Cebu

CAMBODIA

Phnom
Penh

Ho Chi Minh City

Davao

Bandar Seri Begawan

Phuket

Songkhla

BRUNEI

Kota Kinabalu

Ipoh

Manado

M A L A Y S I A

Medan

Kuala Lumpur

Kuching

Borneo

Sorong

Jayapura

*Irian
Jaya*

SINGAPORE

Singapore

Palu

Celebes

New Guinea

Pakanbaru

Pontianak

Samarinda

I N D O N E S I A

Sumatra

Banjarmasin

Palembang

Ujungpandang

AUSTRALIA AND OCEANIA

SOUTH KOREA

JAPAN

ASIA

CHINA

TAIWAN

PHILIPPINE SEA

Wak

NORTHERN MARIANA ISLANDS (U.S.)

Saipan ★

LAOS

PHILIPPINES

Agana ★ *Guam* (U.S.)

VIETNAM

THAILAND

CAMBODIA

Yap Islands

Koror ✪

Caroline Islands

Palikir ✪

M I C R O N E S I A

PALAU

BRUNEI

M A L A Y S I A

Borneo

SINGAPORE

Celebes

Irian Jaya

Wewak

PAPUA NEW GUINEA

I N D O N E S I A

New Guinea

Sumatra

Java

Dili

EAST TIMOR

Port Moresby ✪

Honiara ✪
Guadalcanal

Coral Sea Islands (Australia)

Great Barrier Reef

CORAL SEA

Timor Sea

Darwin

Gulf of Carpentaria

Ashmore and Cartier Islands (Australia)

West Island •

Derby •

Cairns •

Townsville •

INDIAN OCEAN

Mackay •

Rockhampton • Gladstone •

Alice Springs •

Tropic of Capricorn

A U S T R A L I A

Brisbane •

Lord Howe Island (Australia)

Geraldton •

Kalgoorlie •

Broken Hill •

Perth •

Whyalla •

Sydney •

Bunbury •

Esperance •

Adelaide •

Canberra ✪

TASMAN SEA

Melbourne •

Hobart •

Tasmania

GUESS WHAT? The horizontal lines on a globe are called latitude lines. The equator is located at 0° latitude. The latitude of Honolulu, Hawaii, is 31.3°N. The latitude of Wellington, New Zealand, is 41.3°S. The vertical lines on a globe are called longitude lines. They pass through both the North and South Poles.

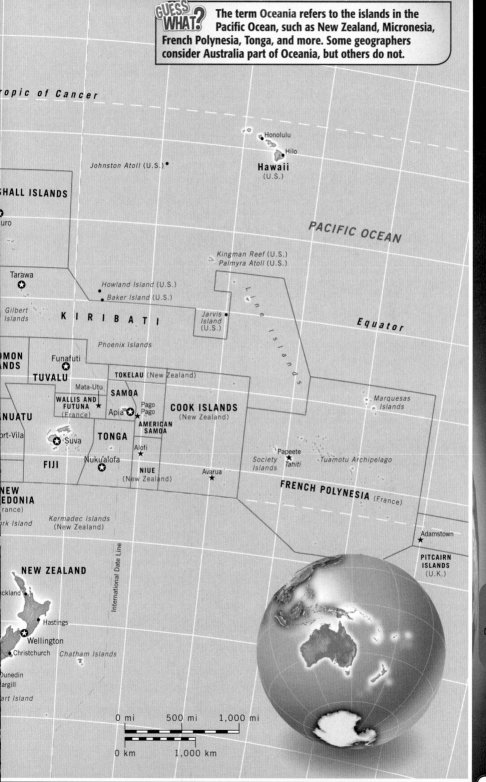

The term Oceania refers to the islands in the Pacific Ocean, such as New Zealand, Micronesia, French Polynesia, Tonga, and more. Some geographers consider Australia part of Oceania, but others do not.

Maps

EUROPE

Reykjavík
ICELAND

Arctic Circle

0 mi   300 mi   600 mi

0 km   300 km   600 km

FAROE ISLANDS
(Denmark)
• Torshavn

SHETLAND ISLANDS

ORKNEY
ISLANDS

HEBRIDES

Trondheim

Bergen

NORWAY

Oslo ✪   Gävle

Stavanger

SWEDEN

• Aberdeen   Göteborg

Glasgow
• Edinburgh   DENMARK   Ålborg

Belfast
UNITED   NORTH   Copenhagen ✪
KINGDOM   SEA   Malmö

Dublin ✪
IRELAND   Liverpool   Leeds
Manchester   Sheffield   Hamburg
Birmingham   Bremen   Berlin
London ✪   NETHERLANDS   Poznań
The Hague ✪ Amsterdam   GERMANY
Rotterdam   Hamburg   Wroc
Calais • Lille   Antwerp • Essen
GUERNSEY (U.K.)   Brussels   Düsseldorf
JERSEY (U.K.)   BELGIUM   Cologne
Le Havre   LUXEMBOURG   Bonn   Prague ✪
Paris ✪   Luxembourg   Frankfurt   CZECH
          Stuttgart   REPUBLIC   Brno   Br

ATLANTIC OCEAN

Nantes   Strasbourg   LIECHTENSTEIN Munich   Vienna ✪

BAY OF   Dijon   Zürich   Vaduz ✪
BISCAY   FRANCE   Bern ✪ Liechtenstein   AUSTRIA   HUN
          Geneva   SWITZERLAND   Ljubljana ✪ SLOVENIA
Bordeaux   Lyon   Turin   Milan   Trieste   Zagreb ✪
          Toulouse   Genoa   CROATIA
Porto   Bilbao   SAN   BOSNIA AN
PORTUGAL   Andorra ✪ Marseille MONACO ✪ Monaco   MARINO   HERZEGOVI
          la Vella   MONACO   Florence ✪   Sarajevo •
Madrid ✪   ANDORRA   Bastia   ITALY   MO
Lisbon ✪   Barcelona   Corsica   Rome •   ADRIATIC SEA
SPAIN   Valencia Majorca   VATICAN   Bari
Faro   Seville   Palma   CITY
          Málaga   Sardinia   Naples •
          Gibraltar   MEDITERRANEAN SEA   Cagliari

MOROCCO   ALGERIA   Palermo Messina
                    Sicily
A F R I C A   TUNISIA   Valletta ✪
                    MALTA

146

Murmansk

Pechora

ASIA

Arkhangel'sk

Oulu

FINLAND

mpere

Helsinki

Tallinn

ESTONIA

ga

LATVIA

HUANIA

Vilnius

Minsk

BELARUS Homyel'

Brest

St. Petersburg

Smolensk

R U S S I A

Izhevsk

Nizhniy Novgorod

Kazan

Moscow

Samara

Lipetsk

Saratov

Voronezh

KAZAKHSTAN

Kiev

Kharkiv

Voroshilovgrad

Volgograd

Lviv

Derazhnya

Gorlovka

UKRAINE

Makeyevka

Zhdanov

Rostov

Chisinau

Iasi

MOLDOVA

Odessa

Mykolayiv

Kerch

Grozny

ROMANIA

Simferopol

Bucharest

Craiova

Sevastopol

Constanta

BLACK SEA

Sofia

Varna

BULGARIA

pje

DONIA

Istanbul

aloniki

T U R K E Y

Volos

ECE

Izmir

Athens

SYRIA

IRAN

Crete

CYPRUS

IRAQ

LEBANON

Maps

147

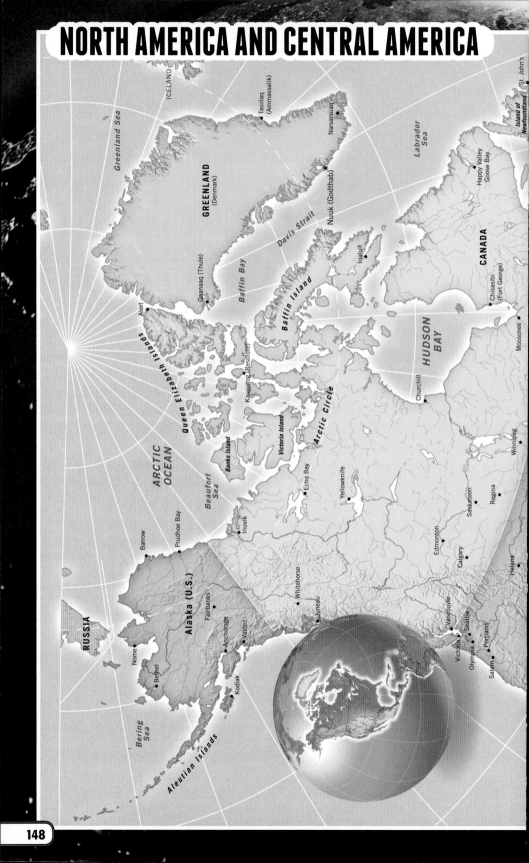

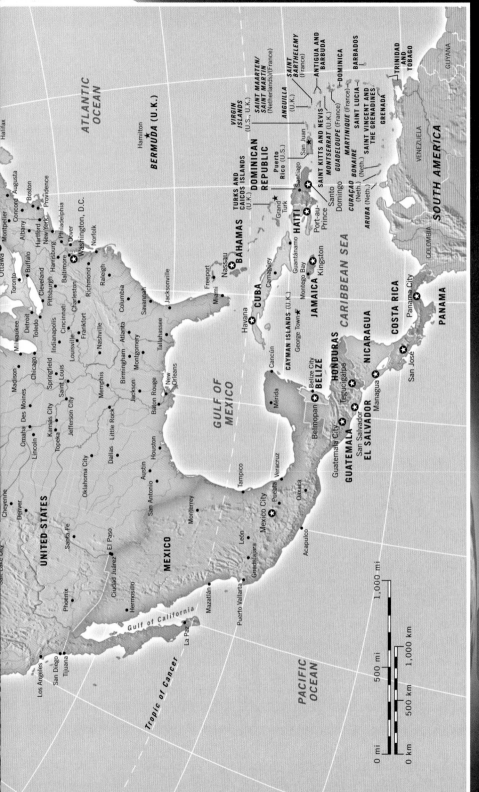

ATLANTIC OCEAN

BERMUDA (U.K.)
Hamilton

VIRGIN ISLANDS (U.S., U.K.)

SAINT MAARTEN/ SAINT MARTIN (Netherlands)/(France)

ANGUILLA (U.K.)

SAINT BARTHÉLEMY (France)

ANTIGUA AND BARBUDA

DOMINICA

BARBADOS

TRINIDAD AND TOBAGO

GUYANA

VENEZUELA

SOUTH AMERICA

GUADELOUPE (France)

MARTINIQUE (France)

SAINT LUCIA

SAINT VINCENT AND THE GRENADINES

GRENADA

BONAIRE (Neth.)

CURAÇAO (Neth.)

ARUBA (Neth.)

COLOMBIA

SAINT KITTS AND NEVIS

MONTSERRAT (U.K.)

San Juan

Puerto Rico (U.S.)

DOMINICAN REPUBLIC

Santiago

Santo Domingo

TURKS AND CAICOS ISLANDS (U.K.)

Grand Turk

HAITI

Port-au-Prince

Guantánamo Bay

BAHAMAS

Nassau

Freeport

CUBA

Camagüey

Havana

Montego Bay

JAMAICA

Kingston

George Town

CAYMAN ISLANDS (U.K.)

CARIBBEAN SEA

Jacksonville

Savannah

Tallahassee

Columbia

Raleigh

Richmond

Norfolk

Washington, D.C.

Dover

Philadelphia

Baltimore

Harrisburg

New York

Hartford

Providence

Boston

Concord

Augusta

Montpelier

Albany

Buffalo

Toronto

Ottawa

Halifax

Detroit

Cleveland

Pittsburgh

Charleston

Frankfort

Cincinnati

Indianapolis

Columbus

Toledo

Milwaukee

Chicago

Madison

Des Moines

Omaha

Lincoln

Topeka

Kansas City

Jefferson City

Saint Louis

Springfield

Nashville

Louisville

Memphis

Birmingham

Atlanta

Montgomery

Jackson

Little Rock

Baton Rouge

New Orleans

GULF OF MEXICO

Oklahoma City

Dallas

Austin

San Antonio

Houston

UNITED STATES

Cheyenne

Denver

Santa Fe

Salt Lake City

Phoenix

Los Angeles

San Diego

Tijuana

Ciudad Juárez

El Paso

Hermosillo

MEXICO

Monterrey

Tampico

Veracruz

Puebla

Mexico City

Oaxaca

Mérida

Cancún

BELIZE

Belmopan

Belize City

GUATEMALA

Guatemala City

EL SALVADOR

San Salvador

HONDURAS

Tegucigalpa

NICARAGUA

Managua

COSTA RICA

San José

PANAMA

Panama City

Acapulco

León

Guadalajara

Puerto Vallarta

Mazatlán

La Paz

Gulf of California

Tropic of Cancer

PACIFIC OCEAN

0 mi   500 mi   1,000 mi
0 km   500 km   1,000 km

CUBA

MEXICO

HAITI DOMINICAN REPUBLIC Puerto Rico (U.S.)

JAMAICA

BELIZE

HONDURAS

NICARAGUA

COSTA RICA PANAMA

ANTIGUA AND BARBUDA

SAINT KITTS AND NEVIS GUADELOUPE

DOMINICA

SAINT LUCIA BARBADOS

GRENADA SAINT VINCENT AND THE GRENADINES

CARIBBEAN SEA

ATLANTIC OCEAN

Aruba

Barranquilla

Cartagena Maracaibo

Lake Maracaibo

Medellín

Cali Bogotá

TRINIDAD AND TOBAGO

Caracas

Orinoco River

Ciudad Guayana

VENEZUELA GUYANA

Georgetown

Paramaribo

SURINAME Cayenne

FRENCH GUIANA (France)

COLOMBIA

Esmeraldas

Equator Quito

ECUADOR

Guayaquil

Putumayo River

Negro River

Macapá

Amazon River

Manaus

Santarém

Belém

São Luís

Parnaíba

Fortaleza

Iquitos

Benjamin Constant

Amazon River

A M A Z O N   B A S I N

Madeira River

Natal

PERU

Piura

Cruzeiro do Sul

Rain Forest

Pôrto Velho

Recife

Maceió

Xingu River

Tapajós River

Araguaia River

Tocantins River

BRAZIL

São Francisco River

Trujillo

Ucayali River

Marañón River

Cobija

Riberalta

Salvador

Lima

Cuzco

Lake Titicaca

A n d e s   M t s .

BOLIVIA

La Paz

Cochabamba

Santa Cruz

Sucre

Brasília

Brazilian Highlands

Belo Horizonte

Arequipa

Arica

Iquique

Antofagasta

PACIFIC OCEAN

San Miguel de Tucumán

Paraguay River

PARAGUAY

Asunción

Formosa

Ciudad del Este

Resistencia Encarnación

Paraná River

São Paulo

Curitiba

Rio de Janeiro

CHILE

Valparaíso

Santiago

Concepción

Córdoba

Rosario

Paraná River

Salto

URUGUAY

Pôrto Alegre

ATLANTIC OCEAN

Buenos Aires

Montevideo

ARGENTINA

Bahía Blanca

Mar del Plata

Río de la Plata

Comodoro Rivadavia

Strait of Magellan

Río Gallegos

Stanley

Punta Arenas

Ushuaia

Falkland Islands (Islas Malvinas) (Administered by U.K., claimed by Argentina)

Cape Horn

0 mi   500 mi   1,000 mi

0 km   500 km   1,000 km

ANTARCTICA

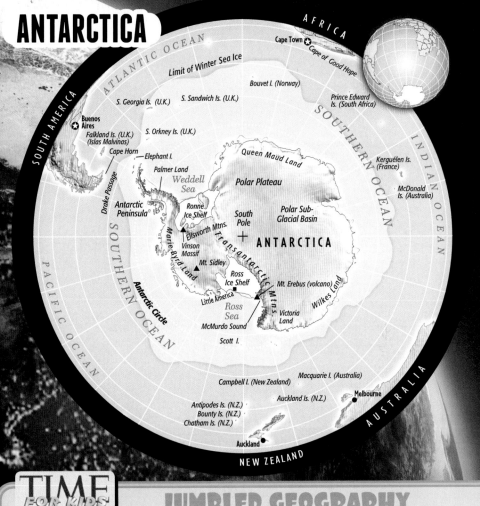

TIME FOR KIDS GAME

JUMBLED GEOGRAPHY

Unscramble the letters below to find the names of three continents, two oceans, the northernmost and southernmost places on Earth, and three types of lines found on a map. Then write the letters in the red spaces in order to answer the riddle below.

OERTQUA   _ _ _ _ _ _

HNTRO PLEO   _ _ _ _ _ _ _ _ _

AASI   _ _ _ _

RCTANITACA   _ _ _ _ _ _ _ _ _ _

ONLUDEGIT   _ _ _ _ _ _ _ _ _

TUHSO LEPO   _ _ _ _ _ _ _ _ _

TUELATDI   _ _ _ _ _ _ _ _

TICANTLA ONECA   _ _ _ _ _ _ _ _ _ _ _ _ _

HOTUS RIMECAA   _ _ _ _ _ _ _ _ _ _ _ _

CFPAIIC ACENO   _ _ _ _ _ _ _ _ _ _ _ _

What always sits in the corner but still makes it all around the world?

⚫ ⚫ ⚫ ⚫ ⚫ ⚫ ⚫ ⚫

⚫ ⚫ ⚫ ⚫ ⚫

ANSWER ON PAGE 245

MOVIES AND TV

Academy Awards ✦ February 24, 2013

At the 85th Annual Academy Awards, in Los Angeles, *Brave* was named Best Animated Feature. *Life of Pi,* the magical tale of a young man stuck at sea in a lifeboat with a ferocious tiger, was one of the night's big winners. It won Oscars for cinematography (how the film looked), original score, and visual effects. And the movie's director, Ang Lee, took home a trophy for directing.

The Youngest Academy Award Nominees

Most Academy Award winners are adults, but some kids have made it onto the list of nominees. Here are a few of the children who've made the list, along with their age when they were nominated, the name of the film, and the year the movie was released. Actors with a 🌠 next to their name were winners.

Actor	Age	Film	Year
Justin Henry	8	*Kramer vs. Kramer*	1979
Jackie Cooper	9	*Skippy*	1931
Quvenzhané Wallis	9	*Beasts of the Southern Wild*	2012
Mary Badham	10	*To Kill a Mockingbird*	1962
Quinn Cummings	10	*The Goodbye Girl*	1977
🌠 Tatum O'Neal	11	*Paper Moon*	1973
Patty McCormack	11	*The Bad Seed*	1956
Brandon De Wilde	11	*Shane*	1953
Haley Joel Osment	11	*The Sixth Sense*	1999
Keisha Castle-Hughes	13	*Whale Rider*	2002
Hailee Steinfeld	14	*True Grit*	2010
🌠 Patty Duke	16	*The Miracle Worker*	1962
Jack Wild	16	*Oliver!*	1968

Quvenzhané Wallis

MYSTERY PERSON

I was born on July 9, 1956, in Concord, California. A two-time Oscar winner, I was also nominated for a best actor Oscar for playing a boy who made a wish that turned him into an adult overnight, in the 1988 film *Big*. More recently, I was the voice of Woody in *Toy Story 3,* which was named the Best Animated Feature of the Year at the 2011 Academy Awards.

Who Am I?

ANSWER ON PAGE 245

Teen Choice Awards ☆ July 22, 2012

MOVIES

Choice Sci-fi/Fantasy Movie: *The Hunger Games*

Choice Actor, Sci-fi/Fantasy: Josh Hutcherson, *The Hunger Games* and *Journey 2: The Mysterious Island*

Choice Actress, Sci-fi/Fantasy: Jennifer Lawrence, *The Hunger Games*

Choice Actress, Drama: Emma Stone, *The Help*

Choice Romance Movie: *The Twilight Saga: Breaking Dawn–Part 1*

Choice Actress, Romance: Kristen Stewart, *The Twilight Saga: Breaking Dawn–Part 1*

Choice Animated Movie Voice: Taylor Swift as Audrey, *Dr. Seuss' The Lorax*

Emma Stone

Choice Movie Villain: Alexander Ludwig, *The Hunger Games*

Choice Movie Scene Stealer, Male: Liam Hemsworth, *The Hunger Games*

Choice Movie Scene Stealer, Female: Ashley Greene, *The Twilight Saga: Breaking Dawn–Part 1*

Choice Summer Movie, Action: *The Avengers*

Josh Hutcherson

Choice Summer Movie, Comedy/Music: *Katy Perry: Part of Me*

Choice Summer Movie Star, Male: Chris Hemsworth, *Snow White and the Huntsman* and *The Avengers*

Choice Summer Movie Star, Female: Kristen Stewart, *Snow White and the Huntsman*

Kristen Stewart

TELEVISION

Choice TV Show, Comedy: *Glee*

Choice TV Actor, Comedy: Chris Colfer, *Glee*

Choice TV Actress, Comedy: Lea Michele, *Glee*

Choice TV Show, Animated: *The Simpsons*

Choice TV Personality, Male: Simon Cowell, *The X Factor*

Choice TV Personality, Female: Jennifer Lopez, *American Idol*

Choice TV Reality Competition Show: *The X Factor*

Choice TV Breakout Show: *The X Factor*

Lea Michele

In 2012, country singer Tate Stevens won the second season of *The X Factor*.

Chris Colfer

Movies and TV

Primetime Emmy Awards ☆ September 23, 2012

Modern Family was the big winner at the Primetime Emmy Awards. It scored wins in the following categories.

Outstanding Comedy Series: *Modern Family*

Outstanding Supporting Actor in a Comedy: Eric Stonestreet, *Modern Family*

Outstanding Supporting Actress in a Comedy: Julie Bowen, *Modern Family*

Outstanding Directing for a Comedy Series: Steven Levitan, *Modern Family*

The Amazing Race was named Outstanding Reality Competition Program. *Game Change,* the fictionalized look at the 2008 presidential campaign, took home a bunch of awards, including Outstanding Mini Series or Movie and Outstanding Lead Actress in a Miniseries or Movie, for Julianne Moore's portrayal of vice presidential nominee Sarah Palin.

Golden Globes ☆ January 28, 2013

Les Misérables was named the Best Comedy or Musical at the 70th Annual Golden Globes. *Les Mis,* as it is known, is based on a popular musical that was based on a book written by Frenchman Victor Hugo. The book was originally published in 1862.

Brave, the tale of a plucky princess who accidentally puts her family under a terrible spell, took home the award for Best Animated Feature. The film was produced by Pixar Animation Studios, which also made *Toy Story* (1995) and its sequels, *Monsters, Inc.* (2001), and *Finding Nemo* (2003).

Brave

TOP 10 Highest-Grossing Kids' Movies

These are the kid-friendly films that have made the most money in the United States.

1. *Star Wars: Episode I–The Phantom Menace* (1999)	$474,544,677
2. *Star Wars* (1977)	$460,935,665
3. *Shrek 2* (2004)	$436,471,036
4. *E.T. the Extra-Terrestrial* (1982)	$434,949,459
5. *The Lion King* (1994)	$422,783,777
6. *Toy Story 3* (2010)	$414,984,497
7. *Finding Nemo* (2003)	$380,838,870
8. *Alice in Wonderland* (2010)	$334,185,206
9. *Shrek the Third* (2007)	$320,706,665
10. *Harry Potter and the Sorcerer's Stone* (2001)	$317,557,891

Source: IMDB.com. This list includes only films rated G or PG.

People's Choice Awards ☆ January 9, 2013

Favorite Movie Actor: Robert Downey Jr.

Favorite Movie Actress: Jennifer Lawrence

Favorite Movie Icon: Meryl Streep

Favorite Action Movie: *The Hunger Games*

Favorite Action Movie Star: Chris Hemsworth

Favorite Face of Heroism: Jennifer Lawrence, *The Hunger Games*

Favorite Comedic Movie Actor: Adam Sandler

Favorite Comedic Movie Actress: Jennifer Aniston

Favorite Dramatic Movie Actor: Zac Efron

Favorite Dramatic Movie Actress: Emma Watson

Favorite Movie Superhero: Robert Downey Jr. as Iron Man

Favorite Movie Fan Following: Twihards

Favorite Movie: *The Hunger Games*

Favorite TV Comedy: *The Big Bang Theory*

Favorite Comedic TV Actor: Chris Colfer

Favorite Comedic TV Actress: Lea Michele

Favorite Daytime TV Host: *The Ellen DeGeneres Show*

Favorite TV Competition Show: *The X Factor*

Favorite Celebrity Judge: Demi Lovato

Jennifer Lawrence

Emma Watson

Nickelodeon Kids' Choice Awards ☆ March 31, 2012 ☆

Favorite TV Show: *Victorious*

Favorite TV Actor: Jake Short

Favorite TV Actress: Selena Gomez

Favorite TV Sidekick: Jennette McCurdy

Favorite Reality Show: *Wipeout*

Favorite Cartoon: *SpongeBob SquarePants*

Favorite Movie: *Alvin and the Chipmunks: Chipwrecked*

Favorite Movie Actor: Adam Sandler

Favorite Movie Actress: Kristen Stewart

Favorite Animated Movie: *Puss in Boots*

Favorite Voice from an Animated Movie: Katy Perry

Adam Sandler

Jake Short

Jennette McCurdy

Victoria Justice, star of *Victorious*

Movies and TV

155

A Chat with One Direction

By TFK Kid Reporter Julia Horbacewicz

One Direction performs on *The X Factor*

One Direction has only one way to go from here: up. The five-member boy band ("1D" to fans) began their climb to fame in the United Kingdom (U.K.) in 2010, after appearing on the British version of the talent show *The X Factor*. Originally, the boys—Niall Horan, Zayn Malik, Liam Payne, Harry Styles, and Louis Tomlinson—each auditioned as solo artists. But the judges suggested they compete as a group. They finished in third place that season, and the rest is history! Some are even calling 1D the new "Fab Five," which is a play on the nickname for rock legends the Beatles.

The band's first single, "What Makes You Beautiful," was released in the U.K. in September 2011 and shot to Number 1 on the charts. Now their popularity has also spread to the United States, thanks to buzz on YouTube and Twitter. They released their first U.S. album, *Up All Night*, on March 13, 2012. It topped the U.S. *Billboard* album chart at Number 1, making them the first British group ever to do this with a debut album. Now, when One Direction visits the United States, wherever they go, thousands of screaming fans are sure to follow. They performed at Nickelodeon's 2012 Kids' Choice Awards, made a special appearance on *iCarly*, and then announced their first North American tour. The guys had an award-filled year in 2012, taking home three MTV Video Music Awards and three Teen Choice Awards. After releasing the album *Take Me Home* in November 2012, they set out on a massive 2013 world tour covering Europe, Australia, and North America.

TFK Kid Reporter Julia Horbacewicz sat down for a chat with the band during a visit to New York City. Read on to find out what the guys had to say about their time in the states.

TFK: When you first auditioned for *The X Factor* in the U.K., did you ever imagine you would become this famous?

NIALL: No! We expected to do an album in the U.K. and see how things go. But you know, the power of YouTube and Twitter has just taken us across the world. It's been absolutely incredible so far.

TFK: How did you become interested in music? Have you all been singing since you were young?

LIAM: We actually all did a little singing at school—in theater productions, choirs, karaoke. So we were all interested in music and performing before, but just not on this scale. It's amazing it's gotten to this.

TFK: What's a typical day for you guys on tour?

ZAYN: Normally, when we're on tour in the U.K., we're kind of chilled out because we just do the shows, and we've got the day to ourselves. But over here [in the U.S.], we have a lot of busy promo days. It depends what we're doing that day. Like, if we're doing something for Nickelodeon, it's not that bad. But if we have a full day of promos, we may be up at 5 a.m., so it's early mornings and late nights.

LIAM: Yeah, quite long days. But you do a lot of exciting things in the day, so it's a lot of fun.

TOP 10 Most Popular Songs of 2012

Billboard.com looked at the songs that were played most often on the radio and streamed most often online to come up with the most popular songs of the year.

1. "Somebody that I Used to Know," by Gotye featuring Kimbra
2. "Call Me Maybe," by Carly Rae Jepsen
3. "We Are Young," by Fun. featuring Janelle Monáe
4. "Payphone," by Maroon 5 featuring Wiz Khalifa
5. "Lights," by Ellie Goulding
6. "Glad You Came," by The Wanted
7. "Stronger (What Doesn't Kill…)," by Kelly Clarkson
8. "We Found Love," by Rihanna featuring Calvin Harris
9. "Starships," by Nicki Minaj
10. "What Makes You Beautiful," by One Direction

HARRY: We travel a lot, so we may wake up somewhere, do a load of work, then drive somewhere else and do it again.

TFK: What are a few interesting facts that the fans don't know about you yet?

LIAM: The thing about us is, we're so truthful, and we say everything.

ZAYN: We've given everything away already. We've got nothing left to give!

TFK: How often do you guys get to see your friends, and what do they think about the band's success?

LIAM: Louis's friend Stan actually came out on tour with us for a few weeks.

LOUIS: *[Laughing]* Liam is so dramatic. My friend came out for one week.

LIAM: I thought he was there longer. Anyway, it's quite nice that we get to invite our friends on tour, and they get to see a bit of backstage. I was speaking to Stan, and he really enjoyed it and said it was a good laugh.

TFK: What's the craziest thing a fan has ever done?

ZAYN: Fans do some crazy things.

LOUIS: Sometimes they chase after the van. We'll be at an event—wherever it is—and they'll run up to the van and start banging on the windows, or kiss the windows.

TFK: What advice can you give to our readers about becoming a singer?

HARRY: I think it's important to just be yourself and have a lot of fun with it. I think a lot of people may take it so seriously that they don't enjoy it. It's important to make sure you're having a good time.

Music

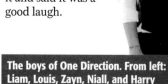

The boys of One Direction. From left: Liam, Louis, Zayn, Niall, and Harry

GRAMMY AWARDS
February 10, 2013

Record of the Year: "Somebody that I Used to Know," Gotye featuring Kimbra

Adele and Beyoncé

Album of the Year: *Babel,* Mumford & Sons

Song of the Year: "We Are Young," Fun. featuring Janelle Monáe

Best New Artist: Fun.

Best Pop Solo Performance: "Set Fire to the Rain [Live]," Adele

Best Pop Duo/Group Performance: "Somebody that I Used to Know," Gotye featuring Kimbra

Best Pop Vocal Album: *Stronger,* Kelly Clarkson

Best Traditional Pop Vocal Album: *Kisses on the Bottom,* Paul McCartney

Best Rock Performance: "Lonely Boy," The Black Keys

Best Rock Song: "Lonely Boy," The Black Keys

Best Rock Album: *El Camino,* The Black Keys

Best Alternative Music Album: *Making Mirrors,* Gotye

Best R&B Performance: "Climax," Usher

Best Traditional R&B Performance: "Love on Top," Beyoncé

Best Country Solo Performance: "Blown Away," Carrie Underwood

Best Country Song: "Blown Away," Carrie Underwood

Best Country Album: *Uncaged,* Zac Brown Band

Best Children's Album: *Can You Canoe?,* The Okee Dokee Music LCC

Best Musical Theater Album: *Once: A New Musical,* Original Broadway Cast

Best Song Written for Visual Media: "Safe & Sound," from *The Hunger Games,* Taylor Swift featuring The Civil Wars

Kelly Clarkson

Fun.

MTV VIDEO MUSIC AWARDS
September 6, 2012

Video of the Year: "We Found Love," Rihanna featuring Calvin Harris

Best New Artist: "What Makes You Beautiful," One Direction

Best Pop Video: "What Makes You Beautiful," One Direction

Best Rock Video: "Paradise," Coldplay

Best Video with a Message: "Skyscraper," Demi Lovato

Best Electronic Dance Music Video: "Feel So Close," Calvin Harris

Most Share-Worthy Video: "What Makes You Beautiful," One Direction

Best Visual Effects: "First of the Year (Equinox)," Skrillex

Best Editing: "Countdown," Beyoncé

Best Art Direction: "Wide Awake," Katy Perry

Rihanna

AMERICAN MUSIC AWARDS
November 18, 2012

Favorite Pop/Rock Female Artist: Katy Perry

Favorite Pop/Rock Male Artist: Justin Bieber

Favorite Country Female Artist: Taylor Swift

Favorite Country Male Artist: Luke Bryan

Favorite Alternative Rock Artist: Linkin Park

Favorite Soul/R&B Male Artist : Usher

Favorite Soul/R&B Female Artist: Beyoncé

Favorite New Artist of the Year: Carly Rae Jepsen

Favorite Country Band, Duo, or Group: Lady Antebellum

Favorite Electronic Dance Music Artist: David Guetta

Favorite Pop/Rock Album: *Believe,* Justin Bieber

Favorite Country Album: *Blown Away,* Carrie Underwood

Artist of the Year: Justin Bieber

Usher

Luke Bryan

Music

Carrie Underwood

Taylor Swift

TEEN CHOICE AWARDS
July 22, 2012

Choice Male Artist: Justin Bieber

Choice Female Artist: Taylor Swift

Choice Music Group: Selena Gomez & The Scene

Choice R&B/Hip-Hop Artist: Nicki Minaj

Choice R&B/Hip-Hop Song: "Starships," Nicki Minaj

Choice Rock Group: Fun.

Choice Rock Song: "Paradise," Coldplay

Choice Electronic Dance Music (EDM) Artist: David Guetta

Choice Single by a Group: "We Are Young," Fun. featuring Janelle Monáe

Choice Single by a Female Artist: "Eyes Open," Taylor Swift

Choice Single by a Male Artist: "Boyfriend," Justin Bieber

Choice Male Country Artist: Hunter Hayes

Choice Female Country Artist: Taylor Swift

Choice Country Song: "Sparks Fly," Taylor Swift

Choice Country Group: Lady Antebellum

Choice Summer Song: "Call Me Maybe," Carly Rae Jepsen

Choice Love Song: "What Makes You Beautiful," One Direction

Choice Breakup Song: "Payphone," Maroon 5 featuring Wiz Khalifa

Choice Summer Music Star, Female: Demi Lovato

Choice Summer Music Star, Male: Justin Bieber

Choice Summer Music Star, Group: One Direction

Choice Breakout Artist: Carly Rae Jepsen

Choice Breakout Group: One Direction

Demi Lovato

Selena Gomez

Justin Bieber

Carly Rae Jepsen

COUNTRY MUSIC AWARDS
November 1, 2012

Hunter Hayes

Entertainer of the Year: Blake Shelton

Female Vocalist of the Year: Miranda Lambert

Male Vocalist of the Year: Blake Shelton

Vocal Group of the Year: Little Big Town

New Artist of the Year: Hunter Hayes

Album of the Year: *Chief,* Eric Church

Song of the Year: "Over You," Miranda Lambert

Vocal Duo of the Year: Thompson Square

Single of the Year: "Pontoon," Little Big Town

Musical Event of the Year: "Feel Like a Rock Star," Kenny Chesney and Tim McGraw

PEOPLE'S CHOICE AWARDS
January 9, 2013

Nicki Minaj

Favorite Male Artist: Jason Mraz

Favorite Female Artist: Katy Perry

Favorite Band: Maroon 5

Favorite Pop Artist: Katy Perry

Favorite R&B Artist: Rihanna

Favorite Hip-Hop Artist: Nicki Minaj

Favorite Country Artist: Taylor Swift

Favorite Breakout Artist: The Wanted

Favorite Song: "What Makes You Beautiful," One Direction

Favorite Album: *Up All Night,* One Direction

Favorite Music Video: "Part of Me," Katy Perry

Favorite Music Fan Following: KatyCats, Katy Perry

Katy Perry

The Wanted

Music

FROM TIME FOR KIDS MAGAZINE

Engraved in Time

By Jonathan Rosenbloom

In April 1861, Jonathan Dillon was fixing an ordinary pocket watch in a store in Washington, D.C. Suddenly, the shop's owner raced up to Dillon and said: "War has begun; the first shot has been fired." The owner was talking about the beginning of the Civil War. Confederate soldiers had fired on Fort Sumter, in Charleston, South Carolina.

Abraham Lincoln

Lincoln's family gave his watch to the National Museum of American History in 1958.

An upset Dillon decided to write down his feelings about this important event. He chose a very unusual place for his words: the inside of the watch he was working on. In tiny script, Dillon engraved: "April 13 - 1861, Fort Sumpter was attacked by the rebels on the above date." He also wrote, "Thank God we have a government." Without telling anyone what he had done, Dillon closed up the watch and it was returned to its owner: the President of the United States, Abraham Lincoln!

Time for a Story

In 1906, a reporter from the *New York Times* heard Dillon's story and interviewed the elderly watchmaker. Dillon said no one, not even Lincoln, ever knew about the inscription. And that's where the tale ended—until 2009. Douglas Stiles, Dillon's great-great grandson, had heard the watch story from an uncle and searched the Internet to see if he could learn more about the secret writing. Stiles found the old *New York Times* article online and then spoke to officials at the National Museum of American History, in Washington, D.C.

Stiles told museum officials that there might be some secret writing in the watch. Since this was a rare chance to learn about American history, officials decided to let the public watch the watch being opened. "It's a moment of discovery, and you can only discover things once," said Harry R. Rubenstein, a curator at the museum. "We wanted to share it."

The Moment of Truth

Working under powerful lighting and using magnifying glasses, George Thomas, a master watchmaker, very carefully opened the back of the watch. "The moment of truth has come," he said. "Is there or is there not an inscription?"

Stiles and his brother, Don, were asked to take the first look. "There is an inscription!" Douglas Stiles shouted. "My goodness, that's Lincoln's watch," he said later on. "My ancestor put graffiti on it."

Historians noted that Dillon had made a couple of mistakes in his message. He misspelled *Sumter* and got the date of the attack wrong. (It was April 12, not April 13.) But does that matter? Not at all! Dillon's secret writing "adds to our understanding of how an ordinary person was affected by the events of the day," said Brent D. Glass, the director of the museum.

THE WHITE HOUSE

Presidents and their families have been living in the White House for more than 200 years. The President's house features 132 rooms, including three kitchens, eight staircases, three elevators, and 35 bathrooms. The rooms are spread over six levels. There are a lot of fun things for the First Family to do in and around the White House. For example, there is a library, a movie theater, and a two-lane bowling alley. In 1975, President Gerald Ford installed a swimming pool on the grounds that is still in use. There is even an underground passage so members of the First Family can reach the pool without walking across the lawn.

This side of the building is the West Wing, which is where many members of the senior staff perform their day-to-day tasks. Here, the President works in the Oval Office. The Situation Room, Roosevelt Room, and Press Briefing Room are all in the West Wing.

The main section of the White House is known as the Executive Residence.

The office of the First Lady is found in the East Wing. All of the White House social events are planned in the offices here. The Family Theater is also found in the East Wing.

FIRST KIDS

Sasha and Malia Obama are not the only kids to enjoy living in the White House. Here are some of the other famous youngsters who grew up at 1600 Pennsylvania Avenue, in Washington, D.C.

GUESS WHAT? Grover Cleveland was the only President who got married in the White House. On June 2, 1886, he wed Frances Folsom in the Blue Room. In 1893, his daughter Esther became the only child of a President to be born in the White House.

President Ford's daughter, Susan Ford, once said that living in the presidential mansion was "like a fairy tale."

◄◄ President Nixon hosted his daughter Tricia Nixon's wedding at the White House, in 1971.

Amy Carter was 9 years old when her parents, Jimmy and Rosalynn Carter, moved to Washington. She famously read a book at the table during a state dinner. Amy attended public school in Washington, D.C. ▶▶▶

Quentin Roosevelt (left) and Archibald Roosevelt (right) were two of Teddy Roosevelt's children. During their first year in the White House, the President's office was on the same floor as the family's quarters.

1 GEORGE WASHINGTON
SERVED 1789–1797

Born: February 22, 1732, in Virginia

Died: December 14, 1799

Political Party: None (first term), Federalist (second term)

Vice President: John Adams

First Lady: Martha Dandridge Custis

GUESS WHAT? When George Washington ran for President in 1788, he did not have an opponent. He is the only President to be elected unanimously.

2 JOHN ADAMS
SERVED 1797–1801

Born: October 30, 1735, in Massachusetts

Died: July 4, 1826

Political Party: Federalist

Vice President: Thomas Jefferson

First Lady: Abigail Smith

GUESS WHAT? In November 1800, before the paint on the walls had even dried, John Adams and his family became the first residents of the White House.

3 THOMAS JEFFERSON
SERVED 1801–1809

Born: April 13, 1743, in Virginia

Died: July 4, 1826

Political Party: Democratic-Republican

Vice Presidents: Aaron Burr, George Clinton

First Lady: Martha Wayles Skelton

GUESS WHAT? Thomas Jefferson was right-handed. But after injuring his right wrist in 1786, he taught himself to write with his left hand.

4 JAMES MADISON
SERVED 1809–1817

Born: March 16, 1751, in Virginia

Died: June 28, 1836

Political Party: Democratic-Republican

Vice Presidents: George Clinton, Elbridge Gerry

First Lady: Dorothy "Dolley" Payne Todd

GUESS WHAT? Before James Madison, Presidents wore short, knee-length pants called knee breeches. Madison was the first President to regularly wear long pants, or trousers.

5 JAMES MONROE
SERVED 1817–1825

Born: April 28, 1758, in Virginia

Died: July 4, 1831

Political Party: Democratic-Republican

Vice President: Daniel D. Tompkins

First Lady: Elizabeth "Eliza" Kortright

GUESS WHAT? In 1817, James Monroe became the first President to ride on a steamboat.

6 JOHN QUINCY ADAMS
SERVED 1825–1829

Born: July 11, 1767, in Massachusetts

Died: February 23, 1848

Political Party: Democratic-Republican

Vice President: John C. Calhoun

First Lady: Louisa Catherine Johnson

GUESS WHAT? In 1826, the Marquis de Lafayette, a French nobleman, gave John Quincy Adams an alligator. President Adams kept his new pet in the East Room of the White House for a few months.

7 ANDREW JACKSON

SERVED 1829–1837

Born: March 15, 1767, in South Carolina

Died: June 8, 1845

Political Party: Democratic

Vice Presidents: John C. Calhoun, Martin Van Buren

First Lady: Rachel Donelson Robards

GUESS WHAT? Andrew Jackson was the first President to face an assassination attempt. The would-be assassin's gun misfired, and the President (who was 67 years old) hit his attacker with his cane.

8 MARTIN VAN BUREN

SERVED 1837–1841

Born: December 5, 1782, in New York

Died: July 24, 1862

Political Party: Democratic

Vice President: Richard M. Johnson

First Lady: Hannah Hoes

GUESS WHAT? One of Martin Van Buren's nicknames was "The Little Magician." Some people believe the nickname referred to his height. Van Buren was only 5 feet 6 inches (168 cm). Others said it was his almost-magical ability to win arguments.

9 WILLIAM HENRY HARRISON

SERVED 1841

Born: February 9, 1773, in Virginia

Died: April 4, 1841

Political Party: Whig

Vice President: John Tyler

First Lady: Anna Tuthill Symmes

GUESS WHAT? William Henry Harrison studied medicine at the University of Pennsylvania for a short time before joining the army. He is the only U.S. President who worked toward becoming a doctor.

10 JOHN TYLER

SERVED 1841–1845

Born: March 29, 1790, in Virginia

Died: January 18, 1862

Political Party: Whig

Vice President: None

First Ladies: Letitia Christian (d. 1842), Julia Gardiner

GUESS WHAT? As President, John Tyler made $25,000 a year (a large salary at the time). But five years after leaving office, he was so poor he could not pay a bill for $1.25 until after he had harvested and sold a crop of corn.

11 JAMES K. POLK

SERVED 1845–1849

Born: November 2, 1795, in North Carolina

Died: June 15, 1849

Political Party: Democratic

Vice President: George M. Dallas

First Lady: Sarah Childress

GUESS WHAT? First Lady Sarah Polk banned dancing in the White House. She would also not allow guests to play cards or drink alcoholic beverages.

12 ZACHARY TAYLOR

SERVED 1849–1850

Born: November 24, 1784, in Virginia

Died: July 9, 1850

Political Party: Whig

Vice President: Millard Fillmore

First Lady: Margaret Mackall Smith

GUESS WHAT? Before becoming President, Zachary Taylor was a soldier and a frontiersman. He and his family moved around a lot. Because he never settled in one place, he never registered to vote—even for his own election!

Presidents

13 MILLARD FILLMORE
SERVED 1850-1853

Born: January 7, 1800, in New York

Died: March 8, 1874

Political Party: Whig

Vice President: None

First Lady: Abigail Powers

 When Millard Fillmore became President, 30 states made up the United States.

14 FRANKLIN PIERCE
SERVED 1853-1857

Born: November 23, 1804, in New Hampshire

Died: October 8, 1869

Political Party: Democratic

Vice President: William R. King

First Lady: Jane Means Appleton

 Franklin Pierce's inaugural address was 3,319 words long. He did not use notes and delivered the entire speech from memory.

15 JAMES BUCHANAN
SERVED 1857-1861

Born: April 23, 1791, in Pennsylvania

Died: June 1, 1868

Political Party: Democratic

Vice President: John C. Breckinridge

First Lady: None

 James Buchanan was farsighted in one eye, which means that he could see things clearly only from a distance. In his other eye, he was nearsighted, which meant he could see things clearly only close-up. Because of this, he often kept one eye closed.

16 ABRAHAM LINCOLN
SERVED 1861-1865

Born: February 12, 1809, in Kentucky

Died: April 15, 1865

Political Party: Republican

Vice Presidents: Hannibal Hamlin, Andrew Johnson

First Lady: Mary Todd

 Mary Todd Lincoln consulted mediums (people who claim to be able to communicate with the dead) and held séances (rituals in which a medium tries to contact spirits) in the White House.

17 ANDREW JOHNSON
SERVED 1865-1869

Born: December 29, 1808, in North Carolina

Died: July 31, 1875

Political Parties: Union, Democratic

Vice President: None

First Lady: Eliza McCardle

Andrew Johnson never went to school and was a tailor before going into politics. Because of his humble upbringing, many people called him the "courageous commoner."

18 ULYSSES S. GRANT
SERVED 1869-1877

Born: April 27, 1822, in Ohio

Died: July 23, 1885

Political Party: Republican

Vice Presidents: Schuyler Colfax, Henry Wilson

First Lady: Julia Boggs Dent

Ulysses S. Grant was the army general who led the Northern army during the U.S. Civil War. He was also a talented painter.

19 RUTHERFORD B. HAYES
SERVED 1877-1881

Born: October 4, 1822, in Ohio

Died: January 17, 1893

Political Party: Republican

Vice President: William A. Wheeler

First Lady: Lucy Ware Webb

GUESS WHAT? In 1879, Rutherford B. Hayes signed the Act to Relieve Certain Legal Disabilities of Women. This act made it possible for female lawyers to argue cases before the Supreme Court.

20 JAMES A. GARFIELD
SERVED 1881

Born: November 19, 1831, in Ohio

Died: September 19, 1881

Political Party: Republican

Vice President: Chester A. Arthur

First Lady: Lucretia Rudolph

GUESS WHAT? Unlike most people who are either right-handed or left-handed, James A. Garfield was ambidextrous, which means that he could use both hands equally well. He could even write in Latin with one hand and Greek with the other—at the same time.

21 CHESTER A. ARTHUR
SERVED 1881-1885

Born: October 5, 1829, in Vermont

Died: November 18, 1886

Political Party: Republican

Vice President: None

First Lady: Ellen Lewis Herndon

GUESS WHAT? One of Chester A. Arthur's favorite pastimes was salmon fishing.

22 GROVER CLEVELAND
SERVED 1885-1889

Born: March 18, 1837, in New Jersey

Died: June 24, 1908

Political Party: Democratic

Vice President: Thomas A. Hendricks

First Lady: Frances Folsom

GUESS WHAT? Grover Cleveland dedicated the Statue of Liberty, in New York Harbor, on October 28, 1886. The famous statue was a gift from France.

23 BENJAMIN HARRISON
SERVED 1889-1893

Born: August 20, 1833, in Ohio

Died: March 13, 1901

Political Party: Republican

Vice President: Levi P. Morton

First Lady: Caroline Lavina Scott (d. 1892)

GUESS WHAT? Socially, Benjamin Harrison was considered stiff and formal. Some people referred to him as "the human iceberg" during his presidency.

24 GROVER CLEVELAND
SERVED 1893-1897

Born: March 18, 1837, in New Jersey

Died: June 24, 1908

Political Party: Democratic

Vice President: Adlai E. Stevenson

First Lady: Frances Folsom

GUESS WHAT? When Grover Cleveland claimed he was going on a fishing trip during the summer of 1893, he was actually having a cancerous growth removed from his mouth. The public did not find out about it until 1917, nearly 10 years after his death.

25 WILLIAM MCKINLEY

SERVED 1897–1901

Born: January 29, 1843, in Ohio

Died: September 14, 1901

Political Party: Republican

Vice Presidents: Garret A. Hobart, Theodore Roosevelt

First Lady: Ida Saxton

GUESS WHAT? William McKinley was shot by a man named Leon Czolgosz in 1901, and later died. After being shot, the President saw his guards attacking his assassin and said, "Don't let them hurt him."

26 THEODORE ROOSEVELT

SERVED 1901–1909

Born: October 27, 1858, in New York

Died: January 6, 1919

Political Party: Republican

Vice President: Charles W. Fairbanks

First Lady: Edith Kermit Carow

GUESS WHAT? In 1905, Theodore Roosevelt helped negotiate a peace treaty that ended the Russo-Japanese War. For this, he became the first President to win the Nobel Peace Prize, an award given to people who promote peace around the world.

27 WILLIAM H. TAFT

SERVED 1909–1913

Born: September 15, 1857, in Ohio

Died: March 8, 1930

Political Party: Republican

Vice President: James S. Sherman

First Lady: Helen Herron

GUESS WHAT? Six years before becoming President, William H. Taft said, "Don't sit up nights thinking about making me President for that will never come, and I have no ambition in that direction."

28 WOODROW WILSON

SERVED 1913–1921

Born: December 28, 1856, in Virginia

Died: February 3, 1924

Political Party: Democratic

Vice President: Thomas R. Marshall

First Ladies: Ellen Louise Axson (d. 1914), Edith Bolling Galt

GUESS WHAT? At birth, Woodrow Wilson was named Thomas Woodrow Wilson. He was called "Tommy" as a young man.

29 WARREN G. HARDING

SERVED 1921–1923

Born: November 2, 1865, in Ohio

Died: August 2, 1923

Political Party: Republican

Vice President: Calvin Coolidge

First Lady: Florence Kling

GUESS WHAT? Warren G. Harding was the first President to be elected by both male and female voters. Women got the right to vote in 1920.

30 CALVIN COOLIDGE

SERVED 1923–1929

Born: July 4, 1872, in Vermont

Died: January 5, 1933

Political Party: Republican

Vice President: Charles G. Dawes

First Lady: Grace Anna Goodhue

GUESS WHAT? First Lady Grace Coolidge had a pet raccoon named Rebecca.

31 HERBERT C. HOOVER

SERVED 1929–1933

Born: August 10, 1874, in Iowa

Died: October 20, 1964

Political Party: Republican

Vice President: Charles Curtis

First Lady: Lou Henry

 GUESS WHAT? Herbert C. Hoover was the first President born west of the Mississippi River.

32 FRANKLIN D. ROOSEVELT

SERVED 1933–1945

Born: January 30, 1882, in New York

Died: April 12, 1945

Political Party: Democratic

Vice Presidents: John Garner, Henry Wallace, Harry S Truman

First Lady: Anna Eleanor Roosevelt

GUESS WHAT? Franklin D. Roosevelt began collecting stamps when he was 8 years old. When he passed away in 1945, he had more than 1,200,000 stamps.

33 HARRY S TRUMAN

SERVED 1945–1953

Born: May 8, 1884, in Missouri

Died: December 26, 1972

Political Party: Democratic

Vice President: Alben W. Barkley

First Lady: Elizabeth "Bess" Virginia Wallace

 GUESS WHAT? Harry S Truman claimed that he had read all of the books in his local library by the time he was 14 years old. That's more than 2,000 books! He once said, "Not all readers are leaders, but all leaders are readers."

34 DWIGHT D. EISENHOWER

SERVED 1953–1961

Born: October 14, 1890, in Texas

Died: March 28, 1969

Political Party: Republican

Vice President: Richard M. Nixon

First Lady: Mamie Geneva Doud

GUESS WHAT? Dwight D. Eisenhower kept a paperweight on his desk with the motto "Gently in manner–strongly in deed" written in Latin.

35 JOHN F. KENNEDY

SERVED 1961–1963

Born: May 29, 1917, in Massachusetts

Died: November 22, 1963

Political Party: Democratic

Vice President: Lyndon B. Johnson

First Lady: Jacqueline Lee Bouvier

GUESS WHAT? John F. Kennedy usually went swimming twice a day. He liked the pool water very warm. He kept the water in the White House pool 90°F (32°C) to help soothe the severe back pain he suffered from.

36 LYNDON B. JOHNSON

SERVED 1963–1969

Born: August 27, 1908, in Texas

Died: January 22, 1973

Political Party: Democratic

Vice President: Hubert H. Humphrey

First Lady: Claudia Alta "Lady Bird" Taylor

 GUESS WHAT? Lyndon and Lady Bird Johnson had many dogs. The most famous were a pair of beagles named Him and Her.

37 RICHARD M. NIXON

SERVED 1969–1974

Born: January 9, 1913, in California

Died: April 22, 1994

Political Party: Republican

Vice Presidents: Spiro T. Agnew, Gerald R. Ford

First Lady: Thelma Catherine "Pat" Ryan

 GUESS WHAT? Richard M. Nixon played both the piano and the violin. He also composed pieces of music to be played on both instruments.

38 GERALD R. FORD

SERVED 1974–1977

Born: July 14, 1913, in Nebraska

Died: December 26, 2006

Political Party: Republican

Vice President: Nelson A. Rockefeller

First Lady: Elizabeth "Betty" Anne Bloomer Warren

GUESS WHAT? Gerald R. Ford survived two assassination attempts, in California, in September 1975. Both would-be assassins, Sara Jane Moore and Lynette "Squeaky" Fromme, were women.

39 JIMMY CARTER

SERVED 1977–1981

Born: October 1, 1924, in Georgia

Political Party: Democratic

Vice President: Walter F. Mondale

First Lady: Rosalynn Smith

GUESS WHAT? Jimmy Carter was the first President born in a hospital.

40 RONALD REAGAN

SERVED 1981–1989

Born: February 6, 1911, in Illinois

Died: June 5, 2004

Political Party: Republican

Vice President: George H.W. Bush

First Lady: Nancy Davis

GUESS WHAT? Ronald Reagan was 69 years old when he became President. He's the oldest person to be elected President of the United States.

41 GEORGE H.W. BUSH

SERVED 1989–1993

Born: June 12, 1924, in Massachusetts

Political Party: Republican

Vice President: J. Danforth Quayle

First Lady: Barbara Pierce

GUESS WHAT? George H.W. Bush is the second President whose son followed in his footsteps. The first father-son pair was John Adams and John Quincy Adams.

42 BILL CLINTON

SERVED 1993–2001

Born: August 19, 1946, in Arkansas

Political Party: Democratic

Vice President: Albert Gore Jr.

First Lady: Hillary Rodham

 GUESS WHAT? The U.S. Secret Service gave Bill Clinton the code name Eagle. Hillary Clinton was known as Evergreen. Their daughter, Chelsea, was referred to as Energy.

43 GEORGE W. BUSH
SERVED 2001–2009

Born: July 6, 1946, in Connecticut
Political Party: Republican
Vice President: Richard B. "Dick" Cheney
First Lady: Laura Welch

GUESS WHAT? From 1989 to 1994, George W. Bush was the managing partner and part owner of the Texas Rangers baseball team.

44 BARACK OBAMA
SERVED 2009–

Born: August 4, 1961, in Hawaii
Political Party: Democratic
Vice President: Joe Biden
First Lady: Michelle Robinson

GUESS WHAT? Of the 50 states that make up the United States, 48 of them are next to one another. These are called the contiguous United States. The two noncontiguous states are Hawaii and Alaska. Barack Obama is the first President born outside of the contiguous United States.

PRESIDENTIAL SUCCESSION

This list shows the order of people who would take over if a sitting President died, resigned, or was removed from office.

1. Vice President
2. Speaker of the House
3. President pro Tempore of the Senate
4. Secretary of State
5. Secretary of the Treasury
6. Secretary of Defense
7. Attorney General
8. Secretary of the Interior
9. Secretary of Agriculture
10. Secretary of Commerce
11. Secretary of Labor
12. Secretary of Health and Human Services
13. Secretary of Housing and Urban Development
14. Secretary of Transportation
15. Secretary of Energy
16. Secretary of Education
17. Secretary of Veterans Affairs
18. Secretary of Homeland Security

TELLING IT LIKE IT IS

Once a year, the President is expected to deliver an important speech before both houses of Congress. In non-election years, this is known as the State of the Union address. Traditionally delivered in January, the speech will include the President's thoughts on how the country is doing and goals for the future. In addition to members of Congress, most members of the Cabinet and the Supreme Court attend, as well as newsworthy guests.

Presidents

MYSTERY PERSON

I was born on October 11, 1884, in New York City. In 1905, I married a man who became the 32nd President of the United States. I was a socially active First Lady. I championed the rights of women, minorities, and the poor.

Who Am I?

ANSWER ON PAGE 245

Case of the Smuggled Dino
By Kyla Oliver

In March 2012, Mark Norell, a paleontologist at New York City's American Museum of Natural History, came across an auction catalog. It featured a *Tarbosaurus bataar* skeleton that was for sale to the highest bidder. According to the catalog, the dino was found in Great Britain. Norell knew immediately that something was wrong. This type of dinosaur, discovered in 1946, roamed the Earth some 70 million years ago in what is now Mongolia, a nation in Asia. And Norell also knew that in Mongolia it is a crime to send fossils out of the country.

Norell wondered what the skeleton—8 feet (2.4 m) high and 24 feet (7.3 m) long—was doing in New York City and why it was up for sale. The fossil scientist wrote a letter to other paleontologists. "As someone who is intimately familiar with [dinosaurs], these specimens were undoubtedly looted from Mongolia," he said. Norell's letter reached the desk of Tsakhiagiin Elbegdorj, the President of Mongolia. He demanded that the skeleton be

> A paleontologist is a type of scientist who studies the remains of organisms that lived long ago.

returned to his country. Soon, American lawyers became involved in the case of the dinosaur skeleton, saying it had been smuggled out of Mongolia and illegally brought into the United States.

Saving the Old Bones

Attempts were made to stop the auction, but it was too late. Someone had bid just over $1 million for *Tarbosaurus bataar*. But the next day, the auction house agreed to hold on to the dino until the legal problems could be solved.

Five experts evaluated the skeleton. They confirmed that it almost certainly was a *Tarbosaurus bataar* that was dug up from the Gobi Desert in Mongolia. The fossil skeleton was then turned over to the United States government for safekeeping. It was stored in a warehouse until a judge ruled who owned it. The *Tarbosaurus bataar* is being returned to its home in Mongolia, where it once roamed the land millions of years ago.

A keen-eyed scientist was able to alert the authorities that this *Tarbosaurus bataar* was being sold illegally at an auction.

THE SCIENTIFIC METHOD

Scientists follow a specific process when asking and answering questions about the world around us. This process is known as the scientific method. It helps scientists make sure that the results of their experiments are accurate and reliable.

You can use the scientific method to study anything, from which foods attract ants to how the phases of the moon affect the ocean's tides.

THE BASIC STEPS:

1. Make an observation and ask a question. Each scientific experiment begins with someone looking around and wondering why something is or acts in a certain way. (Why is the sky blue? Why do cats purr? Where does water go when it's boiled?)

2. Do some background research. Before you begin an experiment, you should see what is already known about that topic. That knowledge will help you design your experiment.

3. Make a hypothesis. A hypothesis is an educated guess about what an experiment might find. It doesn't matter if your guess turns out to be right or wrong.

4. Conduct the experiment. This is how you test your hypothesis. You may need to repeat the experiment more than once to make sure it produces the same results each time.

5. Make a conclusion. After you've conducted your experiment and gathered your data, you then study and analyze those results carefully. Did the data prove or disprove your hypothesis?

WHITE HOUSE SCIENCE FAIR

The first-ever White House Science Fair was held in October 2010. It was such a success that a second fair was held in February 2012. At this event, President Barack Obama met with more than 100 students. Each student had won a different science, technology, engineering, or math competition. Some of the students had won for their research. One girl, for example, had studied the role of special cells in the development of cancer. Another had looked at how mussels living in saltwater marshes are able to fend off crabs, which like to eat them. Other students had won by designing and building new inventions to help solve problems. One student, for example, had invented a dissolvable sugar packet to cut down on paper waste at coffee shops and restaurants. Another had created an environmental-cleanup video game. And a group of students had worked together to build a special motorized chair to help a classmate with disabilities.

All the students got to talk with President Obama about their research and inventions. He even helped one student inventor demonstrate his Extreme Marshmallow Cannon. It can shoot the fluffy sugar-and-gelatin confections more than 170 feet (52 m).

USING SCIENCE TO SOLVE A *TITANIC* MYSTERY

On April 14, 1912, the passenger ship *Titanic* hit an iceberg and later sank in the Atlantic Ocean. It had been making its very first voyage from Southampton, England, to New York City. More than 1,500 of the ship's 2,224 passengers and crew died in the disaster.

Three days later, a ship called the *Mackay-Bennett* sailed from Canada to help recover bodies from the icy waters. The fourth body they pulled out of the water was that of a small boy with blond hair. He looked to be about 2 years old. His clothes included a pair of brown shoes. Many of the 306 bodies found by the *Mackay-Bennett* were buried at sea. But others, including that of the blond-haired boy, were taken back to Canada. No one knew who the boy was, however. So his body was buried in a graveyard in Halifax, Canada, with the words *Unknown Child* carved on his headstone.

Over the years, people made several attempts to identify the boy. For a long time, he was thought to be a little Swedish boy named Gosta Palsson, who had been emigrating to the United States with his family when the *Titanic* sank.

THE WRONG BOY

It took the scientific discovery of DNA to finally unlock the mystery of the *Titanic*'s "Unknown Child." *DNA* stands for deoxyribonucleic acid. It's a special type of molecule that's found in almost all living cells.

In 1998, a **genetic anthropologist** named Ryan Parr decided he would like to help figure out if the unidentified boy from the *Titanic* was Gosta Palsson. Parr got permission from the descendants of the Palsson family to exhume, or dig up, the body of the Unknown Child and examine the DNA. All that remained of the body were three teeth and a piece of bone 2.4 inches (7 cm) long. But that was enough to gather DNA evidence.

> A **genetic anthropologist** is a scientist who uses DNA taken from ancient human remains to learn more about early cultures and societies.

DNA TO THE RESCUE

DNA is shaped like a spiral ladder. Scientists call this shape a double helix. (*Helix* is a fancy name for something that has a spiral shape.) DNA is made up of segments, called genes, which are found on the "rungs" of the ladder. The genes contain the information that determines how living things—including humans—look and act.

Humans have about 25,000 genes, which are grouped together on 23 pairs of threadlike structures called chromosomes. Children inherit their genes from both of their parents. That's why children have many of the same traits as their parents, such as height, skin color, and eye color.

Parr used the bone fragment to get a sample of a special kind of DNA called mitochondrial DNA, or mtDNA. It's passed from generation to generation but only through women in a family. Parr then compared the mtDNA of the Unknown Child with mtDNA samples from women in the Palsson family. The samples didn't match. That meant the Unknown Child was definitely *not* Gosta Palsson.

Ryan Parr

> **GUESS WHAT?** Each of your cells has about 6 feet (1.8 m) of DNA coiled inside it. And you have at least 10 trillion cells in your body. So if you were to line up all your strands of DNA, they would stretch for about 10 billion miles (16 billion km). That's more than 50 round trips from Earth to the sun!

The *Titanic*

A SECOND GUESS

Five other boys under the age of three had died in the *Titanic* disaster. With the help of many other people, Parr tracked down women in all those families. The women agreed to provide samples of their mtDNA. Like Parr, they wanted to solve the mystery of the Unknown Child.

Two families came close to matching the child's mtDNA. One was the family of a Finnish boy named Eino Viljami Panula. He had been 13 months old when the *Titanic* sank. The other was the family of an English toddler named Sidney Leslie Goodwin. He had been 19 months old when the ship slipped into the sea. As the mtDNA was being studied, another group of scientists carefully examined the three teeth that had been found in the grave. They decided that the teeth seemed to be from a child younger than 15 months old. That meant the Unknown Child was probably Eino Panula.

SOLVING THE MYSTERY

Doubts remained. One big reason was the pair of leather shoes that had been found on the Unknown Child's body. A police officer had put the shoes in a desk drawer when the boy was buried. In 2002, the officer's family found the shoes and donated them to the Maritime Museum in Halifax, where many items from the *Titanic* are on display. When researchers looked at the shoes, they quickly realized that they were too big to belong to a child as young as Eino Panula.

In 2007, Parr took a sample of a different section of mtDNA from the bone fragment. He compared this sample with ones collected from women in the Panula and Goodwin families. This time he found a very close match. The DNA showed with 98% certainty that the Unknown Child was Sidney Goodwin.

The mystery was solved. On August 6, 2008, the relatives of Sidney Goodwin held a special memorial service at his grave in Halifax. The little boy from England has become a symbol of all the children who tragically lost their lives during the *Titanic* disaster.

On the 100th anniversary of the disaster, a visitor left a teddy bear on the grave of Sidney Goodwin.

SCIENTISTS AT WORK

There are many, many different scientists at work today. Meet a few of the standouts.

MATH IS FOR THE BIRDS

Scientists used to think that only humans and other primates, like monkeys and apes, could be taught how to put numbers in order. But, in 2011, a behavioral psychologist named Damian Scarf published a study that showed that pigeons could also learn that some numbers are higher than other ones.

A behavioral psychologist studies the behavior of people. Some also study the behavior of animals.

Damian Scarf

Scarf spent a year teaching pigeons to put images that contained one, two, or three objects in lowest-to-highest order. Each time a bird picked—or pecked—the right order for the images, it was rewarded with a piece of wheat.

Once the birds showed they had learned the abstract concepts of one, two, and three, Scarf tested them with pairs of images that contained up to nine objects. Scarf found that the birds were able to correctly order the images 70% of the time, even when both numbers in the paired images were new to them. That's about the same as the results researchers have gotten with macaque monkeys. Scarf and other scientists want to learn if pigeons and monkeys developed this skill from a common ancestor millions of years ago.

SOLVING A MUMMY MURDER MYSTERY

A paleopathologist studies how people in ancient times got ill and died.

In 2012, **paleopathologist** Albert Zink announced that he and a team of scientists had solved part of a 3,000-year-old murder mystery. It involved the death of Ramses III, who was Egypt's pharaoh, or king, from about 1188 to 1157 B.C. Ancient papyrus writings suggest that someone—perhaps one of Ramses's many sons—tried to kill the king in the final year of his reign.

Right after his death, King Ramses's body had been preserved, or mummified, and wrapped tightly in white cloth. Removing the cloth after thousands of years would probably destroy the mummy. So Zink decided to examine the king's body with a computed tomography (CT) scan. The CT scan of King Ramses's mummy showed a deep cut across his throat—a cut deep enough to have killed him instantly. The scan also found an amulet (an object to ward off evil or illness) inside the throat wound. The people who prepared the mummy for burial probably put the amulet there. Ancient Egyptians believed that such objects could help people return to life in another world.

King Ramses was obviously murdered. But who did it? Zink examined another mummy in the king's burial chamber. It had wounds that suggested the person had died from a hanging. In addition, DNA evidence (see page 174) showed that the second mummy was closely related to the king. Could the second mummy be the king's son? And could that son have been the murderer? Probably, says Zink. Most likely the son wanted to be king himself. And when it was discovered that he had murdered his father, the dead king's followers may have captured and killed him. The ancient papyrus writings may have had the story right after all.

Ramses III

THE LEGGIEST ANIMAL IN THE WORLD

In 1928, two scientists found a strange cream-colored millipede in California's mossy woodlands. It seemed to have more legs than most millipedes, so they called it *Illacme plenipes,* which means "the peak of many feet" in Latin. Other scientists tried to find more specimens of *I. plenipes,* but they failed. Many people thought this particular type of millipede must have become extinct.

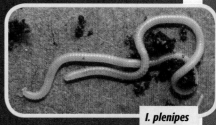

I. plenipes

In 2005, an **evolutionary biologist** named Paul Marek conducted his own search for *I. plenipes.* He and his brother made several trips into the California woodlands where the millipede was last seen. He looked in dark, moist places where he knew millipedes like to hide. Finally, he found several *I. plenipes.* They were crawling around on the undersides of big sandstone boulders.

An evolutionary biologist studies how animals and other living organisms have evolved throughout history.

Marek took the creatures back to his lab, where he could study them under a microscope. He found that *I. plenipes* is quite small, even for a millipede. It's 1.2 inches (3 cm) long. It has hairs on its back that produce a silky substance. And, unlike other millipedes, its mouth can pierce plants and suck fluid from them.

Some of the specimens Marek collected had 750 legs. That made *I. plenipes* the leggiest creature in the animal kingdom. The previous record holder had been a species of millipede with 742 legs.

Today, *I. plenipes* is found only in special areas of Northern California. Its closest relative is in South Africa. The fact that these two species live so far away from each other has led Marek and other scientists to believe that similar species may exist elsewhere in the world. They just may not have been discovered yet.

AN UNDERWATER SPACE STATION

Aquarius Reef Base is the only undersea research station in the world. It's located 63 feet (19 m) under the surface of the ocean in a coral reef that's 8 miles (13 km) off the coast of southern Florida. Since 1992, scientists have gone there to study ocean plants and animals.

A marine biologist studies plants and animals that live in the oceans.

The Aquarius is made of steel. It's 43 feet (13 meters) long and 20 feet (6 m) wide. It has six bunk beds, a shower, a toilet, and a kitchen area with a microwave, refrigerator, and trash compactor. It also has a small laboratory with computers and other equipment. Scientists conduct experiments there.

World-famous marine biologist Sylvia Earle has led many expeditions to this "underwater space station." These trips have helped scientists make important discoveries about the creatures that live in coastal ecosystems. They have also given scientists valuable information about the impact that pollution and climate change are having on the ocean's fragile coral reefs.

Scientists live in Aquarius for up to 10 days at a time.

GUESS WHAT? About 90% of all ocean creatures live in the coastal waters above the continental shelves that surround each of Earth's continents. Farther away from the coasts, the shelves drop off into much deeper waters of the open ocean. Those deep areas support fewer forms of life.

KITCHEN SCIENCE

WHAT MAKES POPCORN POP?

Popcorn is a special type of corn—and the only type that pops. Its scientific name is *Zea mays everta.* It's able to pop because each kernel is hard on the outside and starchy on the inside.

A kernel of popcorn contains a small amount of water. When the kernel is heated to above the boiling point of 212°F (100°C), the water turns to steam. As the steam builds up, it creates pressure inside the kernel. The steam needs a way to escape. Eventually, the pressure causes the outer casing of the kernel to rip open, and the steam rushes out. The explosion of the kernel is what makes the familiar popping noise. The explosion also causes the starchy interior of the kernel to inflate and form a new bumpy shape. A "popped" kernel can swell up to 50 times its original size.

WHAT MAKES MILK TURN SOUR?

Milk contains a sugar called lactose. It's the ingredient that makes milk taste good. Milk also contains a type of harmless bacteria called lactobacillus. The bacteria feed on the lactose for energy so they can reproduce and create more bacteria. As they do so, the sweet-tasting lactose turns into sour-tasting lactic acid. When enough lactic acid builds up in the milk, the milk "turns" and tastes bad.

The milk we buy in grocery stores has been pasteurized, or heated to very high temperatures. Pasteurizing is done to kill harmful bacteria in the milk that might make us sick. But the heating process also kills some of the harmless lactobacilli. That's why pasteurized milk lasts longer in the refrigerator than non-pasteurized milk. There are fewer lactobacilli it in, which means the milk takes longer to turn sour.

GUESS WHAT? Popcorn kernels can pop up to 3 feet (1 m) in the air.

WHY DO ONIONS MAKE US CRY?

Onions belong to a family of plants known as alliums. Other plants in this family include leeks, garlic, and chives. Alliums absorb a chemical called sulfur from the soil in which they're grown. That chemical gets into their cells.

When you cut an onion, you break open some of its cells. The chemicals inside the cells—including the sulfur—are then released into the air, where they join together to create a sulfur gas. The gas floats up through the air and into your eyes. It mixes with the natural water in your eyes to form sulfuric acid. Sulfuric acid stings, which causes your eyes to water. The water—or tears—is your eyes' way of diluting the acid so it will stop stinging.

GUESS WHAT? Chefs have a trick for keeping onions from stinging their eyes. They cool the onions in a refrigerator before cutting them. When an onion is cold, the chemicals in its cells are less likely to form a sulfur gas.

WHY DOES PEPPER MAKE US SNEEZE?

Pepper contains a chemical called piperine. It has properties that can irritate and inflame the nerve endings in the mucous membranes that line the inside of your nose. (The mucous membranes are where mucus, or snot, is made.)

The irritated nerves quickly send a message to your brain, which then orders the muscles of your nose and throat to contract . . . and sneeze! The sneeze forces air, mucus, and, hopefully, the irritating pepper out of your nose.

GUESS WHAT? The rush of air that comes out of the nose during a sneeze can reach speeds of more than 100 miles (161 km) per hour.

WHY DO SOME EGGS FLOAT IN WATER?

Whether an object—like an egg—floats or not depends on its density, or how much it weighs compared with the amount of space it takes up. If an egg's density is higher than the density of the water, then it will sink. If its density is lower than that of the water, then it will float.

Fresh eggs are denser than water, so they sink. But as an egg gets older, two things happen: The water inside the shell begins to evaporate, and the egg begins to rot. Both those things cause gases to form inside the shell. And gases are lighter than water. That's why stale and rotten eggs float when put in water.

You can test an egg for freshness by placing it gently in a bowl of water. Don't eat the egg if it floats!

GUESS WHAT? If you add enough salt to water, even a fresh egg will float in the liquid. That's because salt water has a higher density than freshwater.

WHY DOES A TEAKETTLE GET QUIET RIGHT BEFORE IT STARTS WHISTLING?

Water at the bottom of a teakettle boils first. It turns into bubbles of gas, which rise up toward the surface of the water. But those bubbles meet cooler water on the way up, which makes them collapse and change back into a liquid. The quiet rumbling you hear as the water in the teakettle boils is the sound of those bubbles popping as they collapse. As more water is heated, more bubbles form—and collapse. The rumbling becomes louder and louder.

Eventually, all the water is hot enough so that the bubbles make it to the surface without popping. At that point, the noise from the teakettle stops but only for a few moments. The gas in the bubbles soon forms enough vapor pressure (steam) in the air above the water to set off the teakettle's whistle.

WHY DOES SUGAR DISSOLVE FASTER IN HOT WATER THAN IN COLD WATER?

Like all materials, sugar and water are made of very small particles called molecules. When you mix sugar in water, the water molecules start colliding with the sugar molecules. This action causes the sugar molecules to break apart from each other. As they dissolve, they seem to disappear.

Water molecules move faster when they're hot than when they're cold. That means the sugar gets dissolved faster, too. The sugar is still in the water, though. You can taste it. You just can't see it.

Curious About Mars?

There is no dream too big for NASA's Jet Propulsion Laboratory (JPL). Since it was formed in 1936, JPL has pushed the limits of exploration. By focusing primarily on the construction of robotic spacecraft, the team has repeatedly made history.

This illustration shows the delivery spacecraft lowering Curiosity onto the surface of Mars. The spacecraft landed at a safe distance away.

In 1958, JPL created and launched America's first satellite, Explorer 1. Currently, the Mars Science Laboratory is one of JPL's largest missions. For decades, the team has been sending instruments, devices, and robots to the Red Planet to determine whether there has ever been life on Mars.

JPL had trouble at the beginning of the Mars Science Laboratory. The earliest missions to the Red Planet failed, and equipment did not work properly. The team learned from these errors and developed more-advanced instruments. In November 2011, JPL sent a high-tech rover called Curiosity to Mars. The journey was 285 million miles (459 million km) long and took eight months.

Curiosity has 17 high-powered cameras that serve as eyes on the ground. The rover's arm can scoop up soil and analyze it on board. Chemical sniffers sample the Martian air for carbon compounds, the building blocks and by-products of life. A long-distance laser blasts rocks to study their chemistry. So far, the Curiosity rover has been an extraordinary success. Its cameras have produced the clearest pictures of Mars ever taken.

The Curiosity mission has four main goals.

☆ To find out if there is any life on Mars or if there is any evidence that there once was life on Mars

☆ To collect as much information as possible about the climate and conditions on Mars

☆ To investigate the geology (the rocks and other things that make up the planet) of Mars to learn about how the planet was formed

☆ To prepare for human exploration of Mars

SIMULATING MARS ON EARTH

While the Curiosity rover was on its long voyage to Mars, scientists set up test-drives in the Mojave Desert in California. They used a robot rover called Scarecrow (left) as a stand-in. By studying how Scarecrow moved on various slopes and sandy conditions, they learned some lessons about how Curiosity would move on Mars.

POSTCARDS FROM
MARS

Curiosity's cameras capture magnified images of small areas as well as great wide-angle views of the Martian landscape. Antennas on the roving robot allow Curiosity to beam the photos back to Earth. Here are a few of the photos the rover has taken.

Curiosity took lots of photos of parts of itself using its Mars Hand Lens Imager. Scientists fit the different images together to create this self-portrait.

In October and November 2012, Curiosity explored an area nicknamed Rocknest. This particular rock (known as Rocknest 3) is about 15 inches (40 cm) long and 4 inches (10 cm) tall. Curiosity scooped up some of the dust and sand next to Rocknest 3 to analyze.

This panoramic view was created by piecing together a bunch of pictures taken while Curiosity was at Rocknest.

TOP 5
Planets with the Longest Day

A day on Earth is 24 hours long. That's the average time it takes for the sun to move from its noon position in the sky back to that same position. See which planets have the longest single day.

1. Mercury 175 Earth days, 21.6 hours

2. Venus 116 Earth days, 18 hours

3. Mars 24.7 Earth hours

4. Earth 24 hours

5. Uranus 17.2 Earth hours

Source: NASA's National Space Science Data Center

This image shows the base of Mars's Mount Sharp. The peak in the center of the photo is about 300 feet (100 m) tall.

THE SUN

The sun is a star, a huge ball of gas with no solid surface. The sun's energy comes from burning hydrogen into helium at its core, a process called **nuclear fusion.** The temperature of the core, where nuclear fusion is taking place, is in the tens of millions of degrees. On the surface, this fiery ball is about 10,292°F (5,700°C). The sun's energy shoots off into space, and some of it reaches Earth. This solar energy enables plants to grow and living things to thrive on Earth.

The sun is a vital component of human life. Humans could not exist without it, as the planet would be too cold to sustain human life. The study of how the sun interacts and connects with the Earth is called **heliophysics.** The word *helio* comes from the name of the Greek god of the sun, Helios.

GUESS WHAT? Scientists believe that the sun is about 4.6 billion years old.

Solar flare

SUNSPOTS AND SOLAR FLARES

Inside the sun is a magnetic field. When the magnetic field rises up to the surface, **sunspots** are formed. They appear darker, because they are cooler than the rest of the sun, but they are still hotter than 8,000°F (4,427°C). During periods of high solar activity, the sun will shoot out massive amounts of magnetic energy. These are known as **solar flares.** Some solar flares are so large that the radiation they release can reach Earth's atmosphere. This radiation can disrupt power grids, trains, cell phones, and more. NASA uses satellites such as the **Solar and Heliospheric Observatory (SOHO)** to predict these eruptions and give people time to prepare.

KEEPING THE SOLAR SYSTEM TOGETHER

Gravity is the force of attraction between objects. Earth's gravity pulls on all of the objects on the planet (including people) and keeps them from flying off into space. The sun is so much larger than Earth that its gravitational pull is much, much stronger. It's so strong that it keeps all the planets in our **solar system** from scattering into space or being pulled away by the gravitational pull of another star.

Our solar system is the area of space in which we live. It includes one star (the sun) and its eight large planets, a few dwarf planets, about 170 moons, and a lot of space junk (such as bits of rock and ice).

GUESS WHAT? More than 1 million planets the size of Earth could fit into the sun. That's huge!

ONE HOT VIEW

In 2006, NASA launched the twin Solar Terrestrial Relations Observatory (STEREO) spacecraft. Both circle the sun, just like Earth. STEREO A has a smaller, faster orbit than STEREO B. On September 1, 2012, the two spacecraft formed an equal-sided triangle with the Solar Dynamic Observatory on Earth, allowing scientists to get a real-time, 3-D view of the sun. Never before had they been able to see all sides of the sun at the same time.

THE PLANETS IN OUR SOLAR SYSTEM

Early astronomers were able to see the six closest planets to the sun simply by looking up, but Uranus and Neptune can be seen only by telescope. Mercury, Venus, Earth, and Mars are called terrestrial planets, because they have solid, rocky bodies. Jupiter, Saturn, Uranus, and Neptune are called gas planets, because they are made up of gases.

	Diameter	Distance from the sun	Average surface temperature	Guess what?
MERCURY	3,025 miles (4,868.3 km)	36 million miles (57.9 million km)	354°F (179°C)	Because it's so close to Earth, Mercury can be seen only within one hour or so of the rising or setting of the sun.
VENUS	7,504 miles (12,077 km)	67.2 million miles (108.2 million km)	864°F (462°C)	Venus is similar in size to Earth, but it has no oceans. It is covered by a layer of thick clouds, which trap heat in its atmosphere.
EARTH	7,926 miles (12,756 km)	93 million miles (149.6 million km)	59°F (15°C)	Earth is the only planet known to sustain life. Its atmosphere protects the planet from the worst of the sun's rays. About 70% of Earth is covered with water.
MARS	4,222 miles (6,795 km)	141.7 million miles (228.1 million km)	−82°F (−63°C)	Mars is prone to dust storms that engulf the entire planet.
JUPITER	88,650 miles (142,668 km)	483.6 million miles (778.3 million km)	−238°F (−150°C)	Jupiter is the solar system's biggest planet. Four of its many moons are planet-size themselves.
SATURN	74,732 miles (120,270 km)	885.9 million miles (1.43 billion km)	−285°F (−176°C)	Known as the ringed planet, Saturn spins very quickly. It takes only 11 hours for the planet to rotate fully on its axis. Saturn's famous rings are made up of ice and rock.
URANUS	31,693 miles (51,005 km)	1.78 billion miles (2.87 billion km)	−353°F (−214°C)	Uranus was discovered by William Herschel in 1781.
NEPTUNE	30,707 miles (49,418 km)	2.8 billion miles (4.5 billion km)	−373°F (−225°C)	Neptune was the first planet located by mathematical predictions instead of observations.

Space

WHAT'S IN SPACE?

Outer space isn't just filled up with planets and stars. There are many other objects that scientists may come across when studying the cosmos. Here are a few of them.

Meteoroids are hunks of rock or debris found in space. They are usually fragments of comets or asteroids. When a meteoroid enters Earth's atmosphere, it usually burns up. If it does not, it is known as a **meteor** or a **falling star.** Meteors that hit the ground are called **meteorites.**

Asteroids are rocky objects orbiting the sun that are smaller than planets but larger than meteoroids. Asteroids are most likely the leftover chunks of rock from the formation of the universe. They are usually irregularly shaped and covered with craters. Lots of asteroids can be found between Jupiter and Mars, in an area known as the asteroid belt, or main belt.

GUESS WHAT? The largest meteorite ever recorded was found in Namibia. Known as the Hoba meteorite, it weighs 66 tons (60 m tons).

Humans have been traveling into space for only 50 years, but have already left behind lots of **space junk.** There are old satellites, broken-off pieces of spacecraft, and objects dropped by astronauts. Even tiny particles can damage sensitive equipment. In June 2011, astronauts aboard the International Space Station were forced to evacuate to the Russian *Soyuz* spacecraft docked to the station after spotting space junk headed their way.

A **comet** is made up of frozen gas, rocks, dust, and ice. It's like a cosmic snowball orbiting in space. Comets move in an elliptical (oval-shaped) orbit around the sun. When a comet gets near the sun, it heats up and parts of it begin to melt. Its dust and gases spread out into a formation that can be a few miles, a few hundred miles, or even a few hundred million miles long.

Some scientists say that comets look like big, dirty snowballs.

MYSTERY PERSON

I was born on November 8, 1656, in a town near London, England. I was a noted astronomer and mathematician, and worked closely with another well-known scientist, Isaac Newton. My most famous accomplishment was being the first person to calculate the orbit of a comet. That comet was later named in my honor.

Who Am I?

ANSWER ON PAGE 245

LIFE AND TWEETS IN SPACE

In 1998, the first pieces of the International Space Station (ISS) were launched into orbit. Since 2000, the ISS has been continuously occupied by a rotating crew of astronauts and scientists. From September to November of 2012, that crew included Sunita Williams, commander of expedition 33. Williams and other astronauts and scientists from around the world performed scientific research and collected data about conditions in the Milky Way galaxy and beyond. Many of their experiments focused on humans' ability to live and work in space over long periods of time.

Thanks to a 2010 software upgrade on the ISS, astronauts aboard the station are now able to access the Internet for personal use. This allowed Williams and the other ISS residents to share information about everything from the launch to the landing via Twitter. Williams tweeted about experiments, spacewalks, receiving packages, and more. And she posted lots of pictures. She even did a special "Geo quiz" every week. For each quiz, she uploaded a photo of the area of Earth that the ISS was above and challenged her readers to name the locations.

Sunita Williams

Space

This nighttime view of Baltimore, Maryland, was captured by an astronaut aboard the ISS.

International Space Station

Super Bowl XLVII

On February 3, 2013, the San Francisco 49ers faced the Baltimore Ravens at the New Orleans Superdome in Super Bowl XLVII. In the first half of the game, the Ravens were in total control. They had a comfortable lead, 21–6, at halftime. At the start of the second half, the Ravens' Jacoby Jones caught the opening kickoff and ran 108 yards for yet another touchdown. It looked like lights out for the 49ers. And then the lights actually went out! A power failure blacked out the stadium, and play was delayed for 34 minutes. When the game resumed, the 49ers, led by their exciting young quarterback, Colin Kaepernick, battled back to come within two points of tying. But in the last minutes, the 49ers missed a chance to score, and a Ravens field goal put Baltimore ahead for good. The final score was Ravens 34, 49ers 31.

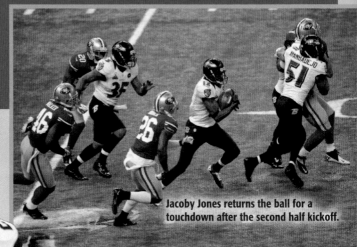

Jacoby Jones returns the ball for a touchdown after the second half kickoff.

2012–2013 NFL AWARD WINNERS

Most Valuable Player
Adrian Peterson, running back, Minnesota Vikings
Offensive Player of the Year
Adrian Peterson, running back, Minnesota Vikings
Defensive Player of the Year
J.J. Watt, defensive end, Houston Texans
Offensive Rookie of the Year
Robert Griffin III, quarterback, Washington Redskins
Defensive Rookie of the Year
Luke Kuechly, linebacker, Carolina Panthers
Coach of the Year
Bruce Arians, Arizona Cardinals
Comeback Player of the Year
Peyton Manning, quarterback, Denver Broncos
Walter Payton Man of the Year
Jason Witten, tight end, Dallas Cowboys

Adrian Peterson

A Record Year

A number of NFL records were tied or set in the 2012 season.

- New Orleans Saints quarterback Drew Brees threw touchdown passes in 54 consecutive games.
- San Francisco 49ers placekicker David Akers tied the record for longest field goal: 63 yards.
- Peyton Manning of the Denver Broncos joined Dan Marino and Brett Favre as the only quarterbacks to throw 400 touchdowns in their careers.
- Colin Kaepernick of the 49ers rushed for 181 yards in a single game, the most ever by a quarterback.

COLLEGE FOOTBALL

BCS Championship Game

The BCS (Bowl Championship Series) Championship Game was played on January 7, 2013, at the Sun Life Stadium, in Miami Gardens, Florida. Alabama handled Notre Dame easily to win its second consecutive BCS championship by a wide margin: 42–14. It is Alabama's third BCS Championship win in four seasons, and its ninth national football title, breaking a tie—with Notre Dame—for the most by any college.

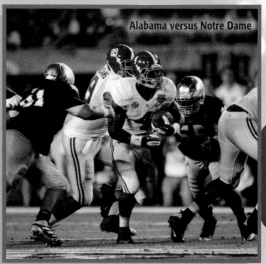
Alabama versus Notre Dame

Sports

Other 2013 Bowl Games

Rose Bowl (Pasadena, California)
January 1, 2013
Stanford 20
Wisconsin 14

Sugar Bowl (New Orleans, Louisiana)
January 2, 2013
Louisville 33
Florida 23

Orange Bowl (Miami, Florida)
January 1, 2013
Florida State 31
Northern Illinois 10

Fiesta Bowl (Glendale, Arizona)
January 3, 2013
Oregon 35
Kansas State 17

The Heisman Trophy

Every year, the Heisman Trophy, named after legendary coach John Heisman, is given to the outstanding player in college football "whose performance best exhibits the pursuit of excellence with integrity." The winner is chosen by a panel of sportswriters from around the country.

The 2012 Heisman went to Texas A&M quarterback Johnny Manziel, who had already earned himself the nickname Johnny Football. He was the first freshman to win the award. In his one year as a starter for Texas A&M, Manziel passed for 3,419 yards and 24 touchdowns, and ran for 1,181 yards and 19 touchdowns.

Johnny Manziel

BASEBALL

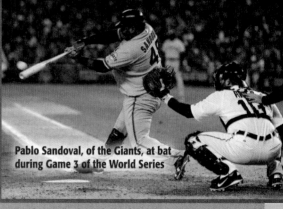

Pablo Sandoval, of the Giants, at bat during Game 3 of the World Series

2012 World Series

In the first two rounds of the playoffs, the San Francisco Giants did things the hard way. They faced elimination twice, battling to defeat the Cincinnati Reds in the first round and coming back from three games to one to beat the St. Louis Cardinals and win the National League championship. It was a bit easier for the American League's Detroit Tigers. They knocked out the Oakland Athletics and then swept the heavily favored New York Yankees in four games. But the Tigers finally met their match in the Giants. The Giants crushed the Tigers in the first game by an 8–3 score, and then held them to no runs in the following two games. The thrilling fourth game went into extra innings. Giants veteran second baseman Marco Scutaro drove in the winning run in the 10th inning to give San Francisco their seventh World Series championship.

2012 MLB League Leaders

BATTING

Home Runs
American League: Miguel Cabrera, Detroit Tigers, 44
National League: Ryan Braun, Milwaukee Brewers, 41

Batting Average
American League: Miguel Cabrera, Detroit Tigers, .330
National League: Buster Posey, San Francisco Giants, .336

Runs Batted In
American League: Miguel Cabrera, Detroit Tigers, 139
National League: Chase Headley, San Diego Padres, 115

PITCHING

R.A. Dickey

Wins
American League: David Price, Tampa Bay Rays, 20
National League: Gio Gonzalez, Washington Nationals, 21

Earned Run Average
American League: David Price, Tampa Bay Rays, 2.56
National League: Clayton Kershaw, Los Angeles Dodgers, 2.53

Strikeouts
American League: Justin Verlander, Detroit Tigers, 239
National League: R.A. Dickey, New York Mets, 230

MYSTERY PERSON

On April 15, 1947, I stepped up to the plate for the Brooklyn Dodgers and became the first African American to play modern Major League Baseball. I spent years fighting for civil rights. In 1962, I was elected to the Baseball Hall of Fame.

Who Am I?

ANSWER ON PAGE 245

2012 Little League World Series

The 2012 Little League World Series championship game was held August 26, 2012, in South Williamsport, Pennsylvania. The team from Tokyo, Japan, pounded the team from Goodlettsville, Tennessee, and won 12–2. The young Japanese and American players had become close friends during the 10-day tournament. In a gesture of camaraderie, Japan's players jogged the traditional postgame victory lap carrying the flags of both countries.

Sports

Miguel Cabrera

2012 MLB Award Winners

Most Valuable Player
American League: Miguel Cabrera, Detroit Tigers
National League: Buster Posey, San Francisco Giants

Cy Young Award (Best Pitcher)
American League: David Price, Tampa Bay Rays
National League: R.A. Dickey, New York Mets

Rookie of the Year
American League: Mike Trout, Los Angeles Angels
National League: Bryce Harper, Washington Nationals

Manager of the Year
American League: Bob Melvin, Oakland Athletics
National League: Davey Johnson, Washington Nationals

Bryce Harper

TOP 5 Oldest Baseball Stadiums

1. **Fenway Park**
   Boston Red Sox, opened in 1912

2. **Wrigley Field**
   Chicago Cubs, 1914

3. **Dodger Stadium**
   Los Angeles Dodgers, 1962

4. **Angel Stadium of Anaheim**
   Los Angeles Angels, 1966

5. **Oakland Alameda County Coliseum**
   Oakland Athletics, 1968

Source: Major League Baseball

Fenway Park

BASKETBALL

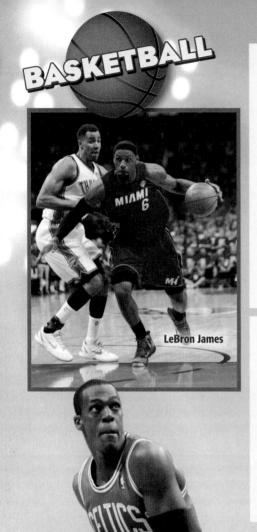

LeBron James

Rajon Rondo

2012 NBA Finals

At the start of the 2011–2012 NBA season, many thought the Miami Heat, led by superstars LeBron James, Dwayne Wade, and Chris Bosh, were the best team in the league. Few would have thought the Oklahoma City Thunder would be the Heat's opponent in the finals. The Thunder, a very young team, surprised everyone by knocking out tough opponents in the playoffs, including the defending champions, the Dallas Mavericks. The finals were a different story, though. LeBron James played a great game and averaged almost 29 points per game. It was all too much for the Thunder, and the Heat won the series and the championship four games to one.

2012 WNBA Finals

When the Minnesota Lynx made it to the 2012 WNBA finals, few were surprised. The Lynx were the defending champions and had the best regular-season record in the league. The Indiana Fever were the second-place team in their conference but were tough throughout the playoffs, even as they worked to overcome injuries to key players. Led by the outstanding play of forward Tamika Catchings, the Fever stunned the Lynx to win their first WNBA championship, three games to one.

2011–2012 NBA Regular Season Leaders

Kevin Durant, Oklahoma City Thunder, averaged 28 points per game. He also had the most total points, with 1,850.

Rajon Rondo, Boston Celtics, averaged 11.7 assists per game.

Steve Nash, Phoenix Suns, had the most total assists, with 664.

Dwight Howard, Orlando Magic, averaged 14.5 rebounds per game. He also had the most total rebounds, with 785.

LeBron James, Miami Heat, was named the season's MVP.

NCAA Division I Championships

The long road to the **NCAA Men's Basketball** National championship began in mid-March, with 64 teams. It ended with number-one-ranked Kentucky squaring off against number-two-ranked Kansas in the New Orleans Superdome. Kentucky was loaded with talent that blocked shots, outrebounded, and ultimately outscored Kansas, to win 67–59. Kentucky's forward Anthony Davis was named the tournament's Most Outstanding Player, only the fourth freshman to win the award. It was Kentucky's eighth NCAA basketball title.

Sometimes, the top-ranked teams don't make it all the way to the **NCAA Women's Basketball** Final Four (the round of games that decide who plays in the championship game). But in 2012, for only the second time in history, all four of the top teams (Baylor, Stanford, Notre Dame, and University of Connecticut) faced off. Baylor and Notre Dame moved on to the championship. Six-foot-eight (203 cm) center Brittney Griner, a junior at Baylor, led her team to an 80–61 victory. The victory gave Baylor an undefeated season—an amazing accomplishment.

2011–2012 WNBA Regular Season Leaders

Angel McCoughtry, Atlanta Dream, averaged 21.4 points per game and had 514 points in total.

Lindsay Whalen, Minnesota Lynx, averaged 5.4 assists per game and had 178 assists in total.

Tina Charles, Connecticut Sun, averaged 10.5 rebounds per game and had 345 rebounds in total. She was named the MVP.

GUESS WHAT? Tina Charles of the Connecticut Sun was drafted first overall in the 2010 WNBA draft and has lived up to those high expectations. In her first season, she was named Rookie of the Year and set all-time league records for rebounds, with 398, and for games with both scoring and rebounds in the double digits (known as a double-double), with 22. She has led the league in rebounds every year she's played.

Tina Charles

Sports

HOCKEY

2012 Stanley Cup

The Los Angeles Kings won their first Stanley Cup in team history, beating the New Jersey Devils in six games. The Kings were the first eighth-seed team in NHL history to defeat the first and second seeds in the playoffs—and to go on to win the Stanley Cup. They were also the first team to ever win the first three games of all four playoff series. The Kings finished the playoffs with an impressive 16–4 record. And 10 of those wins were on the road.

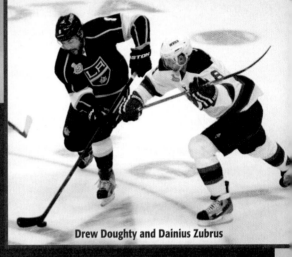

Drew Doughty and Dainius Zubrus

Jeff Carter

2012 NHL Award Winners

AWARD	GIVEN TO . . .	2012 WINNER (TEAM)
Conn Smythe Trophy	Stanley Cup playoffs MVP	Jonathan Quick (Los Angeles Kings)
Hart Memorial Trophy	Most valuable player	Evgeni Malkin (Pittsburgh Penguins)
Ted Lindsay Award	Best player as voted by fellow NHL players	Evgeni Malkin (Pittsburgh Penguins)
Vezina Trophy	Best goaltender	Henrik Lundqvist (New York Rangers)
James Norris Memorial Trophy	Best defenseman	Erik Karlsson (Ottawa Senators)
Calder Memorial Trophy	Best rookie	Gabriel Landeskog (Colorado Avalanche)
Art Ross Trophy	Top point scorer	Evgeni Malkin (Pittsburgh Penguins)
Frank J. Selke Trophy	Best defensive forward	Patrice Bergerson (Boston Bruins)
Jack Adams Award	Best coach	Ken Hitchcock (St. Louis Blues)

Henrik Lundqvist

RECORD BREAKER

New York Rangers goaltender Henrik Lundqvist is the only goaltender in NHL history to begin his career with seven consecutive 30-win seasons.

SOCCER

The **2012 UEFA European Football Championship**, known as Euro 2012 for short, was held in Poland and Ukraine June 8 to July 1. The final featured a showdown between Italy and Spain at the Olympic Stadium in Kiev. Spain scored four goals and shut out Italy.

Jordi Alba (Spain) and Mario Balotelli (Italy)

The **2012 MLS Cup game** was held December 1, in Carson, California. It was a rematch between the Houston Dynamo and the Los Angeles Galaxy, who were the 2011 champs. The Galaxy successfully defended their title by a score of 3–1. Omar Gonzalez was named Man of the Match.

Omar Gonzalez scores a goal with a header.

Sports

2012 Olympics

At the 2012 Olympics, the men's team from Mexico defeated heavily favored Brazil in a close 2–1 match played on August 11. It was Mexico's first gold medal at the London Games and its first significant international soccer trophy of any kind.

The U.S. women beat Japan 2–1 on August 9 to capture their third Olympic gold medal in a row. The U.S. women's team won every game it played in London, and set an Olympic women's team record of 16 goals scored.

Oribe Peralta scores Mexico's second goal.

Alex Morgan, of the U.S. team

Powerful Ladies

The U.S. women's team has been a powerhouse in soccer ever since the sport expanded to include women in international tournaments. It won the first Women's World Cup ever, in 1991, and also the 1999 Women's World Cup. The U.S. women have also won four of the five Olympic gold medals awarded for women's soccer (1996, 2004, 2008, 2012), and eight Algarve Cups (that's an annual global women's invitational tournament). They have been ranked number one in the world by FIFA every year since 2009.

AUTO RACING

Dario Franchitti leads the pack.

2012 Indianapolis 500

The 96th Indianapolis 500 was run on May 27 at the Indianapolis Motor Speedway. The race set an all-time record with 34 lead changes and featured a thrilling finish between Scottish driver Dario Franchitti and Japanese driver Takuma Sato. On the very last lap, Sato was in second and tried to pass Franchetti, who was in the lead. Sato lost control of his car and crashed into an outside wall. Franchetti cruised to his third Indy win.

Dario Franchitti

2012 Chase for the Sprint Cup

The Sprint Cup Series is the top racing series of the National Association for Stock Car Auto Racing (NASCAR). It consists of 36 races. The first 26 make up the regular season, as drivers rack up points for their finishes. After that, the 12 drivers with the most points compete in the last 10 races of the Chase. The driver with the most points after those 10 races is awarded the Sprint Cup, NASCAR's greatest prize. In 2012, the Chase ended on November 18 at Homestead-Miami Speedway. Jeff Gordon won that last race, but it wasn't enough to overtake points leader Brad Keselowski. Though Keselowski finished 15th in that final race, he captured enough points to win the Sprint Cup Championship.

The Final Standings of the Top Three Drivers

1. **Brad Keselowski** — 2,400
2. **Clint Bowyer** — 2,361
3. **Jimmie Johnson** — 2,360

Brad Keselowski

Clint Bowyer

TENNIS

2012 Tennis Champions

In tennis, the four Grand Slam tournaments (also called Majors) are the Australian Open in January, the French Open in May/June, Wimbledon in June/July, and the U.S. Open in August/September. The Australian and U.S. Opens are played on hard courts. The French Open is played on clay, and Wimbledon is played on grass. These competitions offer the most ranking points and prize money, and attract the best players.

Australian Open
Men's Singles: Novak Djokovic
Women's Singles: Victoria Azarenka
Men's Doubles: Leander Paes and Radek Stepanek
Women's Doubles: Svetlana Kuznetsova and Vera Zvonareva
Mixed Doubles: Bethanie Mattek-Sands and Horia Tecau

French Open
Men's Singles: Rafael Nadal
Women's Singles: Maria Sharapova
Men's Doubles: Max Mirnyi and Daniel Nestor
Women's Doubles:
Sara Errani and Roberta Vinci
Mixed Doubles:
Sania Mirza and Mahesh Bhupathi

Wimbledon
Men's Singles: Roger Federer
Women's Singles: Serena Williams
Men's Doubles:
Jonathan Marray and Frederik Nielsen
Women's Doubles:
Serena Williams and Venus Williams
Mixed Doubles: Mike Bryan and Lisa Raymond

Maria Sharapova

U.S. Open
Men's Singles: Andy Murray
Women's Singles: Serena Williams
Men's Doubles: Bob Bryan and Mike Bryan
Women's Doubles: Sara Errani and Roberta Vinci
Mixed Doubles: Ekaterina Makarova and Bruno Soares

Davis Cup (Men's International Team Tennis):
Czech Republic defeated Spain, three matches to two.

Fed Cup (Women's International Team Tennis):
Czech Republic defeated Serbia, three matches to one.

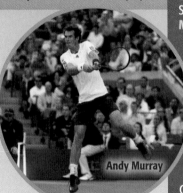

Andy Murray

Sports

SURFING

2012 World Surfing Championships

The Association of Surfing Professionals (ASP) gives out titles every year based on the points surfers receive in competitions on the ASP World Tour. In 2012, Australian surfer Joel Parkinson finally knocked American Kelly Slater out of the top men's position. Fellow Australian Stephanie Gilmore was the women's champion. Hawaii native Kelia Moniz was the women's longboard champ (her first championship), while American Taylor Jensen repeated as the men's longboard champ.

Joel Parkinson

Stephanie Gilmore

GOLF

2012 Golf Champions

Men
Masters: Bubba Watson
U.S. Open: Webb Simpson
British Open: Ernie Els
PGA Championship: Rory McIlroy
U.S. Amateur Championship: Steven Fox

Women
Kraft Nabisco Championship: Sun Young Yoo
LPGA Championship: Shanshan Feng
U.S. Women's Open: Na Yeon Choi
Women's British Open: Jiyai Shin
U.S. Amateur Championship: Lydia Ko

Webb Simpson

Na Yeon Choi

RECORD BREAKER

Two months after record-breaking Olympic swimmer Michael Phelps retired from the pool, he set a record in golf at the Pro-Am Alfred Dunhill Links Championship, at St. Andrew's, in Scotland. Phelps made a 159-foot (48 m) putt—the longest televised putt ever. He broke a record set in 1981 by British broadcaster Terry Wogan, who hit a 99-foot (30 m) put at San Francisco's Gleneagles course.

CYCLING

2012 Tour de France Top Finishes

The Tour de France is an exhausting bike race that takes place every summer. And, in 2012, the race celebrated its 99th anniversary. The race began in Liege, Belgium, and ended 23 days later in Paris, France. Cyclists covered 2,173 miles (3,497 km). Here are the top five finishers.

NAME	COUNTRY	RACE TIME
1. Bradley Wiggins	UK	87:34:47
2. Chris Froome	UK	87:38:08
3. Vincenzo Nibali	Italy	87:41:06
4. Jurgen van den Broeck	Belgium	87:45:02
5. Tejay van Garderen	USA	87:45:51

GUESS WHAT?

A high-tech, super-performance bicycle for the Tour de France can cost from $8,000 to $20,000. The riders don't pay for any of their equipment, though—sponsors donate it to the racers.

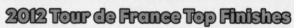

Bradley Wiggins

HORSE RACING

The three most famous horse races in the United States are the Kentucky Derby, at Churchill Downs, in Louisville, Kentucky; the Preakness Stakes, at Pimlico Race Course, in Baltimore, Maryland; and the Belmont Stakes, at Belmont Park, in Elmont, New York. These three races are for 3-year-old horses only and take place within a five-week period from early May to early June. Together, they make up the Triple Crown of Thoroughbred Racing, or Triple Crown for short.

I'll Have Another

2012 Triple Crown Race Results

Kentucky Derby
1. I'll Have Another
2. Bodemeister
3. Dullahan

Preakness Stakes
1. I'll Have Another
2. Bodemeister
3. Creative Cause

Belmont Stakes
1. Union Rags
2. Paynter
3. Atigun

Sports

GUESS WHAT? There has not been a Triple Crown winner (a horse that wins all three races) since June 7, 1978. This is the longest drought in Triple Crown history. Since 1978, 12 horses have won both the Kentucky Derby and the Preakness Stakes but could not finish first in the Belmont. I'll Have Another looked like he had a chance to win the Crown. But a foot injury caused him to be scratched from the Belmont Stakes.

DOGSLEDDING

The Iditarod is an annual dogsled race covering 975 miles (1,570 km) across the mountain ranges, frozen rivers, and icy forests of Alaska, from Anchorage to Nome. It's been called the last great race on Earth. On March 13, 2012, Alaska native Dallas Seavey and his team of Huskies, led by Diesel, rode into Nome after 9 days, 4 hours, 29 minutes, and 26 seconds on the frozen trail. Seavey came in an hour ahead of runner-up Aliy Zirkle. He even interrupted his victory press conference to greet her at the finish line. Seavey credited his veteran dog Guinness (who retired after the race) with making sure the other dogs on his team stayed positive. "Any time I had a dog getting down," he said, "she'd remind them how much fun it is being on the trail."

GUESS WHAT? At age 25, Dallas Seavey was the youngest musher ever to win the Iditarod. He's the son of 2004 Iditarod champion Mitch Seavey and the grandson of Iditarod veteran Dan Seavey. All three competed in the 2012 race.

X GAMES

2012 Summer X Games
June 28–July 1, Los Angeles, California

Moto X
Taka Higashino (Freestyle), **Mike Mason** (Speed & Style), **Vicki Golden** (Women's Racing), **Mike Brown** (Men's Enduro), **Maria Forsberg** (Women's Enduro), **Ronnie Renner** (Step Up), **Jackson Strong** (Best Trick)

Taka Higashino

Skateboard
Bob Burnquist (Big Air), **Pierre-Luc Gagnon** (Vert), **Paul Rodriguez** (Men's Street), **Alexis Sablone** (Women's Street), **Pedro Barros** (Park), **Ryan Decenzo** (Game of SK8)

BMX
Steve McCann (Big Air), **Jamie Bestwick** (Vert), **Scotty Cranmer** (Park), **Garrett Reynolds** (Street)

Rally Car
Sebastian Loeb (RallyCross)

Alexis Sablone

Sebastian Loeb

Nick Goepper

2013 Winter X Games
January 24–27, Aspen, Colorado

Skiing
Henrik Harlaut (Big Air), **Tiril Sjastad Christiansen** (Women's Slopestyle), **Nick Goepper** (Men's Slopestyle), **Maddie Bowman** (Women's SuperPipe), **David Wise** (Men's SuperPipe)

Snowboard
Louis-Felix Paradis (Street), **Torstein Horgmo** (Big Air), **Jamie Anderson** (Women's Slopestyle), **Mark McMorris** (Men's Slopestyle), **Kelly Clark** (Women's SuperPipe), **Shaun White** (Men's SuperPipe)

Snowmobile
Levi LaVallee (Freestyle), **Daniel Bodin** (Best Trick), **Levi LaVallee** (Speed and Style), **Tucker Hibbert** (SnoCross), **Mike Schultz** (SnoCross Adaptive)

On January 26, Elena Hight (above) became the first snowboarder, male or female, to land a double backside alley-oop rodeo during the SuperPipe competition.

RECORD BREAKER

Tucker Hibbert (Snowmobile SnoCross) and Shaun White (Snowboard SuperPipe) became the first Winter X Games athletes to win a gold medal six years in a row.

WINTER SPORTS

Snowboarding

The 2013 FIS Snowboarding World Championships were held in Stoneham-et-Tewkesbury, Quebec, Canada, January 18 to 27.

Men

Big Air	Roope Tonteri
Halfpipe	Iouri Podladtchikov
Slopestyle	Roope Tonteri
Snowboard Cross	Alex Pullin
Parallel Giant Slalom	Benjamin Karl
Parallel Slalom	Rok Marguc

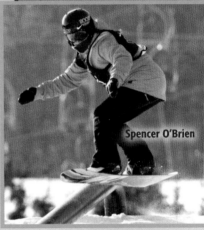

Roope Tonteri

Women

Halfpipe	Arielle Gold
Slopestyle	Spencer O'Brien
Snowboard Cross	Maelle Ricker
Parallel Giant Slalom	Isabella Labock
Parallel Slalom	Ekaterina Tudegesheva

Spencer O'Brien

GUESS WHAT? Carolina Kostner is the first Italian woman to win the World Figure Skating Championships.

Carolina Kostner

Marissa Castelli and Simon Shnapir

Figure Skating

The 2012 World Figure Skating Championships were held in Nice, France, March 26 to April 1.

Men	Patrick Chan	Canada
Women	Carolina Kostner	Italy
Pairs	Aliona Savchenko and Robin Szolkowy	Germany
Ice Dance	Tessa Virtue and Scott Moir	Canada

The 2013 U.S. Figure Skating Championships were held in Omaha, Nebraska, January 20 to 27.

Men	Max Aaron
Women	Ashley Wagner
Pairs	Marissa Castelli and Simon Shnapir
Ice Dance	Meryl Davis and Charlie White

Sports

199

OLYMPICS

London hosted the 2012 Olympics. Here are just a few of the amazing stories that came out of the historic two-and-a-half-week-long competition.

Most Decorated Olympian

American swimmer Michael Phelps won four golds medals and two silver, making him the most successful Olympic athlete for the third Olympics in a row. Phelps had a slow start in London. He did not win a medal in his first race, the 400-meter individual medley, but he medaled in all his other events. Phelps holds Olympic records for:

- The most gold medals. He's won 18 of them. That's twice as many as the second-highest record holder.

- The most gold medals in individual events: 11

- The most medals in individual events for a man: 13

As of March 2013, Phelps is the world-record holder in the 100-meter butterfly, 200-meter butterfly, and 400-meter individual medley.

With a total of 22 medals, Michael Phelps is the most decorated Olympian of all time.

UNSTOPPABLE!

While running in the qualifying heats of the 4x400-meter relay, Manteo Mitchell of the United States broke his left leg. But he kept running, finishing his portion of the race in an amazing 46.1 seconds in an incredible effort. He said he didn't want to disappoint his teammates and let everyone down.

GUESS WHAT? For the first time in its Olympic history, the United States was represented by more female than male athletes.

Blind Archer Sets World Record

The first world record of the 2012 Olympics was set by an archer who is legally classified as blind. Im Dong Hyun, 26, from South Korea, scored 699 in the qualifying round, beating his own record by three points. Then, Im and his teammates, Kim Bub-min and Oh Jin Hyek, set a team world record of 2,087 points. Im has 20/200 vision in his left eye and 20/100 vision in his right eye, which means he needs to be 10 times closer than a person with normal vision to see objects clearly. Yet he successfully shoots at a target 76 yards (69 m) away—three-quarters of the length of a football field—trying to hit a bull's-eye the size of a grapefruit.

ALMOST PERFECT!

Jamie Gray of the United States won the gold medal in women's 50-meter three-position (standing, kneeling, and lying prone) rifle shooting, setting Olympic records in the qualifying and in the final round. Gray finished with 691.9 points, beating the record (690.3) previously set by China's Du Li at the Beijing Games. In the final round she scored 99.9—0.1 away from perfect!

The Fab Five

Going into the Olympics, the American women gymnasts, led by reigning World All-Around Champion Jordyn Wieber, were among the favorites for team gold. But on her first day, Wieber did not score high enough to move on to the individual all-around competition. Her teammates—Gabby Douglas, Aly Raisman, Kyla Ross, and McKayla Maroney—picked up the slack, though, and the United States won the team gold medal by a wide margin. They also won the nickname Fab Five.

After winning the team gold medal, Gabby Douglas scored the top spot in the individual all-around.

Team captain Aly Raisman had the crowd on its feet during her floor exercise routine. She later said it was the best routine she had ever done. She won the gold medal in that event, as well as bronze in the balance beam.

American swimmer Missy Franklin won four Olympic gold medals and a team bronze. She holds the world record in the 200-meter backstroke and the 4x100-meter medley relay. After the Olympics, the 17-year-old was offered sponsorships and endorsements worth millions of dollars. But she turned them all down so that she could maintain her eligibility to swim for her high school team, Regis Jesuit High School, in Aurora, Colorado, and eventually swim in college.

HOMETOWN HERO!

Sports

UNITED STATES

HOW BIG IS THE UNITED STATES?

The United States is about half the size of Russia. It is a little bit bigger than Brazil and China and about half the size of all of South America.

RUSSIA

SOUTH AMERICA

UNITED STATES

CHINA

BRAZIL

HOW MANY PEOPLE?

As of March 7, 2013, there were 315,449,802 people in the United States. That's about 4.5% of the 7,070,664,821 on the planet. Only China and India have more people than the United States does.

WHERE DO WE LIVE?

Busiest Cities

TOP 10

These U.S. cities are the ones with the most people.

CITY	POPULATION
1. New York, NY	8,244,910
2. Los Angeles, CA	3,819,702
3. Chicago, IL	2,707,120
4. Houston, TX	2,145,146
5. Philadelphia, PA	1,536,471
6. Phoenix, AZ	1,469,471
7. San Antonio, TX	1,359,758
8. San Diego, CA	1,326,179
9. Dallas, TX	1,223,229
10. San Jose, CA	967,487

Source: Census.gov

Times Square, New York City

HIGHEST & LOWEST

Mount McKinley, in Alaska, is the country's highest point.

Death Valley, in California, is the country's lowest point.

United States

RECORD-SETTING LAKE

The largest lake in the United States is Lake Superior, on the border of Michigan, Minnesota, and Wisconsin, as well as Ontario, Canada. All of the water in the other Great Lakes (Michigan, Huron, Erie, Ontario) could fit inside Lake Superior—with plenty of room left over. The deepest part of Lake Superior is about 1,333 feet (406 m) below the lake's surface. You could nearly hide the entire Empire State Building underneath the water!

MYSTERY PERSON

I was born on December 10, 1830, in Amherst, Massachusetts. I was quite shy and spent most of my time writing poetry. One of my most famous poems is "I'm Nobody! Who Are You?"

Who Am I?

ANSWER ON PAGE 245

GUESS WHAT? The United States exports more wheat than any other country in the world.

Most Popular U.S. Baby Names

In 2011, parents in the United States picked these names more than any other. To see how popular your name is now and how often it was used every year since 1880, go to *ssa.gov/oact/babynames*.

BOYS

1. Jacob
2. Mason
3. William
4. Jayden
5. Noah
6. Michael
7. Ethan
8. Alexander
9. Aiden
10. Daniel

GIRLS

1. Sophia
2. Isabella
3. Emma
4. Olivia
5. Ava
6. Emily
7. Abigail
8. Madison
9. Mia
10. Chloe

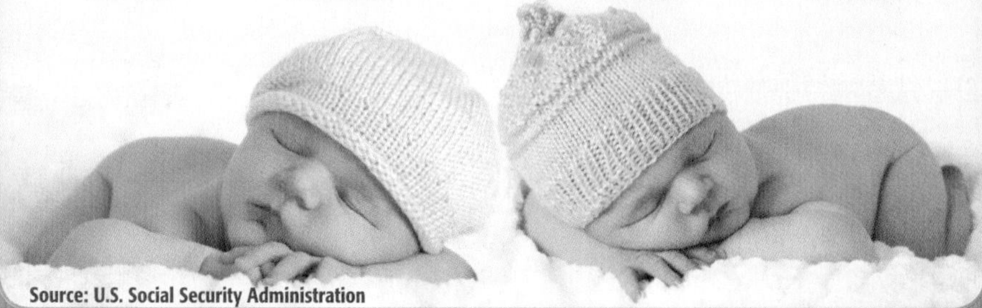

Source: U.S. Social Security Administration

Fastest Roller Coasters

Hold on to your seats! As amusement parks get more and more advanced, roller coasters are getting bigger, faster, and flat-out wilder. Here are the fastest roller coasters in the United States.

1. Kingda Ka
Six Flags Great Adventure;
Jackson, New Jersey
128 mph
(206 kmph)

2. Top Thrill Dragster
Cedar Point; Sandusky, Ohio
120 mph
(193 kmph)

3. Escape from Krypton
Six Flags Magic Mountain;
Valencia, California
100 mph
(160 kmph)

4. Millennium Force
Cedar Point; Sandusky, Ohio
93 mph
(150 kmph)

5. Intimidator 305
Kings Dominion; Doswell, Virginia
90 mph
(145 kmph)

Source: Roller Coaster Database

GUESS WHAT? The Missouri River is the longest river in the United States. It passes through Montana, North Dakota, South Dakota, Nebraska, Iowa, Kansas, and Missouri.

WHERE'S THAT?

Show off your knowledge of U.S. landmarks by matching these cool places to their location.

The Alamo

Independence Hall

Old Faithful

Golden Gate Bridge

1. Washington, D.C.

2. San Francisco, CA

3. Philadelphia, PA

4. San Antonio, TX

5. Nevada-Arizona border

6. Southwestern Colorado

7. Eastern California

8. Yellowstone National Park

The Lincoln Memorial

Mesa Verde

Death Valley

Hoover Dam

United States

THE UNITED STATES

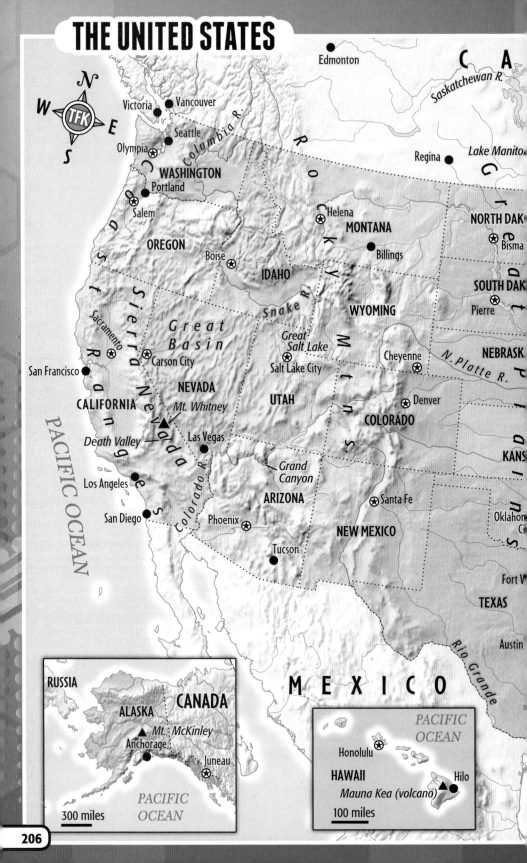

CANADA

Edmonton

Saskatchewan R.

N
W — TFK — E
S

Victoria
Vancouver

Regina

Lake Manito

Seattle

Columbia R.

Olympia

WASHINGTON

Portland

Salem

R
O
C
K
Y

Helena

MONTANA

NORTH DAK

Bisma

OREGON

Boise

Billings

IDAHO

Sierra Nevada

Great
Basin

Snake R.

WYOMING

SOUTH DAK

Pierre

Great
Salt Lake

NEBRASK

N. Platte R.

Sacramento

Carson City

Salt Lake City

Cheyenne

San Francisco

NEVADA

UTAH

Denver

CALIFORNIA

Mt. Whitney

COLORADO

KANS

PACIFIC OCEAN

Death Valley

Las Vegas

Grand
Canyon

Colorado R.

Los Angeles

ARIZONA

Santa Fe

Oklahoma
Ci

San Diego

Phoenix

NEW MEXICO

Range

Tucson

M
t
n
s

Fort W

TEXAS

Rio Grande

Austin

M E X I C O

RUSSIA

CANADA

ALASKA

Mt. McKinley

Anchorage

Juneau

PACIFIC
OCEAN

300 miles

PACIFIC
OCEAN

Honolulu

HAWAII

Mauna Kea (volcano)

Hilo

100 miles

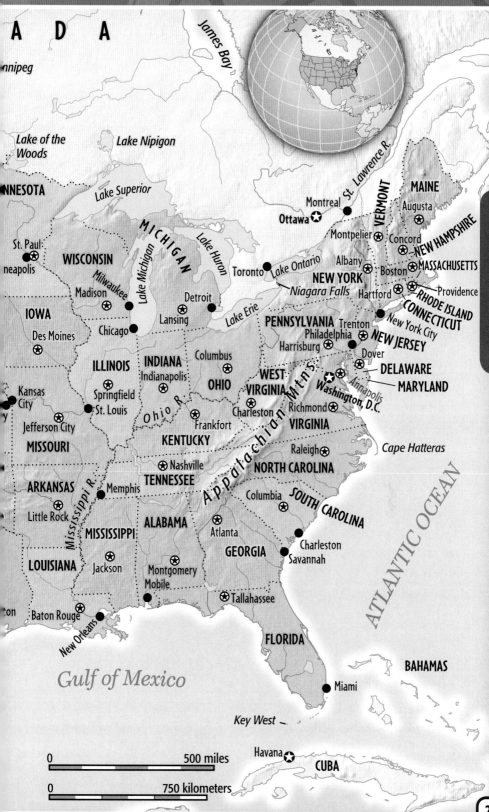

C A N A D A

nnipeg

James Bay

Lake of the Woods

Lake Nipigon

NNESOTA

Lake Superior

Montreal

St. Lawrence R.

VERMONT

MAINE

Augusta

Ottawa

Montpelier

Concord

NEW HAMPSHIRE

St. Paul

neapolis

WISCONSIN

MICHIGAN

Lake Michigan

Lake Huron

Toronto

Lake Ontario

Albany

Boston

MASSACHUSETTS

Milwaukee

Madison

Detroit

Lake Erie

NEW YORK

Niagara Falls

Hartford

Providence

RHODE ISLAND

CONNECTICUT

IOWA

Lansing

PENNSYLVANIA

Trenton

New York City

Des Moines

Chicago

Columbus

Philadelphia

NEW JERSEY

Kansas City

ILLINOIS

INDIANA

Springfield

Indianapolis

OHIO

Harrisburg

Dover

DELAWARE

Jefferson City

St. Louis

Ohio R.

Frankfort

WEST VIRGINIA

Charleston

Washington, D.C.

Annapolis

MARYLAND

MISSOURI

KENTUCKY

Richmond

VIRGINIA

ARKANSAS

Nashville

Raleigh

Cape Hatteras

TENNESSEE

Appalachian Mtns.

NORTH CAROLINA

Memphis

Mississippi R.

Little Rock

Columbia

SOUTH CAROLINA

ALABAMA

Atlanta

MISSISSIPPI

Jackson

Montgomery

GEORGIA

Charleston

Savannah

LOUISIANA

Mobile

Tallahassee

ATLANTIC OCEAN

ton

Baton Rouge

New Orleans

FLORIDA

BAHAMAS

Gulf of Mexico

Miami

Key West

0   500 miles

Havana

0   750 kilometers

CUBA

United States

207

ALABAMA

CAPITAL: Montgomery

LARGEST CITY: Birmingham

POSTAL CODE: AL

LAND AREA:
50,750 square miles
(131,443 sq km)

POPULATION (2012):
4,822,023

ENTERED UNION (RANK):
December 14, 1819 (22)

MOTTO: *Audemus jura nostra defendere.* (We dare maintain our rights.)

TREE: Southern longleaf pine

FLOWER: Camellia

BIRD: Yellowhammer

NICKNAMES: Yellowhammer State, Cotton State, Heart of Dixie

FAMOUS ALABAMIAN: Hank Williams, country singer and songwriter

Birmingham

Montgomery

GUESS WHAT? The first 911 call in the United States was made in Haleyville, Alabama, on February 16, 1968.

Canada

ALASKA

CAPITAL: Juneau

LARGEST CITY: Anchorage

POSTAL CODE: AK

LAND AREA:
570,374 square miles
(1,477,267 sq km)

POPULATION (2012):
731,449

ENTERED UNION (RANK):
January 3, 1959 (49)

MOTTO: North to the future

TREE: Sitka spruce

FLOWER: Forget-me-not

BIRD: Willow ptarmigan

NICKNAMES: The Last Frontier, Land of the Midnight Sun

FAMOUS ALASKAN: Jewel, singer and songwriter

Anchorage

Juneau

GUESS WHAT? Alaska's Point Barrow is the northernmost point of the United States. Amatignak Island, which is part of the Aleutian Islands chain, is the westernmost point of the 50 states.

ARIZONA

CAPITAL: Phoenix

LARGEST CITY: Phoenix

POSTAL CODE: AZ

LAND AREA:
113,642 square miles
(296,400 sq km)

POPULATION (2012):
6,553,255

ENTERED UNION (RANK):
February 14, 1912 (48)

MOTTO: *Ditat deus.*
(God enriches.)

TREE: Palo verde

FLOWER: Saguaro cactus blossom

BIRD: Cactus wren

NICKNAME: Grand Canyon State

FAMOUS ARIZONAN:
Emma Stone, actress

Phoenix

GUESS WHAT? Many people think Tombstone, Arizona, holds some of the last traces of America's Wild West. Miners, gunslinging outlaws, cattle thieves, and gamblers used to roam the streets. Now nearly 500,000 tourists visit Tombstone every year.

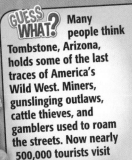

ARKANSAS

CAPITAL: Little Rock

LARGEST CITY: Little Rock

POSTAL CODE: AR

LAND AREA:
52,075 square miles
(134,874 sq km)

POPULATION (2012):
2,949,131

ENTERED UNION (RANK):
June 15, 1836 (25)

MOTTO: *Regnat populus.*
(The people rule.)

TREE: Pine

FLOWER: Apple blossom

BIRD: Mockingbird

NICKNAME: Natural State

FAMOUS ARKANSAN:
Maya Angelou, author and poet

Little Rock

GUESS WHAT? Forests cover more than half of Arkansas. More than half of the forests are hardwoods such as oak. The rest are made up of softwoods such as pine.

CALIFORNIA

CAPITAL: Sacramento

LARGEST CITY: Los Angeles

POSTAL CODE: CA

LAND AREA:
155,973 square miles
(403,970 sq km)

POPULATION (2012):
38,041,430

ENTERED UNION (RANK):
September 9, 1850 (31)

MOTTO: *Eureka!* (I have found it!)

TREE: California redwood

FLOWER: Golden poppy

BIRD: California valley quail

NICKNAME: Golden State

FAMOUS CALIFORNIAN:
Katy Perry, pop singer

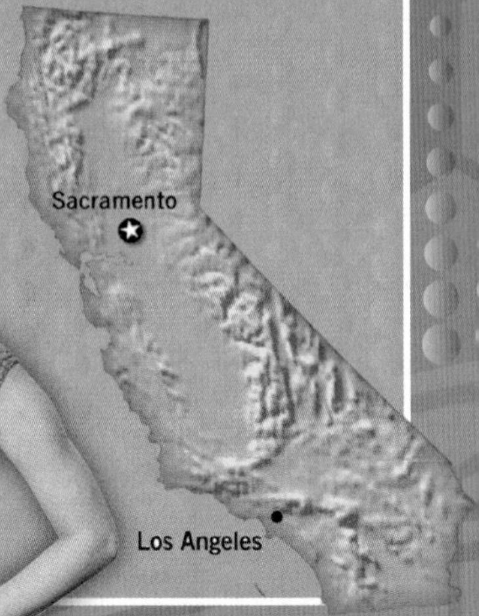

Sacramento

Los Angeles

GUESS WHAT? The hottest, driest place in the United States is Death Valley, California, where summer temperatures often reach more than 115°F (46°C).

COLORADO

CAPITAL: Denver

LARGEST CITY: Denver

POSTAL CODE: CO

LAND AREA:
103,730 square miles
(268,660 sq km)

POPULATION (2012):
5,187,582

ENTERED UNION (RANK):
August 1, 1876 (38)

MOTTO: *Nil sine numine* (Nothing without the deity)

TREE: Colorado blue spruce

FLOWER: Rocky Mountain columbine

BIRD: Lark bunting

NICKNAME: Centennial State

FAMOUS COLORADAN: Roy Halladay, baseball player

Denver

GUESS WHAT? The Kit Carson County Carousel is the oldest wooden merry-go-round in the United States. It originally operated in a Denver amusement park. Now visitors can check it out in Burlington, Colorado.

CONNECTICUT

CAPITAL: Hartford

LARGEST CITY: Bridgeport

POSTAL CODE: CT

LAND AREA:
5,018 square miles
(12,997 sq km)

POPULATION (2012):
3,590,347

ENTERED UNION (RANK):
January 9, 1788 (5)

MOTTO: *Qui transtulit sustinet.* (He who transplanted sustains.)

TREE: White oak

FLOWER: Mountain laurel

BIRD: American robin

NICKNAMES: Constitution State, Nutmeg State

FAMOUS CONNECTICUTER NUTMEGGER: Marcus Camby, basketball player

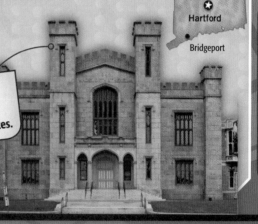

Hartford

Bridgeport

GUESS WHAT? The Wadsworth Atheneum Museum of Art, in Hartford, Connecticut, was built in 1842. It was the first public art museum in the United States.

DELAWARE

CAPITAL: Dover

LARGEST CITY: Wilmington

POSTAL CODE: DE

LAND AREA:
1,955 square miles
(5,063 sq km)

POPULATION (2012):
917,092

ENTERED UNION (RANK):
December 7, 1787 (1)

MOTTO: Liberty and independence

TREE: American holly

FLOWER: Peach blossom

BIRD: Blue hen chicken

NICKNAMES: Diamond State, First State, Small Wonder

FAMOUS DELAWAREAN: Henry Heimlich, doctor and inventor of the Heimlich maneuver

GUESS WHAT? The World Championship Punkin Chunkin contest is held every year in Bridgeville, Delaware. Science lovers and engineers compete to see who can launch pumpkins the farthest.

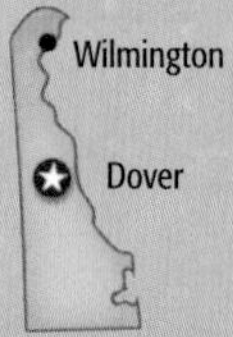

Wilmington

Dover

FLORIDA

CAPITAL: Tallahassee

LARGEST CITY: Jacksonville

POSTAL CODE: FL

LAND AREA:
53,927 square miles
(139,670 sq km)

POPULATION (2012):
19,317,568

ENTERED UNION (RANK):
March 3, 1845 (27)

MOTTO: In God we trust.

TREE: Sabal palm
(cabbage palmetto)

FLOWER: Orange
blossom

BIRD: Mockingbird

NICKNAME: Sunshine State

FAMOUS FLORIDIAN:
Victoria Justice,
actress and singer

GUESS WHAT? Florida's Everglades National Park is home to many rare and endangered species. The Everglades is often called a swamp, but it is actually a shallow, slow-moving river. The water flows southwest at about 0.25 miles (402 m) per day.

GEORGIA

CAPITAL: Atlanta

LARGEST CITY: Atlanta

POSTAL CODE: GA

LAND AREA:
57,919 square miles
(150,010 sq km)

POPULATION (2012):
9,919,945

ENTERED UNION (RANK):
January 2, 1788 (4)

MOTTO: Wisdom, justice,
and moderation

TREE: Live oak

FLOWER: Cherokee rose

BIRD: Brown thrasher

NICKNAMES: Peach State,
Empire State of the South

FAMOUS GEORGIAN:
Dwight Howard,
basketball player

GUESS WHAT? On the final Saturday of the annual Georgia Peach Festival, Peach County employees bake the "World's Largest Peach Cobbler." It takes about 90 pounds (40 kg) of butter to make the 11 by 5 foot (3.4 by 1.5 m) cobbler.

HAWAII

CAPITAL: Honolulu (on the island of Oahu)

LARGEST CITY: Honolulu

POSTAL CODE: HI

LAND AREA:
6,423 square miles
(16,636 sq km)

POPULATION (2012):
1,392,313

ENTERED UNION (RANK):
August 21, 1959 (50)

MOTTO: *Ua mau ke ea o ka aina i ka pono.* (The life of the land is perpetuated in righteousness.)

TREE: Kuku'i (candlenut)

FLOWER:
Yellow hibiscus

BIRD: Nene
(Hawaiian goose)

NICKNAME: Aloha State

FAMOUS HAWAIIAN:
Barack Obama, 44th President of the United States

Honolulu

GUESS WHAT? The Hawaiian language has only 12 letters: A, E, H, I, K, L, M, N, O, P, U, and W. In Hawaiian, the word for friend is *hoaloha*.

IDAHO

CAPITAL: Boise

LARGEST CITY: Boise

POSTAL CODE: ID

LAND AREA:
82,751 square miles
(214,325 sq km)

POPULATION (2012):
1,595,728

ENTERED UNION (RANK):
July 3, 1890 (43)

MOTTO: *Esto perpetua.* (Let it be perpetual.)

TREE: Western white pine

FLOWER: Syringa

BIRD: Mountain bluebird

NICKNAME: Gem State

FAMOUS IDAHOAN:
Gutzon Borglum, Mount Rushmore sculptor

Boise

GUESS WHAT? Idaho's mountains are full of minerals. Alongside these minerals are some rare and beautiful gemstones, including star garnet (the official state gem), opal, zircon, and jade.

213

ILLINOIS

ILLINOIS

CAPITAL: Springfield

LARGEST CITY: Chicago

POSTAL CODE: IL

LAND AREA:
55,593 square miles
(143,986 sq km)

POPULATION (2012):
12,875,255

ENTERED UNION (RANK):
December 3, 1818 (21)

MOTTO: State sovereignty, national union

TREE: White oak

FLOWER: Purple violet

BIRD: Cardinal

NICKNAMES: Prairie State, Land of Lincoln

FAMOUS ILLINOISAN:
Ronald Reagan,
40th U.S. President

GUESS WHAT? Students in the second and third grades at Joliet Elementary School set out to convince the state government to make popcorn the official state snack. In 2003, they succeeded!

Chicago

Springfield

INDIANA

CAPITAL: Indianapolis

LARGEST CITY: Indianapolis

POSTAL CODE: IN

LAND AREA:
35,870 square miles
(92,903 sq km)

POPULATION (2012):
6,537,334

ENTERED UNION (RANK):
December 11, 1816 (19)

MOTTO: The crossroads of America

TREE: Tulip tree (yellow poplar)

FLOWER: Peony

BIRD: Cardinal

NICKNAMES: Hoosier State, Crossroads of America

FAMOUS INDIANAN, OR HOOSIER: Michael Jackson, musician

Indianapolis

GUESS WHAT? One of Indiana's most historic sites is the Levi Coffin Home, which was an important stop on the Underground Railroad. More than 2,000 escaped slaves stayed in the home on their way to Canada.

IOWA

IOWA

CAPITAL: Des Moines

LARGEST CITY: Des Moines

POSTAL CODE: IA

LAND AREA:
55,875 square miles
(144,716 sq km)

POPULATION (2012):
3,074,186

ENTERED UNION (RANK):
December 28, 1846 (29

MOTTO: Our liberties we
prize, and our rights
we will maintain.

TREE: Oak

FLOWER: Wild prairie rose

BIRD: Eastern goldfinch
(American goldfinch)

NICKNAME: Hawkeye State

FAMOUS IOWAN: William
"Buffalo Bill" Cody, scout
and entertainer

Des Moines ⭐

GUESS WHAT? Iowa is the only U.S. state bordered to the east and west by parallel rivers. The Mississippi River is on Iowa's eastern border, and the Missouri River is to the west.

KANSAS

KANSAS

CAPITAL: Topeka

LARGEST CITY: Wichita

POSTAL CODE: KS

LAND AREA:
81,823 square miles
(211,922 sq km)

POPULATION (2012):
2,885,905

ENTERED UNION (RANK):
January 29, 1861 (34)

MOTTO: *Ad astra per
aspera* (To the stars through
difficulties)

TREE: Cottonwood

FLOWER: Sunflower

BIRD: Western
meadowlark

NICKNAMES: Sunflower
State, Jayhawk State,
Wheat State

FAMOUS KANSAN:
Amelia Earhart, first woman
to fly solo across the
Atlantic Ocean

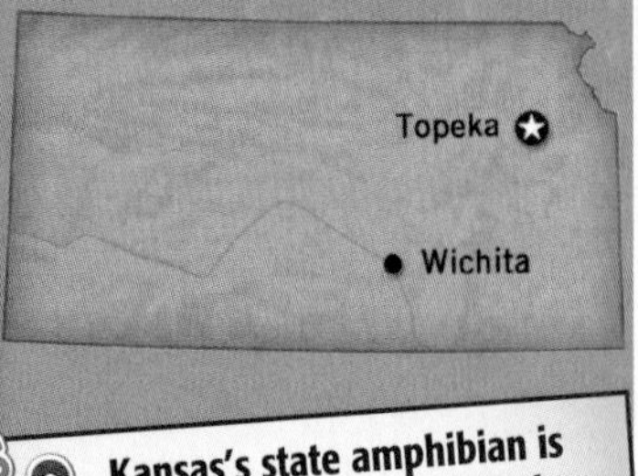

Topeka ⭐

● Wichita

GUESS WHAT? Kansas's state amphibian is the barred tiger salamander.

215

KENTUCKY

CAPITAL: Frankfort

LARGEST CITY: Louisville

POSTAL CODE: KY

LAND AREA:
39,732 square miles
(102,906 sq km)

POPULATION (2012):
4,380,415

ENTERED UNION (RANK):
June 1, 1792 (15)

MOTTO: United we stand, divided we fall.

TREE: Tulip poplar

FLOWER: Goldenrod

BIRD: Cardinal

NICKNAME: Bluegrass State

FAMOUS KENTUCKIAN:
Diane Sawyer, news anchor and journalist

Louisville • Frankfort

GUESS WHAT? Mammoth Cave, in Kentucky, is the longest-known cave system in the world. Objects made and used by people between 2,000 and 4,000 years ago have been found perfectly preserved in the cave.

LOUISIANA

CAPITAL: Baton Rouge

LARGEST CITY:
New Orleans

POSTAL CODE: LA

LAND AREA:
43,566 square miles
(112,836 sq km)

POPULATION (2012):
4,601,893

ENTERED UNION (RANK):
April 30, 1812 (18)

MOTTO: Union, justice, and confidence

TREE: Bald cypress

FLOWER: Magnolia

BIRD: Eastern brown pelican

NICKNAME: Pelican State

FAMOUS LOUISIANAN:
Peyton Manning, football quarterback

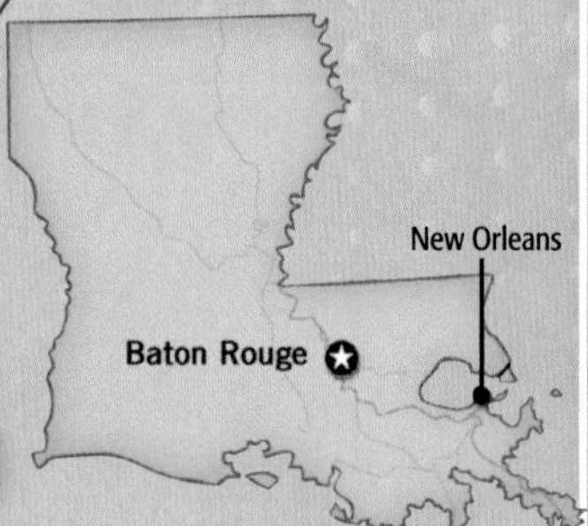

New Orleans

Baton Rouge

GUESS WHAT? The St. Charles streetcar line in New Orleans is the world's oldest continuously operated electric railway line. The streetcars began operating in 1893. Today, they help 20,000 daily commuters and visitors get around.

MAINE

CAPITAL: Augusta

LARGEST CITY: Portland

POSTAL CODE: ME

LAND AREA:
30,865 square miles
(79,940 sq km)

POPULATION (2012):
1,329,192

ENTERED UNION (RANK):
March 15, 1820 (23)

MOTTO: *Dirigo.* (I lead.)

TREE: White pine

FLOWER: White pine cone
and tassel

BIRD: Black-capped
chickadee

NICKNAME: Pine Tree State

FAMOUS MAINER:
Henry Wadsworth
Longfellow, author and poet

Augusta

Portland

GUESS WHAT? Antislavery author Harriet Beecher Stowe wrote the book *Uncle Tom's Cabin* while living in Brunswick, Maine. This famous book helped many Americans realize that slavery was wrong.

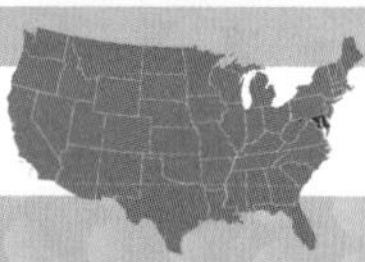

MARYLAND

CAPITAL: Annapolis

LARGEST CITY: Baltimore

POSTAL CODE: MD

LAND AREA:
9,775 square miles
(25,317 sq km)

POPULATION (2012):
5,884,563

ENTERED UNION (RANK):
April 28, 1788 (7)

MOTTO: *Fatti maschii, parole femine* (Manly deeds, womanly words)

TREE: White oak

FLOWER: Black-eyed
Susan

BIRD: Baltimore oriole

NICKNAMES: Free State,
Old Line State

FAMOUS MARYLANDER:
Michael Phelps, swimmer
and Olympic gold medalist

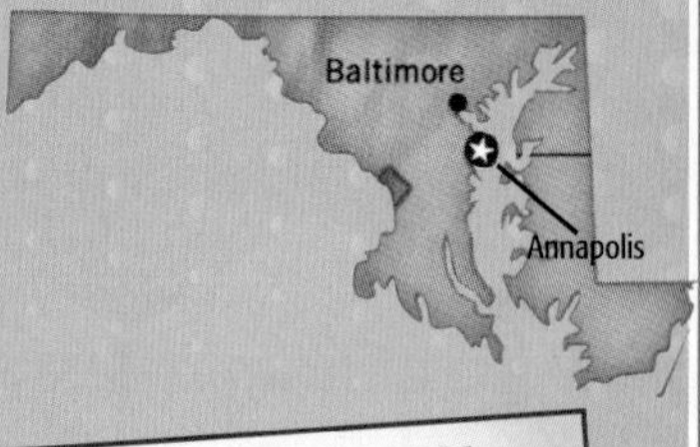

Baltimore

Annapolis

GUESS WHAT? The Baltimore & Ohio Railroad was the first railroad in the United States. Construction began at the Baltimore Harbor, in Maryland, in 1828.

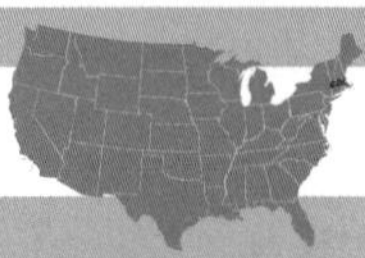

MASSACHUSETTS

CAPITAL: Boston

LARGEST CITY: Boston

POSTAL CODE: MA

LAND AREA: 7,838 square miles (20,300 sq km)

POPULATION (2012): 6,646,144

ENTERED UNION (RANK): February 6, 1788 (6)

MOTTO: *Ense petit placidam sub libertate quietem.* (By the sword we seek peace, but peace only under liberty.)

TREE: American elm

FLOWER: Mayflower

BIRD: Black-capped chickadee

NICKNAMES: Bay State, Old Colony State, Baked Bean State

FAMOUS BAY STATER: Amy Poehler, comedian and actress

Boston ✪

GUESS WHAT? The first subway in the United States, the T, opened in Boston in 1897.

MICHIGAN

CAPITAL: Lansing

LARGEST CITY: Detroit

POSTAL CODE: MI

LAND AREA: 56,809 square miles (147,135 sq km)

POPULATION (2012): 9,883,360

ENTERED UNION (RANK): January 26, 1837 (26)

MOTTO: *Si quaeris peninsulam amoenam circumspice.* (If you seek a pleasant peninsula, look about you.)

TREE: White pine

FLOWER: Apple blossom

BIRD: American robin

NICKNAMES: Wolverine State, Great Lakes State

FAMOUS MICHIGANDER OR MICHIGANIAN: Stevie Wonder, singer

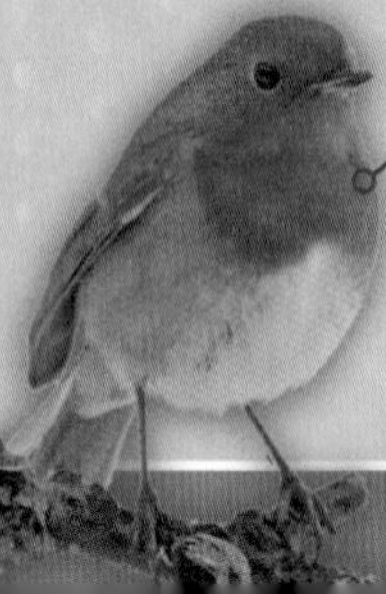

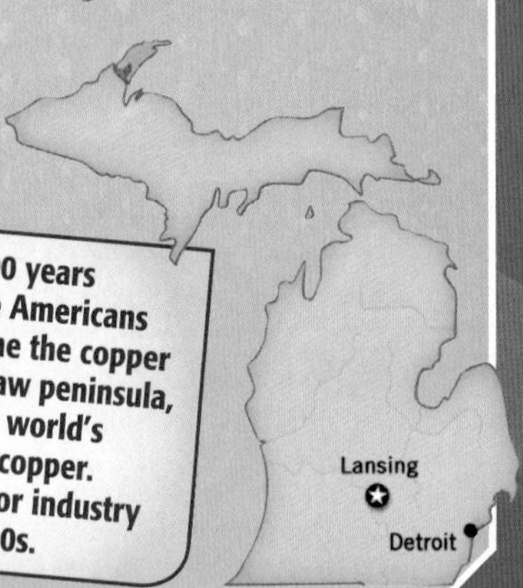

Lansing ✪

Detroit ●

GUESS WHAT? About 7,000 years ago, Native Americans developed ways to mine the copper on Michigan's Keweenaw peninsula, which used to have the world's largest deposit of pure copper. Mining remained a major industry in the area until the 1990s.

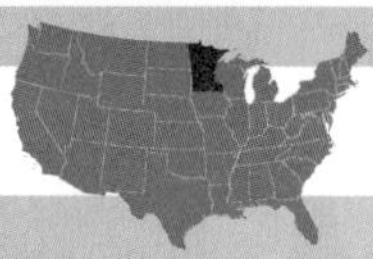

MINNESOTA

CAPITAL: Saint Paul

LARGEST CITY: Minneapolis

POSTAL CODE: MN

LAND AREA:
79,617 square miles
(206,208 sq km)

POPULATION (2012):
5,379,139

ENTERED UNION (RANK):
May 11, 1858 (32)

MOTTO: *L'Etoile du nord*
(Star of the north)

TREE: Red (or Norway) pine

FLOWER: Pink-and-white
lady's-slipper

BIRD: Common loon

NICKNAMES: North Star
State, Gopher State, Land of
10,000 Lakes

FAMOUS MINNESOTAN:
Larry Fitzgerald, football
player

GUESS WHAT? The largest shopping and entertainment complex in the United States is the Mall of America, in Bloomington, Minnesota. The mall has more than 520 stores and 50 restaurants. It also has a miniature golf course, an aquarium, a movie theater, and a spa.

Minneapolis ✪

St. Paul

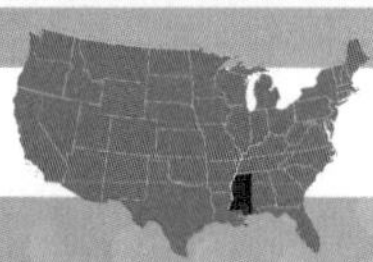

MISSISSIPPI

CAPITAL: Jackson

LARGEST CITY: Jackson

POSTAL CODE: MS

LAND AREA:
46,914 square miles
(121,507 sq km)

POPULATION (2012):
2,984,926

ENTERED UNION (RANK):
December 10, 1817 (20)

MOTTO: *Virtute et armis*
(By valor and arms)

TREE: Magnolia

FLOWER: Magnolia

BIRD: Mockingbird

NICKNAME: Magnolia State

FAMOUS MISSISSIPPIAN:
Jim Henson, *Muppets* creator

GUESS WHAT? Since 1976, the state stone of Mississippi has been petrified wood. Petrified wood is fossilized wood. Over a long period of time, some trees or treelike plants become buried and undergo a big change. Water carrying lots of minerals flows into the tree's cells and basically turns much of the tree to stone.

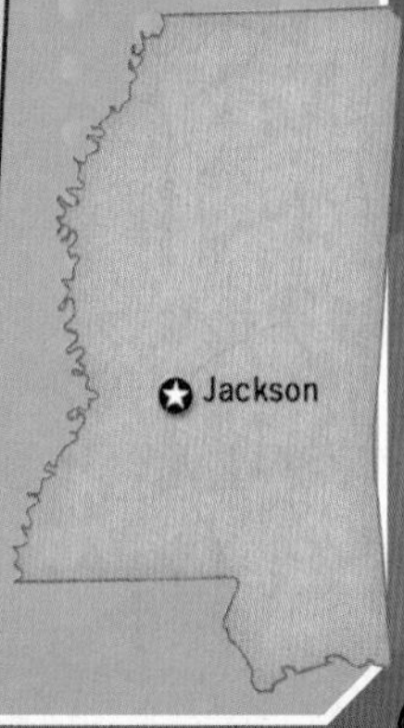

 Jackson

MISSOURI

CAPITAL: Jefferson City

LARGEST CITY: Kansas City

POSTAL CODE: MO

LAND AREA:
68,898 square miles
(178,446 sq km)

POPULATION (2012):
6,021,988

ENTERED UNION (RANK):
August 10, 1821 (24)

MOTTO: *Salus populi suprema lex esto.* (The welfare of the people shall be the supreme law.)

TREE: Flowering dogwood

FLOWER: Hawthorn

BIRD: Bluebird

NICKNAME: Show Me State

FAMOUS MISSOURIAN:
Mark Twain, author of *The Adventures of Tom Sawyer* and *Adventures of Huckleberry Finn*

GUESS WHAT? In 1997, Missouri designated the paddlefish as its official state aquatic animal. The paddlefish is a primitive fish, with a skeleton made of cartilage instead of bone. Cartilage is the type of firm but flexible material that makes up ears and parts of the nose in humans.

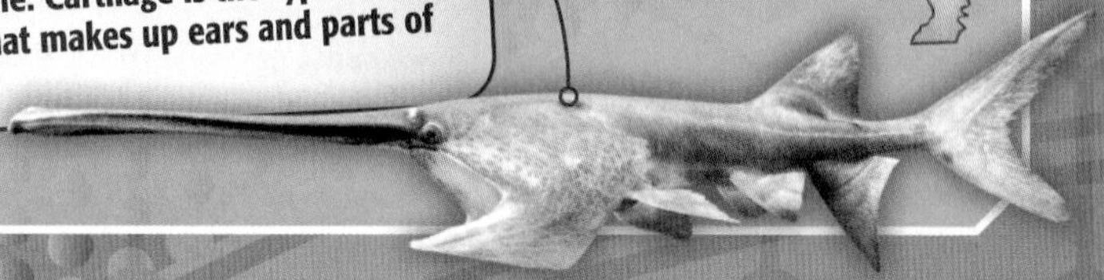

MONTANA

CAPITAL: Helena

LARGEST CITY: Billings

POSTAL CODE: MT

LAND AREA:
145,556 square miles
(376,990 sq km)

POPULATION (2012):
1,005,141

ENTERED UNION (RANK):
November 8, 1889 (41)

MOTTO: *Oro y plata* (Gold and silver)

TREE: Ponderosa pine

FLOWER: Bitterroot

BIRD: Western meadowlark

NICKNAME: Treasure State

FAMOUS MONTANAN:
Evel Knievel, motorcycle daredevil

GUESS WHAT? The state butterfly of Montana is the mourning cloak. Its name refers to the dark clothing people would traditionally wear while in mourning, the period of sadness after the death of a loved one. These butterflies can often blend in with tree bark to hide from predators.

NEBRASKA

CAPITAL: Lincoln

LARGEST CITY: Omaha

POSTAL CODE: NE

LAND AREA:
76,878 square miles
(199,114 sq km)

POPULATION (2012):
1,855,525

ENTERED UNION (RANK):
March 1, 1867 (37)

MOTTO: Equality before the law

TREE: Eastern cottonwood

FLOWER: Goldenrod

BIRD: Western meadowlark

NICKNAMES: Cornhusker State, Beef State

FAMOUS NEBRASKAN:
Standing Bear, Native American civil rights advocate

Omaha
Lincoln

GUESS WHAT? Chimney Rock, in western Nebraska, stands 325 feet (99 m) tall. It was a famous landmark for pioneers crossing the country on the Oregon Trail. The sight of this rock signaled the end of the seemingly endless flat Nebraska plains.

NEVADA

CAPITAL: Carson City

LARGEST CITY: Las Vegas

POSTAL CODE: NV

LAND AREA:
109,806 square miles
(284,397 sq km)

POPULATION (2012):
2,758,931

ENTERED UNION (RANK):
October 31, 1864 (36)

MOTTO: All for our country

TREE: Single-leaf piñon pine

FLOWER: Sagebrush

BIRD: Mountain bluebird

NICKNAMES: Sagebrush State, Silver State, Battle Born State

FAMOUS NEVADAN: Andre Agassi, tennis player

Carson City

Las Vegas

GUESS WHAT? At the end of every summer, tens of thousands of people gather in Nevada's Black Rock Desert for the Burning Man festival. They set up a temporary city and spend a week making music and art, staging performances, and celebrating community. Then they pack up and go home, without leaving any trash or buildings behind.

NEW HAMPSHIRE

CAPITAL: Concord

LARGEST CITY: Manchester

POSTAL CODE: NH

LAND AREA:
8,969 square miles
(23,230 sq km)

POPULATION (2012):
1,320,718

ENTERED UNION (RANK):
June 21, 1788 (9)

MOTTO: Live free or die.

TREE: White birch (canoe birch or paper birch)

FLOWER: Purple lilac

BIRD: Purple finch

NICKNAME: Granite State

FAMOUS NEW HAMPSHIRITE: Bode Miller, skier and Olympic medalist

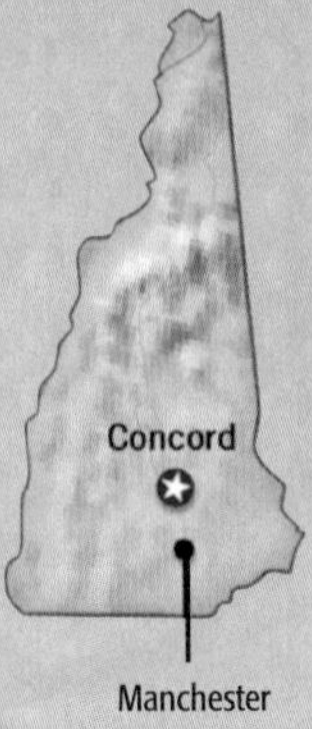

Concord

Manchester

GUESS WHAT? The New Hampshire state dog is the Chinook, which was originally bred to be a working sled dog.

NEW JERSEY

CAPITAL: Trenton

LARGEST CITY: Newark

POSTAL CODE: NJ

LAND AREA:
7,419 square miles
(19,215 sq km)

POPULATION (2012):
8,864,590

ENTERED UNION (RANK):
December 18, 1787 (3)

MOTTO: Liberty and prosperity

TREE: Red oak

FLOWER: Common meadow violet

BIRD: Eastern goldfinch (American goldfinch)

NICKNAME: Garden State

FAMOUS NEW JERSEYITE: Judy Blume, children's book author

Newark

Trenton

GUESS WHAT? In 1870, a boardwalk was built along the beach in Atlantic City, New Jersey. This was the first boardwalk in the world.

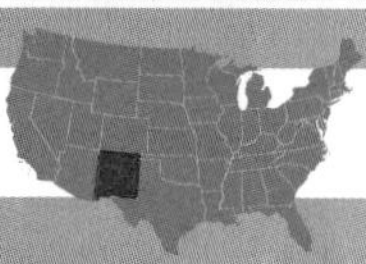

NEW MEXICO

CAPITAL: Santa Fe

LARGEST CITY: Albuquerque

POSTAL CODE: NM

LAND AREA: 121,365 square miles (314,335 sq km)

POPULATION (2012): 2,085,538

ENTERED UNION (RANK): January 6, 1912 (47)

MOTTO: *Crescit eundo.* (It grows as it goes.)

TREE: Piñon pine

FLOWER: Yucca

BIRD: Roadrunner

NICKNAMES: Land of Enchantment, Cactus State

FAMOUS NEW MEXICAN: William Hanna, animator

GUESS WHAT? Every year since 1972, the Albuquerque International Balloon Fiesta is held in Albuquerque, New Mexico. With more than 600 hot-air balloons floating in the sky, it is the largest ballooning event in the world.

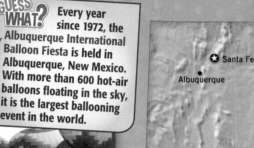

NEW YORK

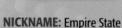

CAPITAL: Albany

LARGEST CITY: New York City

POSTAL CODE: NY

LAND AREA: 47,224 square miles (122,310 sq km)

POPULATION (2012): 19,570,261

ENTERED UNION (RANK): July 26, 1788 (11)

MOTTO: *Excelsior* (Ever upward)

TREE: Sugar maple

FLOWER: Rose

BIRD: Bluebird

NICKNAME: Empire State

FAMOUS NEW YORKER: Lady Gaga (Stefani Germanotta), singer

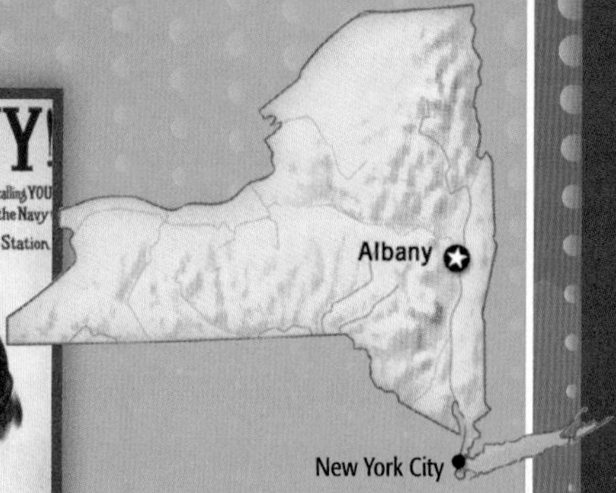

GUESS WHAT? Uncle Sam is a patriotic character that represents the U.S. government. The character is loosely based on Samuel Wilson, a meat-packer from Troy, New York. Sam Wilson's meats helped feed soldiers during the War of 1812.

NORTH CAROLINA

CAPITAL: Raleigh

LARGEST CITY: Charlotte

POSTAL CODE: NC

LAND AREA:
48,708 square miles
(126,154 sq km)

POPULATION (2012):
9,752,073

ENTERED UNION (RANK):
November 21, 1789 (12)

MOTTO: *Esse quam videri*
(To be rather than to seem)

TREE: Pine

FLOWER: Flowering
dogwood

BIRD: Cardinal

NICKNAME: Tar Heel State

**FAMOUS NORTH
CAROLINIAN:** Dale
Earnhardt Jr., race-car driver

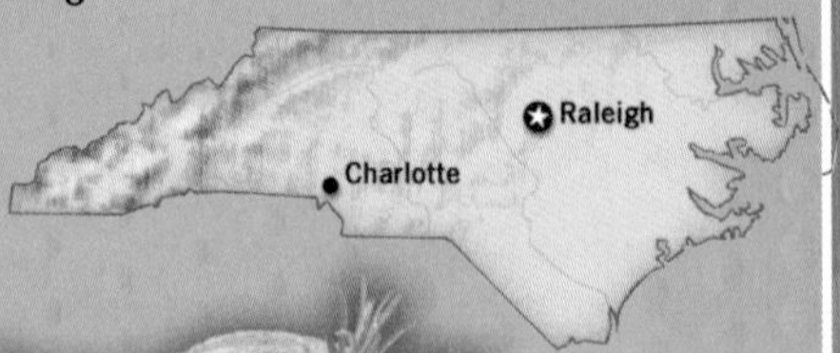

GUESS WHAT? North Carolina produces more sweet potatoes than any other state in the nation.

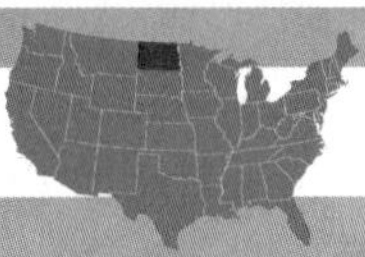

NORTH DAKOTA

CAPITAL: Bismarck

LARGEST CITY: Fargo

POSTAL CODE: ND

LAND AREA:
68,994 square miles
(178,694 sq km)

POPULATION (2012):
699,628

ENTERED UNION (RANK):
November 2, 1889 (39)

MOTTO: Liberty and union,
now and forever, one and
inseparable

TREE: American elm

FLOWER: Wild prairie rose

BIRD: Western meadowlark

NICKNAMES: Sioux State,
Flickertail State, Peace
Garden State, Rough
Rider State

FAMOUS NORTH DAKOTAN:
Louis L'Amour, author

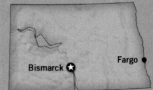

GUESS WHAT? North Dakota is the country's leading producer of sunflowers.

OHIO

CAPITAL: Columbus

LARGEST CITY: Columbus

POSTAL CODE: OH

LAND AREA:
40,953 square miles
(106,068 sq km)

POPULATION (2012):
11,544,225

ENTERED UNION (RANK):
March 1, 1803 (17)

MOTTO: With God, all things are possible.

TREE: Buckeye

FLOWER: Scarlet carnation

BIRD: Cardinal

NICKNAME: Buckeye State

FAMOUS OHIOAN: LeBron James, basketball player

Columbus

GUESS WHAT? The Rock and Roll Hall of Fame is in Cleveland, Ohio. Some of the 2013 inductees were Albert King, Donna Summer, Heart, and Rush.

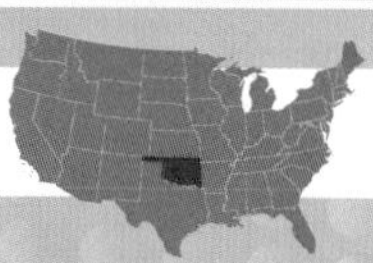

OKLAHOMA

CAPITAL: Oklahoma City

LARGEST CITY:
Oklahoma City

POSTAL CODE: OK

LAND AREA:
68,679 square miles
(177,879 sq km)

POPULATION (2012):
3,814,820

ENTERED UNION (RANK):
November 16, 1907 (46)

MOTTO: *Labor omnia vincit.* (Labor conquers all things.)

TREE: Eastern redbud

FLOWER: Mistletoe

BIRD: Scissor-tailed flycatcher

NICKNAME: Sooner State

FAMOUS OKLAHOMAN:
Carrie Underwood, singer

Oklahoma City

GUESS WHAT? In addition to a state flower, Oklahoma has a state wildflower: the Indian blanket. Shaped like a daisy, this flower has petals that are red with yellow tips.

OREGON

CAPITAL: Salem

LARGEST CITY: Portland

POSTAL CODE: OR

LAND AREA:
96,003 square miles
(248,648 sq km)

POPULATION (2012):
3,899,353

ENTERED UNION (RANK):
February 14, 1859 (33)

MOTTO: *Alis volat propriis.*
(She flies with her
own wings.)

TREE: Douglas fir

FLOWER: Oregon grape

BIRD: Western
meadowlark

NICKNAME: Beaver State

FAMOUS OREGONIAN:
Esperanza Spalding,
jazz musician

Portland

Salem

GUESS WHAT? Every year, Oregon grows and sells more Christmas trees than any other state. It sells about 6.4 million trees a year—almost twice what North Carolina (the second-biggest producer) does.

PENNSYLVANIA

CAPITAL: Harrisburg

LARGEST CITY: Philadelphia

POSTAL CODE: PA

LAND AREA:
44,820 square miles
(116,084 sq km)

POPULATION (2012):
12,763,536

ENTERED UNION (RANK):
December 12, 1787 (2)

MOTTO: Virtue, liberty,
and independence

TREE: Hemlock

FLOWER: Mountain laurel

BIRD: Ruffed grouse

NICKNAME: Keystone State

FAMOUS PENNSYLVANIAN:
Betsy Ross, seamstress who
sewed the first American flag

Harrisburg

Philadelphia

GUESS WHAT? Pennsylvania is sometimes referred to as the Quaker State. Founder William Penn and many of the state's other original settlers belonged to the Quaker sect of Christianity. They moved to the New World to live and practice their faith without persecution.

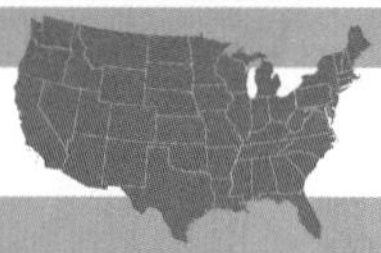

RHODE ISLAND

CAPITAL: Providence

LARGEST CITY: Providence

POSTAL CODE: RI

LAND AREA:
1,045 square miles
(2,707 sq km)

POPULATION (2012):
1,050,292

ENTERED UNION (RANK):
May 29, 1790 (13)

MOTTO: Hope

TREE: Red maple

FLOWER: Violet

BIRD: Rhode Island red
(chicken)

NICKNAME: Ocean State

FAMOUS RHODE ISLANDER: Gilbert Stuart, artist who painted the portrait of George Washington seen on the $1 bill

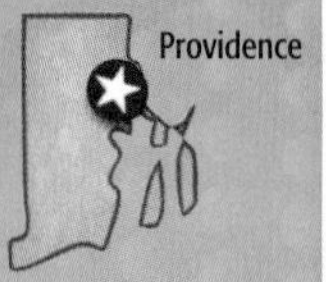

Providence

GUESS WHAT? A topiary is a tree or shrub trimmed into a decorative shape. At the Green Animals Topiary Garden, in Portsmouth, Rhode Island, visitors can see more than 80 incredible topiaries, including an elephant, a teddy bear, a camel, and a giraffe.

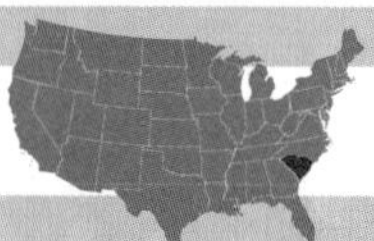

SOUTH CAROLINA

CAPITAL: Columbia

LARGEST CITY: Columbia

POSTAL CODE: SC

LAND AREA:
30,111 square miles
(77,987 sq km)

POPULATION (2012):
4,723,723

ENTERED UNION (RANK):
May 23, 1788 (8)

MOTTOES: *Animis opibusque parati* (Prepared in mind and resources); *Dum spiro spero.* (While I breathe, I hope.)

TREE: Palmetto

FLOWER: Yellow jessamine

BIRD: Carolina wren

NICKNAME: Palmetto State

FAMOUS SOUTH CAROLINIAN: Aziz Ansari, actor and comedian

Columbia

GUESS WHAT? The highest point in South Carolina is Sassafras Mountain. The tallest waterfall is Raven Cliff Falls. Both of these natural landmarks are in the northwestern part of the state, within the Appalachian mountain range.

227

SOUTH DAKOTA

CAPITAL: Pierre

LARGEST CITY: Sioux Falls

POSTAL CODE: SD

LAND AREA:
75,898 square miles
(196,575 sq km)

POPULATION (2012):
833,354

ENTERED UNION (RANK):
November 2, 1889 (40)

MOTTO: Under God the people rule.

TREE: Black Hills spruce

FLOWER: Pasqueflower

BIRD: Ring-necked pheasant

NICKNAMES: Mount Rushmore State, Coyote State

FAMOUS SOUTH DAKOTAN: Sitting Bull, Sioux chief

GUESS WHAT? Badlands National Park, in southwestern South Dakota, was once home to ancient horses, rhinoceroses, and saber-toothed cats. Scientists there have unearthed the remains of ancient camels that were about the size of dogs.

TENNESSEE

CAPITAL: Nashville

LARGEST CITY: Memphis

POSTAL CODE: TN

LAND AREA:
41,220 square miles
(106,760 sq km)

POPULATION (2012):
6,456,243

ENTERED UNION (RANK):
June 1, 1796 (16)

MOTTO: Agriculture and commerce

TREE: Tulip poplar

FLOWER: Iris

BIRD: Mockingbird

NICKNAME: Volunteer State

FAMOUS TENNESSEAN: Dolly Parton, musician and actress

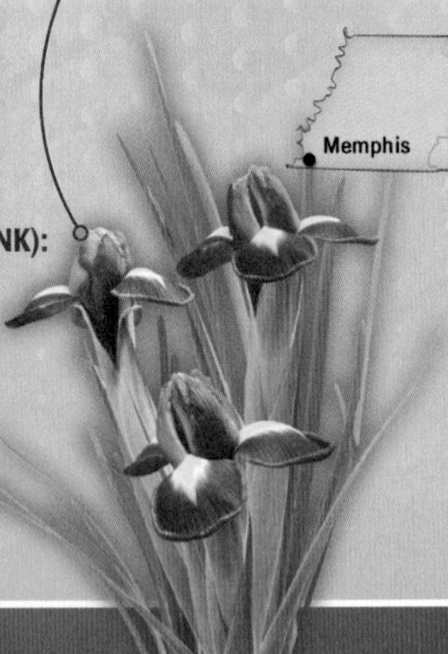

GUESS WHAT? The highest temperature ever recorded in Tennessee occurred on August 9, 1930, in the town of Perryville. It was 113°F (45°C).

TEXAS

CAPITAL: Austin

LARGEST CITY: Houston

POSTAL CODE: TX

LAND AREA:
261,914 square miles
(678,357 sq km)

POPULATION (2012):
26,059,203

ENTERED UNION (RANK):
December 29, 1845 (28)

MOTTO: Friendship

TREE: Pecan

FLOWER: Texas
bluebonnet

BIRD:
Mockingbird

NICKNAME: Lone Star State

FAMOUS TEXAN:
Selena Gomez, actress
and singer

Austin ⊗   Houston

GUESS WHAT? The Texas horned lizard, which is the Texas state reptile, has two spikes on its head and can puff up its body when threatened. Some species of horned lizard can shoot blood out of their eyes to frighten away predators.

UTAH

CAPITAL: Salt Lake City

LARGEST CITY:
Salt Lake City

POSTAL CODE: UT

LAND AREA:
82,168 square miles
(212,815 sq km)

POPULATION (2012):
2,855,287

ENTERED UNION (RANK):
January 4, 1896 (45)

MOTTO: Industry

TREE: Blue spruce

FLOWER: Sego lily

BIRD: California gull

NICKNAME: Beehive State

FAMOUS UTAHN: Philo
Farnsworth, inventor of
the television

Salt Lake City ⊗

GUESS WHAT? Utah was named after the Native American tribe the Utes, who lived in the area when settlers arrived. Today, there about 3,150 Utes in the state.

VERMONT

CAPITAL: Montpelier

LARGEST CITY: Burlington

POSTAL CODE: VT

LAND AREA:
9,249 square miles
(23,956 sq km)

POPULATION (2012):
626,011

ENTERED UNION (RANK):
March 4, 1791 (14)

MOTTO: Freedom and unity

TREE: Sugar maple

FLOWER: Red clover

BIRD: Hermit thrush

NICKNAME: Green Mountain State

FAMOUS VERMONTER:
Joseph Smith, founder of the Mormon Church

Burlington

Montpelier

GUESS WHAT? In 1777, the Vermont territory outlawed slavery. It was the first state to do so.

VIRGINIA

CAPITAL: Richmond

LARGEST CITY:
Virginia Beach

POSTAL CODE: VA

LAND AREA:
39,598 square miles
(102,559 sq km)

POPULATION (2012):
8,185,867

ENTERED UNION (RANK):
June 25, 1788 (10)

MOTTO: *Sic semper tyrannis*
(Thus always to tyrants)

TREE: Flowering dogwood

FLOWER: American dogwood

BIRD: Cardinal

NICKNAMES: The Old Dominion, Mother of Presidents

FAMOUS VIRGINIAN: Katie Couric, news anchor and talk show host

Richmond

Virginia Beach

GUESS WHAT? Colonial Williamsburg, in Williamsburg, Virginia, is a living history museum made up of hundreds of restored and reconstructed buildings filled with furniture from the colonial period. People in costumes tell stories about the lives of the men and women who lived in the 18th-century city. They perform tasks as if they were living and working in the 1700s.

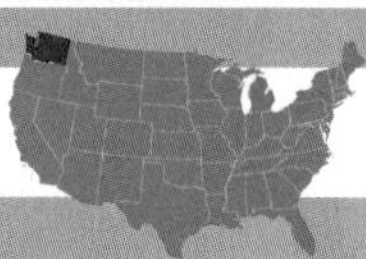

WASHINGTON

CAPITAL: Olympia

LARGEST CITY: Seattle

POSTAL CODE: WA

LAND AREA:
66,582 square miles
(172,447 sq km)

POPULATION (2012):
6,897,012

ENTERED UNION (RANK):
November 11, 1889 (42)

MOTTO: *Al-ki* (an Indian word meaning "by and by" or "hope for the future")

TREE: Western hemlock

FLOWER: Coast rhododendron

BIRD: Willow goldfinch

NICKNAME: Evergreen State

FAMOUS WASHINGTONIAN:
Bill Gates, inventor

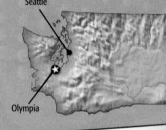

Seattle

Olympia

GUESS WHAT? Washington is known for being rainy. In 1986, a town called Mount Mitchell had 14.26 inches (36 cm) of rain in one day. That's the most rain any one place in Washington has ever had in one day.

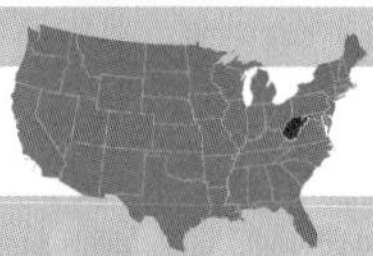

WEST VIRGINIA

CAPITAL: Charleston

LARGEST CITY: Charleston

POSTAL CODE: WV

LAND AREA:
24,087 square miles
(62,385 sq km)

POPULATION (2012):
1,855,413

ENTERED UNION (RANK):
June 20, 1863 (35)

MOTTO: *Montani semper liberi.* (Mountaineers are always free.)

TREE: Sugar maple

FLOWER: Rhododendron

BIRD: Cardinal

NICKNAME: Mountain State

FAMOUS WEST VIRGINIAN:
Brad Paisley, musician

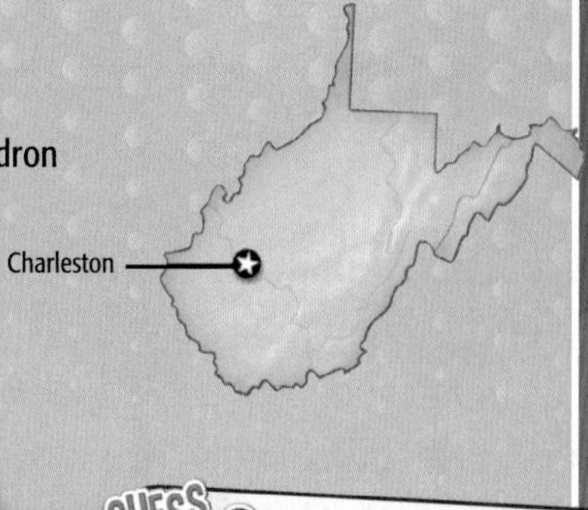

Charleston

Male cardinals are bright red all over. Female cardinals are mostly brown.

GUESS WHAT? Mother's Day was first celebrated in Grafton, West Virginia, in 1908.

WISCONSIN

WISCONSIN
1848

CAPITAL: Madison

LARGEST CITY: Milwaukee

POSTAL CODE: WI

LAND AREA:
54,314 square miles
(140,673 sq km)

POPULATION (2012):
5,726,398

ENTERED UNION (RANK):
May 29, 1848 (30)

MOTTO: Forward

TREE: Sugar maple

FLOWER: Wood violet

BIRD: American robin

NICKNAMES: Badger State, Dairy State

FAMOUS WISCONSINITE:
Georgia O'Keeffe, artist

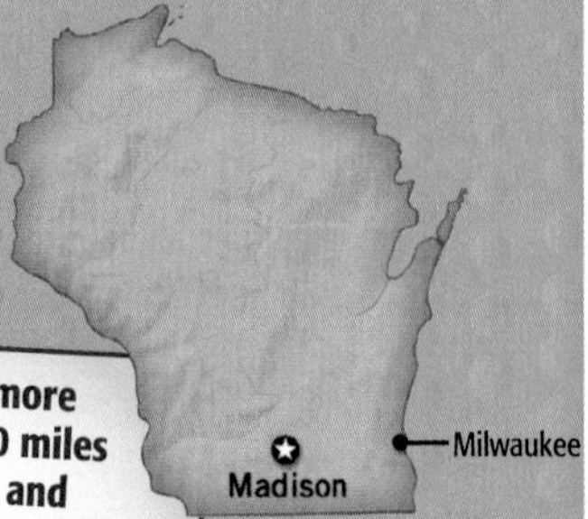

Milwaukee

Madison

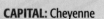

GUESS WHAT? There are more than 13,500 miles (21,726 km) of streams and rivers that can be accessed by boat in Wisconsin. There are also more than 15,000 lakes in the state. The lakes take up nearly 3% of the area of the state.

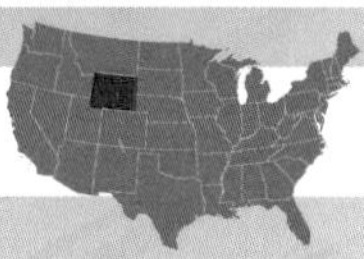

WYOMING

CAPITAL: Cheyenne

LARGEST CITY: Cheyenne

POSTAL CODE: WY

LAND AREA:
97,105 square miles
(251,502 sq km)

POPULATION (2012):
576,412

ENTERED UNION (RANK):
July 10, 1890 (44)

MOTTO: Equal rights

TREE: Plains cottonwood

FLOWER: Indian paintbrush

BIRD: Meadowlark

NICKNAMES: Big Wyoming, Equality State, Cowboy State

FAMOUS WYOMINGITE:
Jackson Pollock, artist

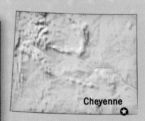

Cheyenne

GUESS WHAT? Wyoming's Yellowstone National Park, which was dedicated in 1872, was America's first national park. There are more than 300 geysers there. A geyser is a naturally occurring hot spring that spouts water and steam into the air.

WASHINGTON, D.C.
THE NATION'S CAPITAL

The District of Columbia, which covers the same area as the city of Washington, is the capital of the United States. The seat of the U.S. government was transferred from Philadelphia, Pennsylvania, to Washington, D.C., on December 1, 1800.

LAND AREA: 68.25 square miles (177 sq km)

POPULATION (2012): 632,323

MOTTO: *Justitia omnibus* (Justice for all)

TREE: Scarlet oak

FLOWER: American beauty rose

BIRD: Wood thrush

FAMOUS WASHINGTONIAN:
John Philip Sousa, composer

U.S. TERRITORIES

In addition to the 50 states and the District of Columbia, the United States government administers some tiny, mostly uninhabited islands around the world, including Kingman Reef, Palmyra Atoll, and Howland Island. The major U.S. territories are Puerto Rico, American Samoa, Guam, the U.S. Virgin Islands, and the Northern Mariana Islands.

PUERTO RICO is in the Caribbean Sea, about 1,000 miles (1,609 km) southeast of Miami, Florida. A U.S. possession since 1898, it consists of the island of Puerto Rico plus the adjacent islets of Vieques, Culebra, and Mona. Both Spanish and English are spoken there. Its capital is San Juan. Puerto Rico has a population of approximately 4 million.

AMERICAN SAMOA, a group of islands in the South Pacific Ocean, is situated about halfway between Hawaii and New Zealand. It has a land area of 76 square miles (199 sq km) and a population of approximately 68,000.

GUAM, in the North Pacific Ocean, was given to the United States by Spain in 1898. It has a land area of 209 square miles (541 sq km) and a population of approximately 186,000.

U.S. VIRGIN ISLANDS, which include Saint Croix, Saint Thomas, Saint John, and many other islands, are located in the Caribbean Sea, east of Puerto Rico. Together, they have a land area of 136 square miles (351 sq km) and a population of approximately 110,000.

THE NORTHERN MARIANA ISLANDS are located in the North Pacific Ocean. They have a land area of 179 square miles (464 sq km) and a population of approximately 45,000.

United States

WEATHER

WEATHER vs. CLIMATE

The atmosphere is the layer of gases that surrounds the Earth—and that's where weather takes place. Weather is the state of the atmosphere at some particular place and time. When people talk about the weather, they might mention the temperature, whether the sky is clear or cloudy, how hard the wind is blowing, or whether it is raining or snowing.

Weather changes from day to day and sometimes even from minute to minute. Climate is not the same as weather. Climate refers to the weather of a specific region averaged over time. For example, a climate might be hot and dry, or cold and dry, or hot and rainy. Climates do change, but those changes usually happen over many, many years.

Tropical rain forests have the warmest, moistest climates. In this climate, there are thunderstorms and rain nearly every day.

WHAT MAKES THE WIND WHoOSH?

Winds are caused by the sun's heat falling on different parts of Earth at different times of the day and year. The temperatures over water and land change at different rates during the day and night. In addition, warm air rises and cool air sinks. These changes cause the movement of air in different patterns called winds.

WHAT IS AIR PRESSURE?

If a friend put her hands on your shoulders, you would feel pressure. If she pushed down, you'd feel more pressure. Air exerts pressure, too.

Air molecules are the tiny, invisible particles that make up air. Air pressure is the force exerted on you by the weight of these miniscule molecules. Air pressure is also called barometric pressure because it is measured with a device called a **barometer**. Clear weather is caused by high pressure. Storms are caused by low pressure. Air pressure tends to decrease the higher up you go.

THERMOMETERS

Thermometers measure temperature. The most common thermometers may contain a column of alcohol or mercury that expands in the presence of heat, or they may be digital and use liquid crystals or electricity.

When it comes to weather, air temperature is important. The air temperature of a location is affected by:

- The heat that is given off by the ground and rises into the air
- How close the area is to a body of water
- The effect of air masses as they pass through

A STORM'S COMING

Thunderstorms occur when a huge mass of warm air collides with a huge mass of cold air. Tall clouds form, and the molecules of water vapor in them freeze and bang into one another. These collisions form electrical fields in the clouds. When the electrical fields get big enough, sparks shoot between them, between the clouds and the electrical fields in the air, or between the clouds and the electrical fields on the ground. These sparks form long paths called lightning. Bolts of lightning can get as hot as 50,000°F (27,760°C). That's hotter than the surface of the sun.

Tornadoes are funnel-shaped clouds made of fast-spinning winds that can reach 300 miles (483 km) per hour. Most large tornadoes form in the central and southern United States, in an area known as Tornado Alley. Though tornadoes do occur in other countries, by far the most occur in the United States: roughly 1,000 a year. The winds that make up a tornado can be strong enough to pick up homes, cars, trees, and anything else in their path. While wind causes most of a tornado's destruction, hail formed in the thunderclouds can also do a lot of damage.

There is a rare weather phenomenon known as thundersnow, wherein thunder and lightning occur during a snowstorm. It generally happens in late winter or early spring and requires a very particular set of air currents. The layer of air closer to the ground must be hotter than the layers above it, but the air must still be cold enough for snow to fall instead of rain. Often during a rainstorm, you can look up and see bolts of lightning clearly flash across the sky, but during thundersnow, the bolts will not be visible. The sky will just be brighter for a moment.

Though thundersnow is rare, when it occurs, there is often heavy snowfall.

Weather

TIME FOR KIDS GAME

SUNSHINE'S SECRET MESSAGE

A proverb is a short saying that often contains a bit of advice or wisdom, or a practical thought. Use the key below to decode the riddle. Fill in the blanks to spell out a proverb about getting through hard times.

A	B	C	D	E	F	G	H	I	J	K	L	M

N	O	P	Q	R	S	T	U	V	W	X	Y	Z

ANSWERS ON PAGE 245

TROPICAL STORMS

Hurricanes, typhoons, and cyclones are all different names for tropical storms with winds stronger than 74 miles (120 km) per hour. They're called **hurricanes** when they form in the northern Atlantic Ocean and the northeastern or southern Pacific Ocean, **typhoons** when they form over the northwestern Pacific, and **cyclones** when they form over the Indian Ocean. These dangerous storms form when tropical winds gather moisture as they pass over water that is at least 80°F (27°C). The winds of a hurricane rotate around the eye, or center, of the storm.

Hurricanes are strongest when they're over water, but they can remain fierce after reaching land, which is where they do the most damage.

Powerful waves caused by a hurricane smash against a pier on the Douro River, in Portugal.

A meteorologist tracks Hurricane Isaac.

THE NAMING OF STORMS

Have you ever wondered how Hurricane Sandy or Hurricane Katrina got its name? For a long time, most hurricanes were named for the location where the storm hit land. Others were named for a holiday they fell on or even a boat they destroyed. In the 1940s, most of the **meteorologists** at the National Hurricane Center were men. They began informally naming the storms after their girlfriends, wives, and mothers. This practice became the formal naming strategy in 1953, when the center started giving women's names to storms that formed over the Atlantic.

In 1979, a new system was put in place that alternated men's and women's names in alphabetical order. Six lists of names were created, which covered six years of storms. The names are repeated in cycles. However, if a storm is particularly noteworthy, such as Katrina in 2005, the name is retired forever. In the future, the name Katrina will be replaced with Katia.

2014 HURRICANE NAMES

ATLANTIC

Arthur	Laura
Bertha	Marco
Cristobal	Nana
Dolly	Omar
Edouard	Paulette
Fay	Rene
Gonzalo	Sally
Hanna	Teddy
Isaias	Vicky
Josephine	Wilfred
Kyle	

EASTERN NORTH PACIFIC

Amanda	Marie
Boris	Norbert
Cristina	Odile
Douglas	Polo
Elida	Rachel
Fausto	Simon
Genevieve	Trudy
Hernan	Vance
Iselle	Winnie
Julio	Xavier
Karina	Yolanda
Lowell	Zeke

GUESS WHAT?

A meteorologist is someone who studies Earth's atmosphere for clues about the weather. Newscasters rely on meteorologists to create the weather forecasts you hear every morning.

CALM IN THE CENTER OF A STORM

The **eye of a hurricane** is the center of the storm. Inside the eye, the weather usually appears quite calm. There often isn't any rain there, and it might even be sunny. A hurricane's eye is usually about 20 to 40 miles (32 m to 64 m) wide, though it can be anywhere from 5 to 120 miles (8 km to 193 km) wide. The area around the eye is called the eye wall. This is where the most intense winds and rainfall occur.

Eye of Hurricane Rita

GUESS WHAT? The Atlantic hurricane season lasts from June 1 to November 30. Some hurricanes take place other times, but most fall within this period. September is often the biggest month for hurricanes.

HURRICANE CATEGORIES

The Saffir-Simpson scale predicts hurricane damage by wind speed. The higher up the scale a hurricane ranks, the more damage it can do to houses and other structures in its path.

CATEGORY 1
74 to 95 miles per hour (119 to 153 kmh)

CATEGORY 2
96 to 110 miles per hour (154 to 177 kmh)

CATEGORY 3
111 to 129 miles per hour (178 to 208 kmh)

CATEGORY 4
130 to 156 miles per hour (209 to 251 kmh)

CATEGORY 5
More than 157 miles per hour (252 kmh)

FROM FLURRIES TO BLIZZARDS

Almost every area of the continental United States, including southern Florida, has had snow. Snowstorms can be deadly. They can lead to traffic accidents, power failures, and 20-foot-tall (6 m) drifts that can bury cars and people. A blizzard is a snowstorm that has winds of more than 35 miles (56 km) per hour for at least three hours. During the Great Blizzard of 1888, most of New England was blanketed with 40 to 50 inches (1 to 1.25 m) of snow. More than 400 people died.

TOP 5 Snowiest Places

Do you live in a snowy place? Here are the U.S. places with the highest average annual snowfall.

1. Valdez, AK
326.3 inches (828.8 cm)

2. Mount Washington, NH
281.2 inches (714.2 cm)

3. Herman, MI
219.6 inches (557.8 cm)

4. Anchorage, AK
218 inches (553.7 cm)

5. Lemolo Lake, OR
217.1 inches (551.4 cm)

Source: National Oceanic and Atmospheric Administration

PRECIPI-WHAT?

Precipitation refers to water that falls from clouds to Earth's surface. Whether precipitation is rain, sleet, snow, or hail is determined by the temperature of the water vapor in a cloud and the temperature of the air between the cloud and Earth. Snow falls when the cloud-to-ground air is consistently below 40°F (4.4°C). Rain falls at higher temperatures. Sleet and hail form when the air temperature fluctuates within the cloud and between the cloud and the ground.

This piece of hail is about the size of a baseball!

THE WATER CYCLE AT WORK

In the lowest layer of the atmosphere, temperature decreases as altitude increases. As a result, water vapor cools as it rises higher in the atmosphere. When water in its gaseous form loses enough heat, **condensation** takes place. The water condenses, or changes back into a liquid. If the air is cold enough, the water freezes and ice particles form. Clouds are made up of tiny bits of water and ice that are so small and light they float on air.

When the heat from the sun warms up the water in rivers, lakes, and oceans, **evaporation** occurs. When water evaporates, it changes from a liquid state into a gas, called water vapor. Water vapor rises into the atmosphere.

As water continues to condense, clouds grow. When so much water has condensed that the cloud droplets are too heavy to float, they fall to Earth as **precipitation.**

RAIN, RAIN, DON'T GO AWAY

A **drought** is an unusually long period of insufficient rain or snowfall. Droughts can last for years, though most last only a few weeks or months. Without water, crops die. As soil dries up and crops wither, the dust is easily picked up by the wind. Whirlwinds of dust, known as **dust storms** or dust devils, sometimes occur in dry areas.

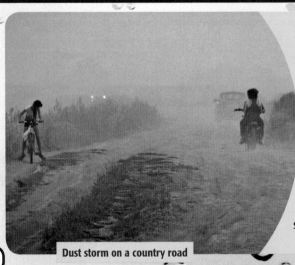

Dust storm on a country road

Going to Extremes

By Julien Hawthorne

Everyone knows that the weather gets hot during the summer, but does it always get as hot as the summers in recent years? According to a report from the National Oceanic and Atmospheric Administration (NOAA), climate change may play a role in extreme weather events.

Released in 2012, NOAA's 2011 *State of the Climate* report was put together by 378 scientists from 48 countries. They looked at a number of extreme weather events that happened around the world in 2011. "2011 will be remembered as a year of extreme events, both in the United States and around the world," said NOAA's Kathryn D. Sullivan. The scientists noted that determining the causes of extreme weather is complicated. They can't blame any single event on global warming. Rather, the purpose of the NOAA study is to help scientists understand how the probability of extreme weather events changes in response to global warming.

According to the report, 2011 was the coolest year since 2008. But it was still one of the 15 warmest years since records began in the late 1800s. Among the extreme weather events scientists looked at was a record heat wave in Texas. In 2011, Texas had the driest seven-month drought ever recorded.

U.S. corn crops suffered because of the drought conditions in 2012.

NOAA found that the Texas heat wave was 20 times more likely to occur today than 50 years ago.

In 2012, the United States experienced extreme weather once again. The 12 months ending in May 2012 were the warmest 12 continuous months on record in the United States. "The frequency of hot days and hot periods has already increased and will increase further," Michael Oppenheimer, a climate expert and a professor at Princeton University's Woodrow Wilson School, told TIME's Bryan Walsh. "What we see now is what global warming really looks like."

Weather

GUESS WHAT? At the end of June 2012, more than 110 million people in the U.S. were living under extreme heat, and more than two-thirds of the country was experiencing drought.

WHAT DOES THE WEATHER HAVE TO DO WITH THE PRICE OF BACON?

Droughts in 2012 led to a smaller corn crop than usual. Because there was less corn in the market, the corn that was for sale was more expensive. Since farmers generally feed corn to their pigs, the higher prices for corn led to higher prices for raising pigs, which led to a higher price for bacon. A 2012 report from Britain's National Pig Association warned breakfast lovers that there could be a global shortage of pork by late 2013. The report led to headlines such as: "The A-pork-alypse Is Coming!" and "Bacon Lovers, Let the Hoarding Begin!" But, experts say, upset meat lovers have nothing to fear. Bacon may be a bit a pricier, but it will still be available at the supermarket.

HEALTH AND THE ENVIRONMENT

Pain-Free Vaccines

Vaccines are made using weak or dead forms of a disease. Once the germs are introduced to a person's system, the immune system kicks into overdrive and creates antibodies, which fight the disease. The antibodies remain in the body, so it is ready to fight if it's ever exposed to the disease again.

Vaccines have saved countless lives, but using needles to administer vaccines has a few downsides. Due to supply shortages, people sometimes reuse needles, which is not safe. And these liquid vaccines generally need to be refrigerated, which can be difficult in developing countries or in disaster zones. Plus, using needles can be painful. Scientists at King's College London, in the United Kingdom, have developed a new type of injection-free method for administering vaccines. It is a small disk with many tiny microneedles made of sugar. These microneedles dissolve when pressed into the skin, and they do not hurt. The vaccine itself is a dried variety, which does not require refrigeration. As vaccines and the ways we use them improve, fewer people around the world will catch diseases that are preventable.

A new vaccine technique does not require the use of a needle.

GUESS WHAT? Today, vaccines protect against polio, measles, mumps, rubella, chicken pox, tetanus, pneumonia, and other illnesses.

Wearable Sensors for Health, Safety, and Sports

Research is being done into how clothing can keep people safe and help them improve their athletic performance. Scientists are experimenting with putting sensors into stretchy clothing that can fit snugly and monitor heart rate and even sweat. These teeny sensors could alert a person with a medical condition to a problem. For example, a person with diabetes might receive a message if the garment detects a drop in blood sugar. The high-tech fabrics could also monitor external factors, like pollen or pollution. Imagine if your sweater could warn you to go inside because the air quality around you was poor and dangerous to your health.

These types of sensors might also show up in exercise clothing. Then an athlete would receive messages about how to adjust his or her position to a hit baseball better or perfect a ballet step. Move over smartphones, smartclothes are on the way!

Tech-enabled clothing could help you improve your golf swing.

No More Wasted Water

Many people around the world are hard at work making sure everyone has access to clean, drinkable water. Some are working on ways to waste less water. Here are just a few cool, new developments in the works.

🔹 In the bathrooms and laundry rooms of tomorrow, water will be reused in inventive ways. For example, water from a shower will be filtered and then reused in a washing machine. Toilet-tank sinks, which reuse sink water in the toilet tank, are already on the market.

A toilet-tank sink

🔹 Trying to get clean using yesterday's dirty water doesn't sound very pleasant. And that's why some engineers are working on a type of shower that captures, filters, cleans, and recirculates water. Reusing shower water could save 20,000 to 32,000 gallons (75,708 to 121,133 L) per household per year. Before these water-saving devices are installed in homes across the United States, they will probably be used in arid areas that are prone to droughts and in regions rebuilding after disasters, when clean water can be hard to find.

🔹 During the water cycle (see page 238), water is continually evaporating and condensing. When the sun's heat makes the water in lakes, rivers, oceans, and even the ground hot enough, the water evaporates, turning into water vapor that rises up into the atmosphere. A company called NBD is developing a device that will draw this vapor from the air and turn it back into water. Their product would be a water bottle that can refill itself using the air around it.

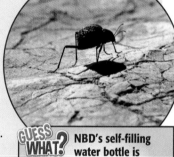

GUESS WHAT? NBD's self-filling water bottle is inspired by the Namib desert beetle, which survives in the desert by collecting tiny droplets of fog.

🔹 Many hot, dry deserts and desertlike areas jut up against coastlines. There is little freshwater to be found in these areas, but plenty of salt water all around them. Inventors are trying to create practical versions of solar-powered seawater greenhouses that will grow crops, generate power, and create drinkable water. Here's how they work. Hot desert air is exposed to the seawater, creating the humid environment plants in a greenhouse need. The humid air is then

A company in Mexico filters and recycles rainwater.

cooled so that the water vapor in it condenses and becomes liquid again. (In this way, the water is transformed from salt water to freshwater, because salt does not evaporate.) This newly harvested freshwater is used to water the plants. The leftover water can be used for drinking water or other uses, and the crops can be used for food and biofuels.

SCIENCE AND TECHNOLOGY

Pack Your Bags ... for Space!

Out-of-this-world voyages will soon be the ultimate high-end vacation. In the near future, travelers willing to spend at least $200,000 will be able to hop aboard *SpaceShipTwo,* a spacecraft operated by Virgin Galactic, to experience weightlessness outside of Earth's

A company called XCOR Aerospace designed this spacecraft for future space tourists.

atmosphere. Other space-travel companies are also preselling vacation packages. More extravagant options for galactic getaways might include weeks-long stays aboard a spacecraft or trips to the International Space Station (see page 185). Eventually, companies will launch private space stations for tourists.

Wait. Who's Driving?

Google and Volvo are just a few of the big-name companies that are pioneers in the field of driverless cars. These futuristic cars come equipped with sensors that can detect any cars, railings, or other objects around them. They are programmed to follow the speed limit and to adjust their speed and direction based on the road and the cars around them. The cars also use radar and ultrasound to sense their surroundings. These vehicles have an override function so that a human driver can resume control at any time. For now, the cars are being readied for highway driving only (and always with an alert driver there and ready to take over). But eventually, driverless cars may be programmed to adapt to traffic patterns on city streets. And since people do not always follow traffic laws, some experts say that driverless cars will be safer than ones driven by humans.

Google's self-driving car

Need a Part? Just Print It

The future looks bright for 3-D printing. Scientists, engineers, and entrepreneurs are experimenting with all sorts of uses for this new technology. Medical researchers are using 3-D printers to print certain kinds of cells that can grow into organs or tissues to help patients. Some cutting-edge 3-D printers can actually work with metal. Just imagine scientists on the International Space Station printing a new part when an old one wears out! These incredible machines might also be used by soldiers who need to fix equipment in the field, far from a supply warehouse.

A 3-D printer creates a plastic object.

SPORTS AND ENTERTAINMENT

Stay tuned! There is another installment of the *Cloudy with a Chance of Meatballs* story headed to the big screen in late 2013.

Coming Soon to a Theater Near You!

The Amazing Spiderman 2
The Book Thief
Captain America: The Winter Soldier
Cloudy with a Chance of Meatballs 2
Planes
Frozen
The Good Dinosaur
The Hobbit: The Desolation of Smaug
The Hobbit: There and Back Again
How to Train Your Dragon 2
The Hunger Games: Catching Fire
The Hunger Games: Mockingjay—Part 1
Lego: The Piece of Resistance
The Muppets . . . Again!
1D3D
Percy Jackson: Sea of Monsters
Rio 2
Stretch Armstrong
Thor: The Dark World
Turkeys
Walking with Dinosaurs 3-D

World Cup Soccer

Soccer fans, get ready! In 2014, the FIFA World Cup will kick off in Brazil in June and July 2014. It's the second time Brazil has hosted the big event. The international tournament was also held there in 1950. Four other countries have hosted twice: Mexico, France, Italy, and Germany.

Cristiano Ronaldo, in the 2010 FIFA World Cup

The Olympics

Olympic fans won't have to wait too long to get their fill of all their favorite Olympic events. In February 2014, the Winter Games will be held in Sochi, Russia. In August 2016, Rio de Janeiro, Brazil, will host the Summer Games. Cities compete to win the honor of hosting the Games. Once a city is chosen, the federal and local governments kick into high gear to get their region ready. Construction is under way in Russia and Brazil. Check out the progress at *olympic.org*.

Allyson Felix, in the 2012 Olympics

GUESS WHAT? Russia used to be part of the Soviet Union, which hosted the 1980 Summer Olympics in Moscow.

PAGE 22:
PENGUIN PAIRS

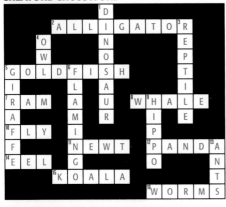

PAGE 40:
MYSTERY PERSON: Charles M. Schulz

PAGE 53:
MYSTERY PERSON: Squanto

PAGE 53:
MERRY MAZE

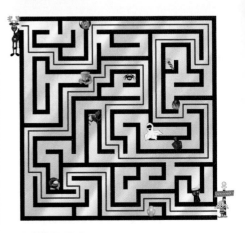

PAGE 23:
MYSTERY PERSON: Anna Sewell

PAGE 27:
CREATURE CROSSWORD

PAGE 54:
MYSTERY PERSON: Michael Dell

PAGE 31:
MORPHING MURAL

PAGE 107:
WORLDLY WORDS

PAGE 116:
MYSTERY PERSON: Hattie Caraway

PAGE 121:
MYSTERY PERSON: Thurgood Marshall

PAGE 124:
MYSTERY PERSON: Marco Polo

PAGE 128:
MYSTERY PERSON: Sacagawea

PAGE 135:
MYSTERY PERSON: Alfred Nobel

PAGE 137:
LETTERS AND STATES: New York

PAGE 139:
THE WISDOM OF WORDS: The quotation is, "If there's a book you really want to read, but it hasn't been written yet, then you must write it."–Toni Morrison

PAGE 151:
JUMBLED GEOGRAPHY
Equator
North Pole
Asia
Antarctica
Longitude
South Pole
Latitude
Atlantic Ocean
South America
Pacific Ocean
RIDDLE ANSWER: A postage stamp

PAGE 152:
MYSTERY PERSON: Tom Hanks

PAGE 171:
MYSTERY PERSON: Eleanor Roosevelt

PAGE 184:
MYSTERY PERSON: Edmond Halley

PAGE 188:
MYSTERY PERSON: Jackie Robinson

PAGE 203:
MYSTERY PERSON: Emily Dickinson

PAGE 205:
WHERE'S THAT?:

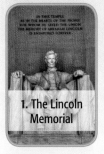
1. The Lincoln Memorial

5. Hoover Dam

2. Golden Gate Bridge

6. Mesa Verde

3. Independence Hall

7. Death Valley

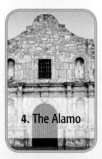
4. The Alamo

8. Old Faithful

PAGE 235:
SUNSHINE'S SECRET MESSAGE:
No matter how long the winter, spring is sure to follow.

FRONT COVER: antishock/Shutterstock.com (background); Ambient Ideas/Shutterstock.com (butterfly); ylq/Shutterstock.com (corner background); Simon_g/Shutterstock.com (zebra); SOHO/ESA/NASA (Solar Heliospheric Observatory); John W. McDonough/Sports Illustrated (Durant); vblinov/Shutterstock.com (monkey); AP Photo/Nancy Palmieri (snowboarder); Todd Williamson/Invision/AP (Lawrence); Jordan Strauss/Invision/AP (One Direction).

CONTENTS: All photos repeated in the interior. See individual pages.

WHAT'S IN THE NEWS: 8: Photo by Andre R. Aragon/FEMA (Hurricane Sandy); AP Photo/Sitthixay Ditthavong (Chicago protest). 9: *The Yomiuri Shimbun* via AP Images (Obamas); AP Photo/Seth Wenig MoMath (MoMath); AP Photo/Rogelio V. Solis (lunch). 10: AP Photo/Khalil Hamra(refugees); AP Photo/Nikolas Giakoumidis (Greece strike); AP Photo/Jung Yeon-je (Geun-hye). 11: AP Photo/*Nasha gazeta*/www.ng.kz (meteorite); AP Photo/Queen Elizabeth Hospital Birmingham (Yousafzai). 12: AP Photo/Red Bull Stratos (Baumgartner); Photo by NASA/Tony Gray and Rick Wetherington (Dragon). 13: SOMKKU/Shutterstock.com (chef); Africa Studio/Shutterstock.com (balloons); AP Photo/Brian Kersey (bionic leg). 14: Todd Williamson/Invision/AP (Lawrence); Todd Williamson/Invision/AP (Wallis); Imaginechina via AP Images (Psy); Evan Agostini/Invision/AP (One Direction). 15: Erick W. Rasco/Sports Illustrated (Williams); Peter Read Miller/Sports Illustrated (Douglas); Bill Frakes/Sports Illustrated (Bolt); AP Photo/Anja Niedringhaus (Attar).

ANIMALS: 16–27: Butterfly Hunter/Shutterstock.com (background). 16: AP Photo/Ethical Expeditions/Eric Fell (Miller's grizzled langur); AP Photo/Galapagos National Park (Galápagos tortoise); AP Photo/Mark A. Klingler/Science (Laotian rock rat); Eric Isselee/Shutterstock.com (ferrets); Enna van Duinen/Shutterstock.com (kangaroos). 17: Aaron Amat/Shutterstock.com (ostrich); Per-Gunnar Ostby/Oxford Scientific/Getty Images (antelope); Darren J. Bradley/Shutterstock.com (tide pool); Peter David/Getty Images (anglerfish). 18: Stella Caraman/Shutterstock.com (vertebra); bogdan ionescu/Shutterstock.com (salamander); Henk Bentlage/Shutterstock.com (meerkat); Mircea BEZERGHEANU/Shutterstock.com (puffin); Comstock/Photos.com (stingray); Cameramannz/Shutterstock.com (tuataras). 19: Vilainecrevette/Shutterstock.com (jellyfish); Joze Maucec/Shutterstock.com (sea urchin); srdjan draskovic/Shutterstock.com (snail); dive-hive/Shutterstock.com (sponge); Cbenjasuwan/Shutterstock.com (butterfly); Mircea BEZERGHEANU/Shutterstock.com (leech); Mohammed Suleiman Ismail/Shutterstock.com (spider). 20: Lee319/Shutterstock.com (birds); Gelpi/Shutterstock.com (Labrador retriever); 315 studio by khunaspix/Shutterstock.com (beagle); viki2win/Shutterstock.com (German shepherd, center); Erik Lam/Shutterstock.com (golden retriever); Eric Isselee/Shutterstock.com (Yorkshire terrier); Dora Zett/Shutterstock.com (boxer); WilleeCole/Shutterstock.com (English bulldog); Toloubaev Stanislav/Shutterstock.com (poodle); Luis Carlos Torres/Shutterstock.com (dachshund); cynoclub/Shutterstock.com (Rottweiler); Eric Fahrner/Shutterstock.com (cat); jurra8/Shutterstock.com (German shepherd, bottom right). 21: AP Photo/Craig Lassig (film festival); Vasiliy Koval/Shutterstock.com (Siamese); Dudarev Mikhail/Shutterstock.com (Persian); ©National Geographic Crittercam/University of Georgia (kitty cam). 22: Nigel Dennis/Gallo Images/Getty Images (aardvark); stockpix4u/Shutterstock.com (clownfish); Kira Kaplinski/Photos.com (sociable weavers nest); Simon Greig/Shutterstock.com (termite mound); Neale Cousland/Shutterstock.com (penguins from left to right, top to bottom: 1, 4, 8, 11); Anna Kucherova/Shutterstock.com (penguins from left to right, top to bottom: 2, 3, 5, 6, 7, 9, 10). 23: AP Photo/PRNewsFoto/Scholastic (hippo and tortoise); Eric Gevaert/Shutterstock.com (chimpanzees); ©Pantheon/SuperStock (Sewell). 24–25: Potapov Alexander/Shutterstock.com (animal tracks). 24: AP Photo (Lolong); AP Photo/Joern Koehler/dapd (*Brookesia micra*). 25: Hung Chung Chih/Shutterstock.com (giant panda); AP Photo/Fiona Hanson/PA (Polynesian tree snail). 26: winnond/Shutterstock.com (elephant skin background); AP Photo/Ahn Young-joon (Koshik); AP Photo/Apichart Weerawong (coffee); AP Photo (tusks). 27: schankz/Shutterstock.com (worm); Gubin Yury/Shutterstock.com (flamingo); Alexandra Lande/Shutterstock.com (goldfish); Eric Isselee/Shutterstock.com (newt); paulrommer/Shutterstock.com (fly); Curioso/Shutterstock.com (koala).

ART: 28–31: kiya-nochka/Shutterstock.com (background). 28: AP Photo/Antonio Calanni (*The Last Supper*); AP Photo/Metropolitan Museum of Art (*The Milkmaid*). 29: Bangkokhappiness/Shutterstock.com (paintbrush); AP Photo/Christie's New York (*Water Lilies*); Namuth Hans/Photo Researchers/Getty Images (Pollock). 30: Press Association via AP Images (*RedBall*); AP Photo/Beth A. Keiser (*Puppy*); Scott Barbour/Getty Images (Jansen creation). 31: AP Photo/Torsten Silz/DAPD (*Obliteration Room*); Jacek Chabraszewski/Shutterstock.com (mural girl); Art Allianz/Shutterstock.com (mural bracelet); Kitch Bain/Shutterstock.com (mural paintbrush).

BODY AND HEALTH: 32–37: Libellule/Shutterstock.com (background). 32: Roblan/Shutterstock.com (spoon of sugar); AP Photo/Bob Bird (vending machine); Elena Schweitzer/Shutterstock.com (donuts); Valeriy Lebedev/Shutterstock.com (boy); HamsterMan/Shutterstock.com (sugar cubes); Seregam/Shutterstock.com (honey); Daniel Wiedemann/Shutterstock.com (syrup). 33: Jacek Chabraszewski/Photos.com (snorkel girl); ©iStockphoto.com/Juanmonino (sleeping boy); Monkey Business Images/Shutterstock.com (eating fruit); Jorg Hackemann/Shutterstock.com (scooter). 34: Eliks/Shutterstock.com (graph paper); Ilya Andriyanov/Shutterstock.com (checking pulse); Rob Hainer/Shutterstock.com (soccer); alekso94/Shutterstock.com (fruit); Ivonne Wierink/Shutterstock.com (lifting weights). 35: Sebastian Kaulitzki/Shutterstock.com (bacteria); leungchopan/Shutterstock.com (boy blowing nose); Ana Blazic Pavlovic/Shutterstock.com (girl); Arvind Balaraman/Shutterstock.com (boy with inhaler). 36: keki/Shutterstock.com (x-ray and cast); CREATISTA/Shutterstock.com (boy); BaLL LunLa/Shutterstock.com (toilet sign). 37: CLIPAREA I Custom media/Shutterstock.com (left brain); FCG/Shutterstock.com (tongue close-up); Zametalov/Shutterstock.com (sticking out tongue).

BOOKS AND LITERATURE: 38–41: smithbaker/Shutterstock.com (background). 38: *THIS IS NOT MY HAT* Copyright ©2012 by Jon Klassen Reproduced by permission of the publisher, Candlewick Press, Inc, Somerville, MA (*This Is Not My Hat*); Courtesy of Macmillan (*Bomb*); Courtesy of HarperCollins Publishers (*The One and Only Ivan, Chickadee*); Disney-Jump at the Sun, an imprint of Disney Book Group (*Hand in Hand*); Chloe Foglia/Courtesy of Simon & Schuster (*Aristotle and Dante Discover the Secrets of the Universe*). 39: Debra Sfetsios-Conover/Courtesy of Simon & Schuster (*Goblin Secrets*); Courtesy Penguin Young Readers Group (*Between Shades of Gray*); Russell Gordon/Courtesy of Simon & Schuster (*Alanna: Song of the Lioness, Book 1*); Jeka/Shutterstock.com (girl); freesoulproduction/Shutterstock.com (book shelves). 40: Courtesy of Random House Children's Books (*Liar & Spy, The*

Mighty Miss Malone); Courtesy of HarperCollins Publishers (*Crunch*); Karin Poprocki/Courtesy of Simon & Schuster (*From the Mixed-up Files of Mrs. Basil E. Frankweiler*); Library of Congress, Prints and Photographs Division (Shultz). 41: *Chuck Close: Face Book,* Abrams Books for Young Readers (*Chuck Close: Face Book*); Courtesy of Macmillan (*Energy Island*); Courtesy Houghton Mifflin Harcourt Books for Young Readers (*The Elephant Scientist*); Workman Publishing Company (*The World Record Paper Airplane Book*); Courtesy of Random House Children's Books (*The Black Stallion, Eragon*); Courtesy Penguin Young Readers Group (*The Outsiders*).

BUILDINGS AND ARCHITECTURE: 42–47: ildogesto/Shutterstock.com (background). 42: ©Reitserof/Dreamstime.com (Canterbury Cathedral); naten/Shutterstock.com (Mosque of Uqba); SeanPavonePhoto/Shutterstock.com (Dome of the Rock); Tatiana Popova/Shutterstock.com (Temple of Apollo); Kristen Hammelbo/Photos.com (National Cathedral); Guy Erwood/Shutterstock.com (St. Mary's Church). 43: RHIMAGE/Shutterstock.com (Eiffel Tower); David Carillet/Shutterstock.com (Pantheon); JGW Images/Shutterstock.com (Town Hall); Ffooter/Shutterstock.com (Willis Tower); Vlad G/Shutterstock.com (St. Peter's Basilica); kornilov007/Shutterstock.com (all columns). 44: littlewormy/Shutterstock.com (Petronus Towers); Anastasios71/Shutterstock.com (Burj Khalifa); chuyu/Shutterstock.com (Shanghai World Financial Center). 45: haraldmuc/Shutterstock.com (beam bridge); Thomas Morrison/Shutterstock.com (arch bridge); SeanPavonePhoto/Shutterstock.com (suspension bridge); z0w/Shutterstock.com (wooden bridge model); Aneese/Shutterstock.com (Margaret Hunt Hill Bridge). 46: S.Borisov/Shutterstock.com (Alhambra); onairda/Shutterstock.com (Versailles); Alexey Stiop/Shutterstock.com (Angkor Wat). 47: Artifan/Shutterstock.com (Space Needle); Lukiyanova Natalia/frenta/Shutterstock.com (Leaning Tower); vvoe/Shutterstock.com (Guggenheim); Arcaid/UIG via Getty Images (container houses).

CALENDARS AND HOLIDAYS: 48–53: Nik Merkulov/Shutterstock.com (background). 49: U.S. Marine Corps photo by Pfc. Cory D. Polom. 50: Steve Pepple/Shutterstock.com (hat and horn); design56/Shutterstock.com (gold bowl); Digital Storm/Shutterstock.com (Earth); Bochkarev Photography/Shutterstock.com (turkey); robertlamphoto/Shutterstock.com (snowman); Noam Armonn/Shutterstock.com (dreidel); Ariene Studio/Shutterstock.com (bear); leungchopan/Shutterstock.com (eggs); JeniFoto/Shutterstock.com (flowers and present); Lisa F. Young/Shutterstock.com (kids in costume). 51: AP Photo/The White House, Susan Sterner, HO (Bush); AP Photo/*The Olympian*, Ron Soliman (Native American). 52: bellenixe/Shutterstock.com (arrow sphere); AGCuesta/Shutterstock.com (Day of the Dead altar); ryabuhina/Shutterstock.com (Holi). 53: North Wind Picture Archives via AP Images (Squanto); Hunter Fitch/Shutterstock.com (pie); newyear/Shutterstock.com (maze background); Robert F. Balazik/Shutterstock.com (reindeer); Yayayoyo/Shutterstock.com (blue vampire, elf); Tetiana Savitska aka Solaie/Shutterstock.com (Leprechaun hat); YurkaImmortal/Shutterstock.com (spider, ghost); Basheera Designs/Shutterstock.com (firecracker, turkey); Christos Georghiou/Shutterstock.com (both eggs); Marish/Shutterstock.com (Cupid, dreidel); BooHoo/Shutterstock.com (drum); Kuttly/Shutterstock.com (North Pole).

COMPUTERS AND COMMUNICATION: 54–59: fotographic1980/Shutterstock.com (background). 54: 3Dstock/Shutterstock.com (phone); foto Arts/Shutterstock.com (boy); Courtesy of Dell Inc. (Dell). 55: Courtesy of Skype, Inc. (Skype); Courtesy of Foodily (Foodily.com); Peredniankina/Shutterstock.com (boy). 56: AP Photo/Paul Sakuma (video chat); Imaginechina via AP Images (Angry Birds Space). 57: PRNewsFoto/Nickelodeon & Viacom Consumer Products via AP Images (Neopets); Courtesy of Arkadium (Mahjongg Dark Dimensions); Richard Hutchings/Photo Researchers/Getty Images (girls on laptop); Photo by Margrett Andrews/Courtesy of Burghard family (Burghard).

COUNTRIES: 60: Jarno Gonzalez Zarraonandia/Shutterstock.com (background); Imaginechina via AP Images (archaeologists); Imaginechina via AP Images (Terracotta Army); feiyuezhangjie/Shutterstock.com (Great Wall). 61–95: Friedrichan/Shutterstock.com (background). 94: Stephen Coburn/Shutterstock.com (Hollywood Walk of Fame); Songquan Deng/Shutterstock.com (Empire State Building); Nikonaft/Shutterstock.com (Eiffel Tower); Yu Lan/Shutterstock.com (Nazca lines); Elder Vieira Salles/Shutterstock.com (Niterói Contemporary Art Museum). 95: Dan Breckwoldt/Shutterstock.com (Temple of Abu Simbel); Dimon/Shutterstock.com (St. Basil's Cathedral); Huyangshu/Shutterstock.com (Potala Palace); gnomeandi/Shutterstock.com (Shwedagon Pagoda); Neale Cousland/Shutterstock.com (Itsukushima Shrine); Przemyslaw Skibinski/Shutterstock.com (Victoria Falls); Chris Howey/Shutterstock.com (Sydney Opera House).

ENERGY: 96–101: artizarus/Shutterstock.com (background). 96: nostal6ie/Shutterstock.com (wood chips); lvalin/Shutterstock.com (volcano); Press Association via AP Images (hydrogen car). 97: CreativeNature.nl/Shutterstock.com (solar panel); Aleksandr Kurganov/Shutterstock.com (hydropower station); Jesus Keller/Shutterstock.com (wind tower); Courtesy of Biolite (Biolite stove). 98: James Jones Jr/Shutterstock.com (offshore drill); digitalconsumator/Shutterstock.com (oil barrels); Thaiview/Shutterstock.com (oil pump). 99: Thorsten Schier/Shutterstock.com (steam stacks); Anton Foltin/Shutterstock.com (strip mall); Rihardzz/Shutterstock.com (tractor); PhotoStocker/Shutterstock.com (apartment); MiloVad/Shutterstock.com (bike). 100: Courtesy of Pavegen Systems (London tiles); YOSHIKAZU TSUNO/AFP/Getty Images (Tokyo); SustainableDanceClub.com/Anneke Hymmen (dance floor). 101: Virunja/Shutterstock.com (algae); STAN HONDA/AFP/Getty Images (exercise class); Courtesy of WeWatt (We-Bike table).

ENVIRONMENT: 102–107: luckypic/shutterstock.com (background). 102: ©iStockphoto.com/Fotolinchen (garden); BMJ/Shutterstock.com (compost). 103: IDAK/Shutterstock.com (desert); Oleksandr Berezko/Shutterstock.com (fennec fox); leungchopan/Shutterstock.com (tropical rain forest); Juriah Mosin/Shutterstock.com (macaws); Tatiana Grozetskaya/Shutterstock.com (taiga); NancyS/Shutterstock.com (gray wolf); yuriy kulik/Shutterstock.com (grassland); NUMAX3D/Shutterstock.com (zebras); Cristian Gusa/Shutterstock.com (temperate forest); Benedikt Saxler/Shutterstock.com (deer); R. Vickers/Shutterstock.com (tundra); Sergey Uryadnikov/Shutterstock.com (polar bears). 104: Luka Veselinovic/Shutterstock.com. 105: Imaginechina via AP Images (smog); forestpath/Shutterstock.com (oil spill); Carolina K. Smith MD/Shutterstock.com (crop dusting); zebrik/Shutterstock.com (trash). 106: Courtesy of Anna Suslova (Suslova); AP Photo/UN Photo/John McIlwaine/dapd (Finkbeiner); Courtesy of Olivia Bouler (Bouler); AP Photo/Mark Humphrey (Loorz). 107: Courtesy of Arvind Gupta (simple motor, Matchstick Meccano).

GEOGRAPHY: 108–113: Tischenko Irina/Shutterstock.com (background). 108: Peteri/Shutterstock.com. 109: Patrick Poendl/Shutterstock.com (oasis); Thomas Nord/Shutterstock.com (archipelago); Dorn1530/Shutterstock.com (Grand Canyon); Sally Scott/Shutterstock.com (butte). 110: AP Photo/Arctic Sounder/Beth Ipsen (Arctic); Andrey Starostin/Shutterstock.com (Atlantic); cdelacy/Shutterstock.com (Indian); Andrea Izzotti/Shutterstock.com (Pacific); AP Photo/Sea Shepherd Conservation Society/Barbara Veiga (Southern). 111: Regien Paassen/Shutterstock.com (geyser); Rich Carey/Shutterstock.com (coral reef); ProfStocker/Shutterstock.com (Dead Sea). 112: AP Photo/Dar Yasin (Muslim women); AP Photo/Ignat Kozlov (voting). 113: Eugene Sergeev/Shutterstock.com.

GOVERNMENT: 114–121: VICTOR TORRES/Shutterstock.com (background). 114: AP Photo/Office of the Supreme Leader (Iran's leaders); AP Photo (Adulyadej). 115: Rich Koele/Shutterstock.com (Constitution); Library of Congress, Prints and Photographs Division (Madison); AP Photo/Jason DeCrow (police). 116: Orhan Cam/Shutterstock.com (Capitol building); AP Photo/J. Scott Applewhite (Leahy); Andre Adams/Shutterstock.com (illustration); Library of Congress, Prints and Photographs Division (Caraway). 117: AP Photo/J. Scott Applewhite (Boehner); AP Photo/Evan Vucci (Pelosi); Andre Adams/Shutterstock.com (illustration). 118: Official White House Photo by Pete Souza (Obama). 119: Official White House Photo by David Lienemann (Biden); AP Photo/*Tulsa World*, Matt Barnard (Holder); Official White House Photo by Pete Souza (Sebelius). 120: AFP/Getty Images (Justices); Sean D/Shutterstock.com (boys). 121: AP Photo/David Goldman (citizens); Library of Congress, Prints and Photographs Division (Marshall).

HISTORY: 122–131: Ssokolov/Shutterstock.com (background). 122: jsp/Shutterstock.com (Hammurabi's Code); zhuhe2343603/Shutterstock.com (Confucius). 123: AP Photo/Manuel Balce Ceneta (Magna Carta); Jeremy Reddington/Shutterstock.com (El Castillo). 124: Steve Wynn/Photos.com (Polo); ©SuperStock/SuperStock (Simón Bolívar). 125: Library of Congress, Prints and Photographs Division (Columbian Exposition); AP Photo (Farnsworth). 126: AP Photo (The Six-Day War); Hung Chung Chih/Shutterstock.com (Zedong). 127: AP Photo/Gerald Herbert (oil spill); AP Photo (Honda Insight). 128: MPI/Getty Images (Sacagawea); Ian Danbury/Photos.com (Drake). 129: Library of Congress, Prints and Photographs Division (railroad); NeonLight/Shutterstock.com (Pearl Harbor). 130: AP Photo (Nixon); Library of Congress, Prints and Photographs Division (integrated classroom). 131: U.S. Air Force photo by Saff Sgt. Jason Robertson (service members); AP Photo/Ron Edmonds (Bush and Gore).

INVENTIONS: 132–135: Zlatko Guzmic/shutterstock.com (background). 132: Photo Courtesy of Potential Energy (fuel-efficient stove); AP Photo/Bela Szandelszky (Gadgil). 133: Courtesy of Makerbot (Replicator 2); Daniel Wiedemann/Shutterstock.com (submarine); Photo Courtesy of Rethink Robotics, Inc, All Rights Reserved (Baxter); Berndnaut Smilde/*Nimbus NP3*/2012/digital C-type print on dibond/125x185 cm/Courtesy the artist and Ronchini Gallery (White Cloud). 134: ©World Wingsuit League (WWL)/Kristian Schmidt (Wingsuit); Bounce Imaging/Carlos Aguilar (Bounce); Courtesy of Bandai America (TechPet); Courtesy of Google, Inc. (Google Glass); Courtesy of Open Source Ecology (Tractor). 135: Photo by NASA (Z-1 space suit); AP Photo/PRNewsFoto/Microsoft Corp. (Enable Talk); Courtesy of Stanley Black & Decker (Max Gyro); Courtesy of Liquiglide (Liquiglide); Photos.com (Nobel).

LANGUAGE: 136–139: hans.slegers/Shutterstock.com (background). 136: Gautier Willaume/Shutterstock.com (Chinese language); AP Photo/Jacquelyn Martin (Nandipati). 137: Michael C. Gray/Shutterstock.com (writing girl); Alex and Anna/Shutterstock.com (United States); Iakov Filimonov/Shutterstock.com (wolf); ©iStockphoto.com/karlkotasinc (illustration). 138: calvindexter/Shutterstock.com (Lincoln); Erika Cross/Shutterstock.com (eating pasta); akiradesigns/Shutterstock.com (rat and girl); Nico Traut/Shutterstock.com (girl with binoculars). 139: Knumina Studios/Shutterstock.com (chicken); VectorForever/Shutterstock.com (all game icons).

MAPS: 140–151: Digital Storm/Shutterstock.com (background); Joe Lemonnier and Joe Lertola (maps).

MOVIES AND TV: 152–155: Vectomart/Shutterstock.com (background). 152: Todd Williamson/Invision/AP Photo (Wallis); Joe Seer/Shutterstock.com (Hanks). 153: John Shearer/Invision/AP Photo (Stone); Jason LaVeris/FilmMagic/Getty Images (Stewart); Jon Kopaloff/FilmMagic/Getty Images (Hutcherson); Jason Merritt/Getty Images (Colfer, Michele); FOX via Getty Images (Stevens). 154: AP Photo/Disney/Pixar (*Brave*); AP Photo/Universal Pictures (*E.T. the Extra-Terrestrial*). 155: Jordan Strauss/Invision/AP Photo (Watson, Lawrence); Jason Merritt/Getty Images (Short); Jon Kopaloff/FilmMagic/Getty Images (McCurdy); Steve Granitz/WireImage/Getty Images (Justice); Jeff Kravitz/FilmMagic/Getty Images (Sandler).

MUSIC: 156–161: pavalena/Shutterstock.com (background). 156–157: FOX via Getty Images. 157: Jon Furniss/Invision for Children in Need/AP Images. 158: Christopher Polk/Getty Images for NARAS (Beyoncé and Adele, Fun.); John Shearer/Invision/AP Photo (Clarkson). 159: John Shearer/Invision for MTV.com/AP Photo (Rihanna); John Shearer/Invision/AP Photo (Usher); Jordan Strauss/Invision/AP Photo (Bryan); Matt Sayles/Invision/AP Photo (Swift, Underwood). 160: Jordan Strauss/Invision/AP Photo (Lovato); Jon Kopaloff/FilmMagic/Getty Images (Gomez); Kevin Winter/Getty Images (Bieber); Kevin Mazur/TCA 2012/WireImage/Getty Images (Jepsen). 161: Chris Pizzello/Invision/AP Photo (Hayes); Jeff Kravitz/FilmMagic/Getty Images (Perry); Jonathan Short/AP Photo/dapd (Minaj); Jordan Strauss/Invision/AP Photo (The Wanted).

PRESIDENTS: 162–171: Anastasiia Kucherenko/Shutterstock.com (background). 162: Library of Congress, Prints and Photographs Division (Lincoln); AP Photo/via Smithsonian Institution (watch). 163: Vacclav/Shutterstock.com (White House); Library of Congress, Prints and Photographs Division (Nixon, Roosevelt); AP Photo/CWH (Carter). 164–171: Viktor Vector/Shutterstock.com (box pattern; Library of Congress, Prints and Photographs Division (presidential portraits, Eleanor Roosevelt).

SCIENCE: 172–179: kentoh/Shutterstock.com (background). 172: AP Photo/U.S. Attorney Office for the Southern District of New York. 173: Image Source/Getty Images (girl with eyedropper, two girls); Rex Features via AP Images (Extreme Marshmallow Cannon). 174–175: stephan kerkhofs/Shutterstock.com (background). 174: AP Photo/*The New York Times* (newspaper); LHF Graphics/Shutterstock.com (DNA); AP Photo/*Canadian Press*, Andrew Vaughan (Ryan Parr). 175: Press Association via AP Images (the *Titanic*); AP Photo/Lefteris Pitarakis (grave). 176: Courtesy of Damien Scarf (Damian Scarf); Patrick Landmann/Getty Images (Ramses III). 177: Courtesy of Paul Marek (*I. plenipes*); Courtesy of Thomas Potts/Aquarius Reef Base/Florida International University (Aquarius). 178: Lorelyn Medina/Shutterstock.com (shelf); freesoulproduction/Shutterstock.com (beakers); Africa Studio/Shutterstock.com (popcorn); dragon_fang/Shutterstock.com (boy); Anneka/Shutterstock.com (girl). 179: Bloom Image/Getty Images (sneeze); Africa Studio/Shutterstock.com (eggs); Kitch Bain/Shutterstock.com (kettle); Stephen Beaumont/Shutterstock.com (sugar).

SPACE: 180–185: Cardens Design/Shutterstock.com (background). 180: NASA/JPL-Caltech (all). 181: NASA/JPL-Caltech/Malin Space Science Systems (all). 182: SOHO/ESA/NASA (sun, Solar Heliospheric Observatory); NASA (solar flair). 183: fluidworkshop/Shutterstock.com. 184: NASA/JPL-Caltech (background); AP Photo/*Fayetteville Observer-Times*, Johnny Horne (comet); Georgios Kollidas/Photos.com (Halley). 185: NASA (all).

SPORTS: 186–201: silvae/Shutterstock.com (background). 186: Yuliyan Velchev/Shutterstock.com (football); David E. Klutho/Sports Illustrated (Jones, Peterson). 187: Al Tielemans/Sports Illustrated (Alabama vs. Notre Dame); John W. McDonough/Sports Illustrated (Manziel). 188: stiven/Shutterstock.com (baseball); Al Tielemans/Sports Illustrated (Sandoval); Chuck Solomon/Sports Illustrated (Dickey); AP Photo (Robinson). 189: AP Photo/Matt Slocum (Little League); Al Tielemans/Sports Illustrated (Cabrera, Harper); Michael Ivins/Boston Red Sox (Fenway). 190: Yuliyan Velchev/Shutterstock.com (basketball); John W. McDonough/Sports Illustrated (James); Heinz Kluetmeier/Sports Illustrated (Rondo). 191: John W. McDonough/Sports Illustrated (NCAA Men's Basketball); Bill

INDEX